PETERSON'S

THE ULTIMATE HIGH SCHOOL SURVIVAL GUIDE

JULIANNE DUEBER

Peterson's
Thomson Learning

Australia • Canada • Denmark • Japan • Mexico • New Zealand • Philippines
Puerto Rico • Singapore • South Africa • Spain • United Kingdom • United States

About Peterson's

Peterson's is the country's largest educational information/communications company, providing the academic, consumer, and professional communities with books, software, and online services in support of lifelong education access and career choice. Well-known references include Peterson's annual guides to private schools, summer programs, colleges and universities, graduate and professional programs, financial aid, international study, adult learning, and career guidance. Peterson's Web site at petersons.com is the only comprehensive—and most heavily traveled—education resource on the Internet. The site carries all of Peterson's fully searchable major databases and includes financial aid sources, test-prep help, job postings, direct inquiry and application features, and specially created Virtual Campuses for every accredited academic institution and summer program in the U.S. and Canada that offers in-depth narratives, announcements, and multimedia features.

Visit Peterson's Education Center on the Internet (World Wide Web) at www.petersons.com

For permission to use material from this text or product, contact us by
- Web: www.thomsonrights.com
- Phone: 1-800-730-2214
- Fax: 1-800-730-2215

ISBN 0-7689-0241-X

Printed in Canada

10   9   8   7   6   5   4   3   2   1

DEDICATION

For Rosemary Lough, my high school Latin teacher

ACKNOWLEDGMENTS

I would like to thank many people for helping me write this book. Special thanks to high school guidance counselor Alissa Parrish for her special insights on what students need and for making editing suggestions. Thanks also to Mary Jane Lyle, Jeanene Dueber, Marian Allbee, Kate Allbee, Anita Correnti, Michael Cundiff, Susan Wagner, Ann Broyles, John Gaal, Stuart Suchland, Connie Williams, Bonnie Wagner, Brian Elliot, Barbara Vilimek, Elaine Steinbrecker, Daniel Lyle, Danielle Owens, and countless other people too numerous to mention for their helpful comments.

I would also like to thank my students both past and present for all of your help as I was writing this book. Your comments were invaluable. You have taught me a lot. Thanks also to the many teenagers who wrote about their school and life experiences for the book.

Thanks to Michael and Patricia Snell, my agents, for their skilled help in the initial stages of the manuscript; to Kate Foster of Peterson's for her editing expertise; and to Heather McCarron of Peterson's for her copy editing and book production skills. A special thanks to Executive Editor Karen Hansen of Peterson's for her special people skills in helping me navigate my way through this manuscript. You asked me to finish the book in a very short time, but you were so calm, kind, and convincing, that I really believed I could make the deadline and I did.

CONTENTS

INTRODUCTION

Dear Student,

Picture this: It's dark outside. You're in a car careening down a road that you've never been on before. Some person you've never met is behind the wheel, making random turns and ignoring stop signs and street lights. This is crazy. You want out, but which way is that? Sound like a nightmare or a scene from a late-night movie? It's what high school feels like to lots of students. When you start your journey, so much is new and unfamiliar; you don't feel in control. There are so many things that teachers, parents, and even older students will assume you know.

The Ultimate High School Survival Guide addresses the typical problems you will have when you start high school. Being in the "big leagues" can be scary. But why let someone else take the wheel? Instead of being confused or ashamed by what you don't know, you can be in the driver's seat. This book will take the mystery out of high school situations that could otherwise be difficult—or unbearable.

You might be saying, "Who wants to read a book written by a teacher? They're the ones who dump too much homework on us at the last minute and think their class is our only class." I can understand your hesitation to believe what I say, but I was once a high school student, too, and I remember my experiences very clearly. I went through many of the things you will be going through. I will show you that when you focus on what you are supposed to be doing in high school, it isn't so difficult to relax and do well.

It makes me sad to see how many students are not thriving in high school. I've been teaching for 33 years, so I've seen this a lot. I believe that many of you have much more potential than you are using. If you discover the key to successful actions in high school, you will not only survive, you will *thrive*. This is the goal of this book—to help you focus on your job of being a high school student and come out feeling good about it. By using this book, you will learn how to make your journey a success.

Remember that you are driving the car; you control your life. Only you can decide what turns to take, but everyone needs a good road map. So turn the page and start on the journey to a better and happier life in high school and beyond.

Sincerely,

Julianne Dueber, Student Advocate

P.S. If you are a freshman just starting out in high school and plan to go to college, be sure to read Chapter 14 on preparing for college. Ask your parents to read it, too, because there's a lot of information in the chapter that they need to know. If you don't plan to go to college, you still will need extra education to get a good job. Read Chapter 13 for options other than college.

School is Your Job

Let's get one thing straight from this moment forward—you're really going to work every day when you go to school. Like a job, you say? Yes, when you go to school every day, you are going to work. Your job is to learn as much as you can in order to prepare for your future. Students always protest, "But I'm not getting paid to do this!" Yes, that's true, but if you prepare yourself now, you'll be able to get a good job instead of having to flip burgers for the rest of your life. Fast food jobs are great when you're young and just starting out, but you want more out of life when you're older, right? Keep in mind that your parents won't always be around to take care of you. Someday you may even be taking care of them or your own children. One thing is certain—you will need all of the skills possible to have a happy and successful life.

Now, you may be thinking, "What's the use, I never do well in school." I have seen that *all* students can learn if they put their minds to it. If you're still not convinced, give it a chance. This book is designed to help you change your focus and learn what you need to survive and to be proud of the work you do. Remember, you are in control. You are in the driver's seat.

PART 1

SCHOOL SKILLS

CHAPTER 1

Strategies for Survival And Success

WHICH SCHOOL IS BEST FOR ME?

Although there are many different types of schools from which to choose, most people attend their neighborhood public school. There are also private school options. The following is a summary of the advantages and disadvantages of attending each type of school.

It is a good idea to use the following information as a starting point in your search for the right school. Ultimately, you need to make your own decision, because every school is unique.

Public vs. Private High Schools

There are public schools and many different kinds of private schools: religious, nonsectarian, military, and boarding. In order to decide which is most suitable for you, you and your parents will need to visit them and gather more information about them. Many schools have an Open House day, where you can get to know some of the students and teachers at the school and ask a lot of questions, such as:

- What is the school size?
- What is the tuition?
- Is there financial aid for students who cannot afford to attend?
- What are the strengths of the school?
- What are the weaknesses of the school?
- What percentage of students continue on to college?
- What are the average ACT and SAT scores for the school?
- Does the school have full accreditation?
- Does the school have a diversified student body?
- What are the school's values? Be sure and find out what makes the school tick. Does it ask its students to

do a service project for others? Are students encouraged to take their place in society as responsible citizens?

- Is it possible to make a visit during a typical day of classes to get a better feel for the school?
- What is the school admission policy? Is it highly competitive?
- Are there programs for students with special needs?
- When are applications for admission and financial aid due?

Advantages of Public High Schools

Money. Because public schools are supported by the taxpayers of your district, your parents will not have to pay tuition.

Diversity. There could be well over 1,000 students in the total school population. In a school of this size, you will encounter kids of diverse religions, races, and nationalities. You will get an opportunity to meet people totally unlike yourself. This will prepare you for the working world you will encounter when you get your first job.

More options. Because the choice of courses you can take will be larger and more varied, you will probably be able to find more classes that will be of interest to you.

Choosing a School Requires Lots of Research

Magnet schools. Your district might have magnet schools that focus on specialized programs such as the arts, foreign languages, or technology. You might be eligible to transfer to such a school within your district. Call your district office to ask for complete information. Some students find attending a magnet school the best way to attend public school because the classes are smaller and geared toward their particular interests. Your district might even have a school within a school for students with special interests or problems or for students in an accelerated program.

Special programs. Many public high schools have a special school within the school for accelerated students, such as the International Baccalaureate Program (IBP). These schools are generally very competitive with a lot of homework and challenging classes. The students in these programs are definitely college-bound. Here are some comments from IBP students.

THE INSIDE SCOOP FROM STUDENTS

At its beginning, the International Baccalaureate Program was composed of the best teachers and was allocated immense resources. Students received more time with their teachers than students who were not enrolled in the program because IBP teachers taught fewer classes. Now, however, there is no special treatment other than that the program is composed of the best students. From my point of view, it was a major detriment. The teachers pretty much assumed that since we were the best students, we didn't need any guidance or help (even though I ended up getting a C) and proceeded to not do much teaching at all. *David*

I feel that I got a better education in English and history than any non-IBP student in my class. This is most evident in my writing skills. Not only do I write fairly well, but I also feel confident about my writing skills. I know that if I dedicate the time to it, I can write a paper that is well organized, makes sense, and is easy to read. But just as important are the friendships that I have developed with several members of my class, friendships that have lasted throughout my college years. It is probably this that I will be most grateful for in the years to come. *Marcie*

Extracurricular activities. The list of extracurricular activities available after school is much greater than that of a private school. You will have more choices. In addition, public schools generally field many sports teams, such as ice hockey and lacrosse.

Disadvantages of Public High Schools

Size. Because the school might be much larger than the environment you are used to, you could feel lost in such a big place. Seeking out an activity or club can make a large school feel less daunting. This is the time to find out what your talents are and to use them, perhaps in drama or peer teaching. In a large school, a student must be his or her own advocate. You can't expect people to just know you. You have to make yourself known if you want to be included.

Possible discipline problems. Unless you are in honors classes, you might find yourself in a class with disengaged students who hate school, aren't interested in learning, and act up so that the teacher can't teach. This won't bother you if you can block out their disruptive behavior. Please note that this only happens in a minority of public school classes.

Advantages of Private Schools

Size. Often, classes are smaller and students get more individual attention.

Fewer discipline problems. Since students' parents pay for them to attend the school, they are less likely to disrupt classes. If disruptive students don't adhere to school rules, the private school can and will expel them.

Opportunity to focus better. Those students who go to all-girl or all-boy schools often say they like the fact that the opposite sex is not present because they can better concentrate on their studies.

Less competition. Sometimes you can be a big fish in a small pond. You won't have as much competition for spaces on sports teams, the debate team, and other extracurricular activities. It may be easier to stand out in a private school.

Disadvantages of Private Schools

Money. The tuition could put your parents in the poor house. If your parents can afford the tuition, then you won't have to worry. Some private schools award partial or full scholarships for people who cannot afford the tuition.

Possible lack of diversity. Many private schools have a student body composed of students of different religions and races. In some cases, though, a private school might have a homogeneous student body—all of the students might belong to the same socioeconomic background. This could be a big disadvantage because you won't benefit from learning about other people's world views.

Homesickness at boarding school. If you go to a boarding school, you probably won't know a soul when you get there. This could be difficult if you have a hard time meeting people. You could also experience some homesickness during the first several weeks.

Military school discipline. If you go to a military school, you might be turned off by the discipline and strict rules. You need to visit a school before you enroll. See how it feels to you. Picture yourself in the environment. If you think you would like it, great. If not, then you need to check out other options.

Wrap-Up

When you visit prospective schools, keep the above information in mind. You and your parents should ask a lot of questions at each school you visit. Each school will be different and will have unique strengths and problems. Have an open mind when you check out a school. After you gather all of the information, you can get to the bottom line: Where would you feel most comfortable? Are the reasons for your choice good ones? If you decide on a private school, can your parents afford it?

Decisions, decisions. Don't panic. There's plenty of information to help you.

THE INSIDE SCOOP FROM PUBLIC SCHOOL STUDENTS

In private schools the teachers push the students pretty hard to get the "good grade." In public schools I have seen a lack of effort on the part of some teachers to push the students to do well. Overall, I really enjoy the diversity of the public school, but I also miss the private school environment. *Rebecca*

Public schools are more in tune with real life and give you a look at reality. Private schools are much more pampered and sheltered. No uniforms either in public school. You also have a more diverse group of people in public schools. You'll know more people than just upper-class white kids. *Jon*

One main advantage for public schools is you pick up street smarts—something you probably couldn't get from a private school. Private schools are maybe a little safer, but in public schools you do get a little bit more freedom. *Abrahem*

I like the public schools because you can get the same education as in a private school without spending a fortune and because public schools allow you to make your own decisions on what classes you take. They let you become more independent. *Natalie*

When I changed to a public school, I instantly fell in love. I met people who were different than me in many ways, which aided me in discovering a wider perspective about life. Having friends with contrary views to mine showed me that I wasn't always right, that there were other ways of looking at things, and that others viewed issues differently because of what background they came from. *Christy*

THE INSIDE SCOOP FROM PRIVATE SCHOOL STUDENTS

Public schools get lots of money from the government, so they have better equipment. But at my school, I am able to make more choices and decisions than at a public school. I also don't have to worry about metal detectors, and I never go to school in fear. *Meg*

The smaller school makes it easier to know everyone in the entire class. The public schools have a variety of classes to choose from. *Katie*

Private school students have an advantage over public school students. The teachers are closer to the students here. The teachers could work at a public school for more money, but they don't. That shows they care. Many public schools have more problems than private, such as drugs and violence. I have never *once* seen drugs or physical violence in a private school. My friends at public schools see that every day. *Tanisha*

Private schools have more one-on-one contact with teachers and smaller classes. The curriculum is more challenging and enriching. Uniforms don't exclude those less fortunate—they don't need to buy a lot of clothes. *Amy*

Everyone knows you in a private school and knows your business, and it can sometimes be too conservative. Public schools have better science and math programs. Students are exposed to more situations and aren't sheltered. If they use what they are given, they can have a great education. But in public schools, kids can also slip through the cracks if they don't take advantage of what they are given. *Jamie*

REGISTRATION AND COURSE SELECTION

After you have decided what school you will attend, you can celebrate that a decision has been made. After your celebration, it's time to register. You and your parents will need to be armed with information to make wise choices for your future. The decisions you make will have a lasting effect on the path you choose. You need to ask the following questions:

- What courses are required for graduating?
- What are your plans for after graduation
- Are there courses that can help you explore your future career plans?
- Are you eligible for honors classes?
- Are you prepared academically to take each class?
- What are the prerequisites for each course?
- What does your high school four-year plan look like?

Planning for Your Future

Where do you want to go for training after high school? A four-year college is not the best choice for everyone. Many students attend a two-year community college or a technical school or obtain on-the-job training through an apprenticeship or internship. No matter which direction you take, considering entrance requirements, career interests, and your abilities will allow you to create a high school plan that will meet your current and future needs.

Read books about careers to give yourself an idea of what you want to do after high school. If you decide on a technical school or a community college, find out what schools offer the courses for the career you want. Visit them to get an idea of what the requirements are for admission.

If you know you want to go to college, read about different colleges. If you already know what college you want to attend after high school, you should check with its admission office to find out what the requirements are for a graduating high school senior. You will learn how many years of English,

Learn in high school so you don't have to take remedial courses in college. That will cost you big bucks.

Freshmen: You have a great opportunity to start fresh and build a good reputation in school. Have a "can-do" attitude and enjoy school.

science, math, and foreign language you will need to be admitted to their college. They will also tell you the average ACT/SAT scores of their current freshman class. It is very important that you take this step *before* freshman year, or as soon as possible after that, so that you will know what classes you need to take.

If you're not sure where you want to go to college, find out the requirements for admission of several colleges you might be interested in. Include the state schools or regional schools in your area.

Be flexible in the classes you take. Recognize that any decisions you make about your high school plan can be adjusted each year. If you choose classes that turn out to be too easy or too hard for you, you can make a change the following year. Be sure, however, that you think things through before you make changes. It is always overwhelming to start out at a new school. If your classes seem to be very hard, give them some time—chances are you will be able to make the adjustment to the workload and succeed. You'll just have to raise the bar a few notches. Don't underestimate yourself and give up too easily. It's important to make your high school years as academically challenging as possible so that you will be better prepared for post–high school training. Too many high school students end up having to take remedial English and math courses in college because they did not work hard enough in high school—and college tuition is NOT cheap.

Plan so you can get ahead. With good planning, you can buck the current trend of taking five years to graduate from college. You *can* graduate in four years or less if you take advantage of the advanced courses for college credit offered in your high school. It is smart to plan ahead so that you don't waste time spinning your wheels or going down the wrong path.

ATTENTION, FRESHMEN: ALL HANDS ON DECK

25 Essential Freshman Survival Strategies

You are starting off on a new road that will have a big effect on your future. You know the grades you earn during your high school years will be very important. Are you afraid of the unknown? You bet, but all freshmen get that queasy feeling in their stomachs before they start high school. Some just don't show it as much. Read the following tips for how to have a more stress-free beginning.

1. **Orientation.** If your high school has an orientation session for freshmen, GO. The more familiar you become with your new school, the better.

2. **Visit the school.** When you get your class schedule, ask an older high school student if he or she can take you to school to see where your classes, the bathrooms, and the cafeteria are. This is an important step. Don't wait until the first day, because then you will feel stressed.

3. **Meet your teachers early.** Ask an older student to introduce you to some of your new teachers or go with a younger sister or brother. They always like to do new things. I have met many new freshmen this way while I am preparing my classroom for the start of the new school year. It is fun for me to meet them. Believe it or not, teachers get nervous, too! Sounds crazy, I know, but it's true. So you will be doing yourself and your teachers a favor by breaking the ice before the start of the year.

4. **Review what you studied last year.** If you are continuing in a course such as a foreign language, review your notes from the year before. Then, when the teacher starts reviewing last year's work, you will remember more and give your teacher a favorable impression.

5. **Ask for periodic updates of your grade.** During the first several weeks of freshman year, ask each of your teachers how you're doing. It doesn't hurt to get an update from them. That way, you'll know if you need to do anything differently. Warning: Be sure and ask your teacher when he is NOT teaching. I've had students ask me about their grades in the middle of class, which is not a good idea. You have interrupted and sidetracked the teacher from teaching his class. Use common sense. Put yourself in your teacher's place and see if what you are doing would irritate you. This usually helps you see the right thing to do.

6. **Make a promise to yourself.** If you were a lackadaisical student in junior high, resolve to do better in high school. You're in the big leagues now, heading toward adulthood and living independently of your parents. Time has a way of slipping through your fingers, so make the most of it and do your very best.

7. **Read this book.** If you can, read this book before you start high school and whenever you are having difficulties in any of your classes. There is a lot of

Read your high school's handbook and course guide, even if it is painfully boring. It has lots of important information to help you survive.

information that will help you get through the typical rocky terrain that trips up teenagers. The last two chapters of this book are on college and other ways you can develop a good future. After you have read these chapters, you will know how serious your high school education is for you. You must do your best!

8. **Read the high school handbook and course guide.** Be sure to read your school's handbook from cover to cover. The handbook will tell you about the school's rules, expectations of you, services available, and many other things.

9. **Check graduation requirements.** Find out how many credits you will need to graduate. Have your parents read the handbook and course guide, too, because they will need to be involved in the courses you select. Talk to your school counselor about the decisions you have to make.

    Most schools measure credits in Carnegie units. Simply put, if you take a social studies class for one year and get a passing grade, you receive one credit. If you take a semester course, you receive ½ credit. A passing grade is an A, B, C, or D. If you fail a required class, you must retake it.

10. **Understand the GPA.** Be aware of what the GPA (grade point average) is and how it will affect your future. See the section on how to figure out your GPA in Chapter 5.

11. **Keep track of your own credits.** Remember, you (with the help of your parents) are responsible for making sure you take all of the courses required for gradua- tion. Your counselor will be watching this, too, but occasionally a student will slip through the cracks because a counselor has to take care of so many students. Always be in charge of your own destiny. Don't assume someone else will take care of it for you. If you fail courses, be especially mindful of what you need to do to make up the classes before you graduate.

    IMPORTANT: Be sure your parents get involved in mapping out your four years in high school. They will be able to help you think through many of the decisions you need to make about your future. Remember that you can change your electives (courses that are not required but that you choose to take) whenever you want. But be certain that you get all of your requirements for graduation fulfilled.

    Check out the charts on the following pages. Photocopy these pages and keep updating them for your reference to be sure you fulfill all of the graduation requirements. You don't want to get to your last semester of senior year and find out you still need a half credit to graduate!

12. **Ask lots of questions: You won't know unless you find out.** If you are ever unsure about what classes to take or whether a certain class fulfills a requirement, ask your school counselor. Your counselor knows better than anyone else the classes you need to take. Besides, your counselor will get to know you during your freshman year and will be better prepared to write letters of recommendation for you for admission to college or technical school or for employment. Read the section about counselors in Chapter 5 to find out more about how they can help you.

13. **Keep a firm grip on the steering wheel.** Don't ever just sit there and let things happen to you. Remember, you are driving your own car. Take charge of your own life and don't count on your parents and your counselor to do it for you. In doing so, you will be preparing yourself for the time when you are on your own—in college or out in the workplace.

14. **Typical minimum requirements for graduation.**
    3 credits of English
    3 credits of history/social studies/government
    2 credits of math
    2 credits of science
    1 credit of fine arts
    1 credit of physical education
    1 credit of practical arts
    ½ credit of health

    Note that these are only minimal requirements for high school graduation. Competitive universities may require more credits in English, social studies, math, science, and foreign language for admission.

15. **Lose those labels!** Were you labeled slow or diagnosed with a learning disability in grade school or junior high? Many such students go on to become successful in many careers because they learn how to compensate for what is difficult for them. They use their creativity to find a better way to learn. You can, too. I have seen many people labeled "special" who have the tenacity to learn and do a great job.

16. **Refuse to be typecast.** By working hard, you can do much better than anyone ever gave you credit for. Remember that many successful people in life were not

Don't let someone else decide who you should be—take control!

Requirements Checklist

	Credits Required	9th Grade	10th Grade	11th Grade	12th Grade	# of credits completed
English						
Math						
Science						
Social Studies						
Foreign Language						
Fine Arts						
Practical Arts						
Physical Education						
Electives						

Be sure that all of the classes you take for required credits will be accepted by the school as fulfilling its requirements. If in doubt, ASK.

Freshman Year

Subject	Class Name	Grade Earned	Credits Earned
English			
Math			
Social Studies			
Science			
Foreign Language			
Electives:			

Sophomore Year

Subject	Class Name	Grade Earned	Credits Earned
English			
Math			
Social Studies			
Science			
Foreign Language			
Electives:			

Junior Year

Subject	Class Name	Grade Earned	Credits Earned
English			
Math			
Social Studies			
Science			
Foreign Language			
Electives:			

Senior Year

Subject	Class Name	Grade Earned	Credits Earned
English			
Math			
Social Studies			
Science			
Foreign Language			
Electives:			

straight-A students. You are starting a new life in high school, so now is a good time to change things for yourself. Ask for help when you need it. Ask your teachers to show you how you can do better. And keep going back. Sometimes it is our negative image of ourselves that holds us back. Beware of the phrase, "I can't." It is self-fulfilling. Maybe you didn't do well in grade school. Do you think it's fair that your bad record should follow you to high school and throughout your life? Of course not. Fight back. I know a student whose high school teachers told him he'd never make it in college. It made him so mad that he fought back and graduated with honors. So, know that with heart and determination, you can succeed.

17. **Learn how to play the game.** If you are having trouble with classes, watch what other students are doing. Don't forget: This is like a game, and the better you play, the more points you get. Make it a fun experience and a challenge.

18. **Smile.** Even if you are terrified inside, smile. Other kids are probably feeling the same way you are. They will want to make friends with you because you look approachable. If you frown or look too serious, people may think you don't want to be friends.

19. **Follow your dream.** If you want to do something badly enough, keep your goal in mind so you can realize your dream. If you are determined enough and have the basic potential to succeed, you will. Don't let anyone hold you back by saying that you can't do it. That's nonsense.

20. **Strive for balance in your course load.** Don't attempt too many honors courses at one time. Many students find that two or three are all they can handle. Find one or two fun courses that sound interesting to you and that will not tax you too much, especially if you are feeling a lot of pressure from your difficult classes. Even if you do not take honors courses, it is still important to have a balanced schedule.

21. **If you're bored in school, sign up for harder classes.** I have seen far too many students who are content to get low grades because they just don't care, and I *know* they're a lot smarter than their C and D grades seem to suggest. If you are daydreaming every day, thinking of escaping and skipping classes, challenge yourself. Keeping yourself busy will make you far happier in the long run. Don't take the easy way out.

Attitude is everything. Be positive. Smile.

22. **Take a typing or keyboarding class.** You will need this skill for the rest of your working life and, of course, for college when you have to type umpteen papers. Discard the "hunt and peck" way of typing. You will save yourself lots of hours in the future, and besides, your sister won't have to type all of your papers the way I did when my siblings were in college. Be self-sufficient because you might not always be able to find someone to do your typing for you.

    P.S. Typing is no longer considered a "girl's skill." Men and women are using their keyboarding skills in their jobs every day. It's a lot faster to type what you want to say than to write it out and then have a secretary type it.

23. **Get your required courses out of the way.** Take as many of your required courses as soon as possible—especially English, math, science, and social studies. They will help you do better on the SAT and ACT, especially if you take the more difficult classes. Then, after you have finished taking the relevant classes, you can take your SAT II in different subject areas. This usually happens in your junior and senior years. See Chapter 13 for more information on all of the college entrance exams.

24. **Consider taking junior college courses,** correspondence courses, or summer school enrichment classes for high school students at your local university. If your high school does not offer classes that are rigorous enough, these opportunities can help you stay in competition with students from the more competitive high schools. Maybe a course at the college level will get you pumped about learning.

25. **Enjoy your high school years.** Using this book will help you keep that car on the road. You won't be pulled over by your teachers because you will be doing things the right way and the easy way. Have fun.

TRY THIS!

Throughout this book, you will be given ideas that can help you learn new behaviors for doing well in school. Note: These are *not* homework assignments. They are merely included to give you practice. Try those that interest you. After each suggested experiment, share what you learned with a friend or a parent or write about it in a journal. Remember that the work you do while using this book will help you in your future classwork and interpersonal relationships.

Don't get to your senior year and say, "If only I had . . ."

1. **Write down all of the fears you have about being in high school.** What are the things you are most afraid of? Is it being with the older students? Is it because you've had trouble with certain subjects? Is it because you are about to venture into an unknown world? Brainstorm with your parents and friends about ways you can conquer these fears. Maybe you will find you just need to relax and be more confident. Maybe you will see that you could work a little harder and do your homework. Put your solutions into action on your first day of school. Write these things down and think of them often. High school can—and should—be fun. Make it work for *you*.

2. **Brainstorm about the things you need to do to make yourself feel comfortable and confident on the first day of school.** Do you need to get some new clothes? Do you want to be different in high school? Keep a record of all of your ideas. Many students have found it helpful to write down the things that concern them in a journal. Try it. It's lots of fun to go back when you're a senior and read what you wrote in your freshman year. You will be pleased to see what giant steps you have taken to learn and succeed.

THE INSIDE SCOOP FROM SENIORS

Author's Note: I have talked to many of my former students who are now high school seniors about what advice they would give incoming freshmen. They have made a lot of mistakes they would like you to avoid. Listen to them talk about what they wish they had known when they were freshmen.

I wish I had started studying during freshman year. I mostly goofed off and didn't do any work unless I had to. My parents were always mad at me, and my grades were terrible. I wasted too much time, and now I find myself in a situation where the only school I can attend is a junior college. I blew it. *Pete*

My first years were spent raising hell in classes. I never listened to my teachers. I thought they were all boring. I just didn't care. "Who needs high school?" I thought. Not me, that's for sure. Well, here I am now wishing I hadn't been so stupid. I wish I could start all over again with what I know now. *Steve*

When I was a freshman, I wanted to act and dress like everyone else. I was afraid to be me. Now I know that I don't have to please others. Now I ask myself what *I* want to wear and who *I* am. I am happier than ever now that I'm a senior and ready to graduate. Thank God I already passed through that phase. It wasn't fun.
Jessica

MATH ANXIETY

Nothing is more supercharged with anxiety in a typical student's mind than problems with math. There are many things you can do to combat your anxiety. Attitude is everything. Do you walk into a math class at the beginning of the school year thinking, "I'm going to fail this class"? Lots of kids do. It's a self-fulfilling prophecy. You help make this failure come true when you think those thoughts. Read on for some of the ways you can confront this demon, get it off your back, and hurl it into outer space.

Mental Strategies for Conquering Math Anxiety

Start off each math class with a positive attitude. Having a negative attitude will get you off on the wrong foot. One year I was having a terrible time in a math class and would sit at my desk for hours saying, "I can't do this." Well, that was true. When I gave myself that message, I became paralyzed and couldn't do anything. You could have called me "Julianne, the deer caught in headlights." One night, feeling very frustrated with myself because I knew I was no dummy, I got mad and said, "You CAN do this. Wake up and get moving!" Once I finally settled down and gave myself permission to be able to "get it," I was able to do much better and actually enjoyed the math course.

Let the information sink in. When you are calm and not stressing out, you will be able to do much better.

Try some relaxation techniques. See Chapter 7 on stress for some ideas. Learning to relax will help you focus on what your job is—to understand the stuff you need to learn.

Act as if you like math. Sometimes, if we act as if we like something, we end up acutally liking it. I've tried this many times in my life when I've had to do something painful or unpleasant. Try it. Along with your positive, relaxed attitude, you will be much better positioned to get on the right track.

Go crazy. What? Yes, I mean it. Turn on some loud music and dance your heart out. "What's the catch?" you ask. While you're dancing, scream your lungs out singing the tune to get yourself psychologically prepared to learn your math. Or, you could jog around the block to get psyched to do your homework. Scream a little while you run or just pretend to scream and don't let the sound come out. You've heard of silent screams, haven't you?

Okay, okay, what if you're a guy or girl who NEVER dances? Well, simple. Lock the bedroom door and go for it. No witnesses, no one will ever know. It's a great feeling to let yourself be free and dance. Try it.

Practical Tips to Better Understand Math Class

Do all the homework exercises that your teacher assigns you. Get a jump on your homework that same day, before you forget what you learned. I used to delay doing my math homework as long as I could. Then, when I would look at the problems and formulas, I would go blank and not remember a thing. Remember that practice is the key to mastering each math concept. Practice, practice, practice—and do it NOW. Oh, one more thing: If the answers are in the back of the book, wait until you have finished your work before you look at them. Then, go back and check. You will never learn if you look at the answers first.

Run, don't walk, to get help from your teacher. The first time you see you're having trouble, ask for help. If you wait a month or longer, you will be helplessly lost.

Take good notes in class. Write down the examples the teacher uses. Take lots of notes. Don't just sit there, assuming you'll remember it all later. And don't forget that you will have several other classes that day—telling yourself you will remember everything you learned without writing anything down is a fantasy. Plus, the class will go faster if you take notes because you will be more involved in the learning process.

Try to never miss a math class. When you are sick and miss one or two classes in a row, you will probably come back feeling lost. The best defense is a good offense. Make attending math class a priority. With all of the energy you can summon, go to class for help. See your teacher for help. Ask other kids in the class for help.

P.S. Two girls were once absent from one of my classes for more than a week. They came after school for help and in ten minutes I went through the *entire* chapter. They listened to me carefully while I explained everything and they understood it all. The girls were grateful for my help, and I was glad they could grasp it so fast. When students are truly focused on their job, they can do anything. Focus and the desire to

Before you ask for help, make sure you've done your homework. Will your textbook provide you with the answers you need?

Remember, math is like a foreign language—you won't understand until your teacher shows you how to unlock its secrets.

survive and thrive are a powerful team that can fight any problems you have in a class. Cultivate that desire—it will be a good friend in math class and any other classes that are tough for you.

Practice each type of problem many times until you nail the concept. Stay with that type of problem until you understand it. Repetition in math homework is very beneficial, because you get into the habit of doing the problems correctly. The little bit of extra time it takes you to work out the problem will be well worth it when test-time comes. Always keep your goal in mind when you are doing your work. Make it fun. See how fast you can do each problem, and do it *accurately.* At first, you will go slowly, but as you understand the concept and how to put it into action, you will be able to do it faster and faster.

Refresh your memory. Every once in a while, go back over the previous chapters' tests. If you're not doing some of these problems every day, you might forget them. Go back and review the information. You'll be in better shape for learning new concepts and for final exams.

Read over the next chapter in your book so that you know what is going to be covered. You will have an advantage because you will have some familiarity with the terminology and what you need to know. If your teacher jumps around in the book, ask what chapter you will be studying next. Your teacher is going to be impressed with you and will want to help you even more. It's a win-win situation. Be aggressive in your quest for success.

Help a classmate. When you see someone else is struggling with the stuff you're learning, try to help. If you can explain it as if you were the teacher, you will be ready to take the test and do well. I used to tutor some classmates in Latin. Because I was teaching it to them, I had the responsibility to know what I was doing and was better prepared when it came time to take tests.

Don't try to memorize a math formula until you understand the concept. The formula will mean absolutely nothing to you until you understand why you're doing it that way. Then, memorizing the formula will be a snap because you'll already know it. Realizing that math is a foreign language helps. The more you practice a language, the better you'll be able to use it.

Oh No, It's Test Time!

First of all, be positive. When you have a can-do attitude, you'll perform much better.

Write the formulas being tested in the margin of your test as soon as your teacher gives it to you.

Prepare for your test several days in advance. If you practice the type of problems that will be on the exam every day, you will be much more comfortable when test time comes.

Pace yourself on the exam. Look over the entire exam and see what you have to do. Then, start to work steadily on the problems. Keep track of your time. Do the easiest problems first, and then move on to the harder ones until you get the job done.

Go over your test with a fine-tooth comb. A lot of students get math problems wrong because they do not proofread. Double-check your answers. Do you have any "careless" errors? Did you reverse any numbers? Did you write down the right stuff? Are your figures written carefully and neatly?

Ignore the hot-doggers. Those kids who whip through the test and hand it in before you've even warmed up often don't do so well. They may look good, but they have a far better chance of making careless errors. Don't let them fluster you. Use all of the test time you are given. Do not rush. Remember, slow and steady wins the race.

Stay away from nervous students before the test. You want to be calm and focused. Panicked students can upset you.

Trust that you have done what you needed to do. Good luck, but if you have prepared yourself well, you won't need luck. You'll do great.

Watch out for careless mistakes. Check your work every time.

TRY THIS!

1. **If you suffer from math anxiety, keep a journal record of each day in class.** If you had trouble understanding the material, what did you do about it? Did you ask another student for help? Did you see the teacher? Keep a running account of what is going on in math class. Read what you wrote once a week. If you see that you haven't done anything to cure your math anxiety, get busy making things happen. Don't sit there frustrated and say, "What's the use?" Fight back.

2. **In your journal, be sure and write about your successes.** Remember that success tends to bring more success. Once you get on a roll, you can keep going. Be active in your own education.

ATTENDANCE

Your high school attendance record can help you if you go to classes. It can haunt you if you don't. Check out the following reasons why your attendance in class is so important.

A good attendance record shows your general attitude toward life. It is evidence that you're doing what you need to and are supposed to do—that is, you accept your responsibility to be present at school as if it were a job.

If you stay home because you just don't feel like going to school, you will have trouble with your grades. You will be hassled by your administrator, parents, and teachers. The reality is that your lot in life will be a tough one if you don't go to class.

Your attendance record will follow you to your next job. Employers will want to see your attendance patterns. If they see that you do not show up regularly for school, chances are they will not hire you. They view this as a pattern that will show up in other areas of your life as well.

If you're not in class, you won't learn. You won't hear your teacher's explanations of the subject matter. You'll be behind in your homework and tests. The longer you skip classes, the more hopeless you will feel about being able to pass.

School attendance policies are there for a reason. Schools know that you won't learn unless you're in class. Don't waste your time hating the policies. Accept what you can't change and realize that those policies are in effect because they're what's best for you.

Even if you hate a particular teacher, still go to the class. Skipping class to spite a teacher only hurts you. Look at the section on how to deal with teachers to get an idea of how you can handle the problem.

Poor attendance can keep you from participating in special programs such as co-op classes where you go to school half the day and to work the other half. The teacher in charge of the program will be afraid to take a chance on you and will only want students who are reliable. Your poor attendance record brands you as unreliable in the teacher's mind.

What to do when you really are sick. If you have been sick for a long time, it will be next to impossible to make up all of the work you missed for six or seven classes. Talk to your teachers about how you can catch up. Ask your counselor to intervene for you. Counselors can ask your teachers if it would be possible to have you do only the most important things to make up your work.

Here's the bottom line: Attend classes, learn, get your credits, and get on with your life.

Enjoy being an independent learner. The buck stops with you.

HELP FOR HOME SCHOOLERS

Most of what is included in this book will be helpful even to those students who get their schooling at home. Check out the following additional tips for things that will help make your high school years happy ones.

Because you will not be at school, you will have to work harder to make friends. Join a youth group or an athletic team so that you will be with people of your own age. You will be more likely to enjoy your home schooling when you do this. Friends are very important to you and will help you learn how to develop relationships.

Keep close track of dates for taking the PSAT, the SAT, and the ACT. You will need to take one or all of these exams to get into college. Read the last two chapters of this book on colleges and other careers. Check out Chapter 13 for detailed information on the exams themselves and books you can buy to practice for them.

In addition to your regular schoolwork, read, read, read. The more you read, the more likely you will do well on the college admissions exams and in college.

Practice writing every day. Start a journal. You can write about more than just what you do every day. Write about your concerns, about your philosophical views, and about anything you can think of that will help you choose your future direction in life. Make a resolve to study in depth the world in which you live.

School districts often do not accept credit for work done at home. Be sure you are committed to completing your high school years at home because you risk the danger of not getting any credit for the work you have already done. This is a big decision for you and your parents. You must weigh all of the consequences before you start.

SHORTCUT TO ACTION

1. Plan out your schedule for all four years of high school. Get your parents to help you.
2. Mentally prepare yourself for high school *before you start.*
3. Make a decision to do your best work, and work to your potential.
4. Know your high school handbook.
5. Your grades in freshman year *are* important. They affect your future.
6. Have a positive attitude in all you do.
7. Practice, practice, practice your math problems.
8. Go to every class. If you're not in class, you won't learn.
9. Do *all* of your homework. Homework points are easy points to get and help your grade.
10. Start preparing for your tests in advance. Then, you'll know what you don't know and can get help long before the exam.
11. Get help from your teachers when you need it.
12. Pay attention in class. It pays off.

CHAPTER 2

How to Get Along with Teachers

I can just hear you groaning and saying, "You want me to work on getting along with teachers?" You bet—it's a critical part of surviving and thriving in high school. How you handle yourself in the classroom determines how well you do in your classes. You will understand the many reasons for this after you have read this chapter.

Before we get down to the nitty-gritty of getting along with teachers, remember this phrase: **You can catch more flies with honey than you can with vinegar.** Yes, you know honey is sweet and vinegar is sour, and maybe you've heard your grandmother or father say this, but what does it mean? Simply put, if you treat others, including teachers, kindly, they will treat you kindly in return. I like all of my students, but I am more comfortable with the students who are pleasant to me than with the students who are always ragging on me. I will go out of my way to help the pleasant student, but I will be less inclined to "go the extra mile" with the kid who complains all of the time and generally has a bad attitude.

Because this book will help you see how best to get through high school, I will be totally honest with you in order to give you the "real story." Put yourself in the teacher's place. Look around your classroom at different students. Would you rather teach someone who's sarcastic and unreceptive or someone who is friendly and interested? Just remember, the teacher's job isn't any easier than yours. Yes, you have to take the exams, but we have to create them and grade them. That is not fun. For me, it's the most boring part of teaching, but it's also a means to an end. It's what I have to do to help you learn all you can. Generally speaking, teachers care about you and want you to have an enjoyable learning experience and get the most out of your classes. Your success is our reward for teaching you and caring about you.

IMPORTANT: Avoid "kissing up" to a teacher at all costs. Your classmates will razz you mercilessly and your teacher will feel that you are simply being nice to get a good grade and may feel manipulated. Be an honorable person and do the right thing for the *right* reason. Come to school to learn, to become a better person, and to work with your teachers.

I thought I would begin by telling you the things teachers hate to hear from kids and why, so that you can see things from our viewpoint. Even though we are on different sides of the fence, we need to break it down so we can thrive together. It's always a good idea to step into someone else's shoes to see how he or she feels. It helps everyone get along better. And yes, teachers need to understand how students feel, too!

"No, you're not in my personal jail. This is my wonderful classroom!"

DON'T SAY THESE THINGS TO TEACHERS

''Are we doing anything important in class today?''

Look at what you are really saying to the teacher: that the teacher doesn't do anything worthwhile in class. I know, I can hear you protesting, "But that's true, they don't." Sometimes students don't understand why we're doing a certain activity, and so they just assume it's a waste of time. In my own experience, I have had good reasons for almost all of the things I have done and said in the classroom. Yes, I admit that occasionally I veer off the subject and waste a few minutes here and there, but not often. The best thing you can do is trust your teachers and believe that they must have good reasons for the things they do. Sometimes you simply have to go along because the teacher is running the show.

If you feel a teacher is goofing off and that you are not learning the subject, ask *politely* why you are doing a certain activity—and please, please, please keep the "you are really a dumb idiot" tone out of your voice. You might be surprised. Your teacher might have a really good reason—maybe it will help you be more focused in the class. You can at least ask, but one word of advice: It is always better to ask a teacher this kind of question after class because it can be very disruptive during class. Also, ask the question without prejudging the teacher. If you don't find the answer satisfactory, talk to another student you respect who does well in the class—maybe that student can help you see what you're missing. And if no one seems to understand the teacher's approach, you may want to talk to your counselor.

''When do we get out of here?''

Now, come on, kids. You're treating your teacher like she's a jailer. I know you often feel that way, especially when you're sitting all day in six or seven classes. If I were in your shoes, I would think the same thing because it *is* hard, but it's better not to say so out loud. Whenever I have to go to all-day workshops, I am ready to jump out of my skin after six hours. So I always understand how my students feel. Remember what I said earlier about honey and vinegar and try to get interested in the class. It will go faster. It's also better not to watch the clock. That will kill you every time. The monotony of the tick-tock, tick-tock, tick-tock will send you over the edge. My advice to you: If a teacher's going over something for the millionth time and you understand it, you could start preparing your battle strategy to study for the next test. I am not telling you to zone out and go to sleep. Be sure you "come back" after the teacher is done with the explanation, or you might miss something important.

"We had homework last night?"

Don't ever advertise your deficiencies out loud in front of your teachers. Quietly ask a student who is already sitting down if there was any homework. If you find out you forgot to do it, sit down immediately and start it. Sometimes you can even get it done before the bell rings or while the teacher is taking attendance, but at least you'll have something to hand in. Sometimes the teacher doesn't even collect the homework. If he's going over it orally in class and it is your turn, don't say, "I didn't do it." That will irritate the teacher. I have a lot more respect for a student who, even when he realizes that he forgot to do the homework, still tries to answer the question. Learn how to fly by the seat of your pants.

"Can I go to the bathroom?"

My nephew told me that he always asked if he could go to the bathroom when he really wanted to walk around the school and see his friends. A teacher doesn't mind if you ask him maybe once or twice a semester, but some kids do it almost every day, which interrupts the class. You are no longer in grade school. You know how to control your bladder. And if you carry the books for several of your classes with you so that you don't have to go to your locker, you'll have more time to use the bathroom in between class periods. Having said all of this, if you need to use a bathroom at unexpected times because of a medical problem, be sure and tell your teacher *before* class so that he will understand.

"Can we go to lunch early?"

The one and only time I gave permission to my students to go to lunch early, the principal came marching a whole line of them back, telling me the third lunch period had not started yet. So, don't ask if you can go early, because teachers don't want to be embarrassed like that. Is it fair that we should get in trouble because our students are hungry and want to beat everyone else to the lunch line? By the way, did you eat breakfast today?

Guess what? Your teacher probably wants to go to lunch as much as you do.

"I hate this class/I hate math."

WRONG—bad move. Your teacher went into the field because she actually likes math. Yes, I know that sounds really weird to you, but it's a fact. This can be taken as a personal insult. One time I had a student storm out of my class saying, "I hate this class, and I hate this school." I chose to ignore him, but some senior girls asked me if I had heard him. I said that I had, but that we were going to have him loving the class by the end of the year. I was glad I didn't get angry with him, because he eventually came around, actually had a good time, and learned a lot.

"Will this count on our grade?"

Oh, how I hate this! No teacher wants his subject reduced solely to a calculator and points. Grades are important, but they should not be the *only* reason why you are in a classroom—you should enjoy learning, too. Your life will be more enjoyable and less stressful with that kind of positive attitude.

THE SCOOP ON TEACHERS

Yes, teachers can seem really bizarre. We can have our distracting peculiarities. Does one teacher scratch his mosquito bites with unabashed passion? Do you wonder why he didn't put insect repellent on *before* he hiked in the woods? Does another teacher clear her throat and then *swallow* it? Try to remember that teachers are only human and what we do is magnified because it's in front of 25 to 30 teenagers who look at us as if we were insects under a microscope. Sometimes I feel I should call myself "teacher species (also known as) bug under glass." Once, while I was writing on the board, I heard a girl say, "Ms. Dueber, I can see your panty line." I nearly dropped my chalk, I was so embarrassed. What does a teacher say to a comment like that? I was rendered speechless. She was a nice kid, so I gave

Every teacher has a long list of embarrassing things that have happened, as have you. So, give your teachers a break.

her the benefit of the doubt—she was just one of those people who blurts out her thoughts.

Another time my zipper broke (in front, no less) and I didn't realize it for a long time. A sweet girl came up and whispered in my ear, "Your zipper is broken." I spent the rest of the class with a folder in front of me and had to go to the ladies' room between classes to sew up my pants so that I could finish the rest of the day. The kids loved it, but I was embarrassed. And just like you, teachers don't like to be embarrassed.

IMPORTANT: Please read this cautionary information carefully. If you have a teacher you absolutely hate because he embarrasses you or because you just can't stand his personality, don't shoot yourself in the foot by doing poorly in the class. I have heard too many students describe how they can't stand a teacher and then proceed to fail the class because they won't do the work. I always ask them, "Are you actually getting even with the teacher, or are you only hurting yourself?" The teacher will move on next year to new classes of students, but you'll have to live with the grade you get. Learn how to tolerate the teacher, and remember that he's a human being, too, with his own set of problems. We all need to accept each other and take care of ourselves by doing what's best for us. Failing a class is not the answer. It's a crazy way out and doesn't make any sense.

TIPS FOR MAKING YOUR TEACHER'S DAY

You may be saying, "Why on earth would I want to make a teacher's day?" Well, the truth is that a happy teacher is a heck of a lot easier to deal with than an angry or isolated teacher. Treat teachers as people and you will see a big difference in their attitude. Try out some of these techniques to see if you can "soften up" your teachers.

Say "Good morning," "Good afternoon," or "Hi" every day when you walk in to class. Teachers like that. It makes us feel like we're important in your life and not invisible human beings.

Take an interest in your teacher as a person. On Monday morning, ask your teacher if he had a good weekend or a nice vacation. If you're lucky, he'll say yes and you won't have to hear a tale of woe.

Listen to your teacher's full explanation before you ask her questions.

Repeat every day, "My teacher is a human being," before you enter each class.

Most importantly of all: Do your work. Nothing is more frustrating to a teacher than to knock herself out teaching only to have you not do your job.

Okay, now I know there are some mean teachers out there. I had my share when I was in school and know you aren't lying when you say that some teachers are difficult. Some teachers are very hard to get along with, but just try the five things I recommended above. You might be surprised. Be the kind of person who treats others as you want to be treated. It's a good thing to practice in all of your relationships with others—parents, bosses, friends, school administrators, and strangers on the street—no matter how they act toward you.

Just remember, your teacher is a PERSON. This will help you get along with her better. Talk to her—you might find out she's really very nice.

WHEN YOU FEEL A TEACHER IS ABUSIVE

When you feel a teacher is treating you unfairly and you are emotionally traumatized as a result, follow these steps *in order.*

Try the five tips for getting along with teachers that I just gave you. In most cases, this should do the trick.

If that doesn't work, first talk to the teacher after class. Tell him how he makes you feel. Be careful of your tone of voice. Be as unemotional as possible and stick to the facts when you talk to him. Often, a teacher will better understand what you are trying to say if you speak in a nonthreatening way. Don't start out saying something like, "You treat me like garbage, and I hate this class." Instead, try, "I feel that you dislike me, and I'd like to talk about it." Tell your teacher how you feel about what is happening to you in class. Are you willing to listen to what he has to say, also? Be open-minded when you hear his version of the situation. Be strong, stick to your purpose, and hopefully the two of you will be able to resolve your problems with this step.

Talk to your parents and your counselor about your situation. You have probably already spoken to your parents and gotten some good advice on your predicament. Now is the time to ask them to help you resolve the situation. They can ask to set up a conference between themselves, your counselor, the teacher, and the principal. It is best to try to remain in the class if you can stand it—otherwise, your entire class schedule may have to be changed. If you already like five out of six of your teachers, you may not want to give them up to get out of the one class. You will have to weigh the pros and cons of each option before you make a final decision. Do it carefully, because it's an important one.

Hey, sometimes it just takes a little creativity to figure out how you're going to play the school game. Use your imagination to do the job.

A SAD NOTE

If you look at the dedication page of the book, you will note that this book is dedicated to my high school Latin teacher, Rosemary Lough, who died just as I was starting to write this book. She had a profound impact on my life, but I never went back to tell her what she meant to me. My excuse was that she had changed schools and I didn't know where she was. Learn from my mistake and go back and thank those special teachers who meant a lot to you when you have been out of high school for several years.

Mrs. Lough was my favorite teacher, because she had a great sense of humor, was an excellent teacher, and had a flair for drama. One day in May, my entire class was feeling frisky and changed rooms to try to trick her. We were laughing at our joke, congratulating ourselves on being so funny when we heard her loud, booming laugh. She had been looking at us through an open window and we didn't realize it. She knew how to enjoy life. She taught me that school could be interesting and fun.

TRY THIS!

1. **Study your least favorite teacher for a week.** Watch what she does during the class. Try to figure out why she acts like she does. See if you can look at the situation from her point of view.
2. **Try saying "good morning" and "good afternoon" to all of your teachers for a week.** Exchange some casual conversation with them about the weather, the local sports team, or about something that is happening in school. Did it make a difference in your relationship? Share your discoveries with a friend.
3. **When a teacher is obviously angry when you walk into class, say something nice to him and see if it gets him out of his bad mood.**

SHORTCUT TO ACTION

1. Be nice to your teachers. You will do better.
2. Learn to ignore your teachers' weird habits and mannerisms.
3. Do your work. Teachers get tired of students not doing what they're supposed to. **Play the game!**
4. Pay attention in class.
5. When you have trouble with a teacher, talk to him first—when you are both calm. Best time: after school when neither of you has to go to class.
6. If you keep having trouble with a teacher, see your counselor for help.
7. Think of creative ways to like your teacher.
8. Forget about how much you hate a teacher. You don't like all of the students in your school, either, do you?

CHAPTER 3

Who Me—Successful in School?

This first section of the book contains most of the down-and-dirty tips on how to do better in high school. For many of you, just hearing the word *school* makes you groan or get depressed. You often have a feeling of impending doom and a fear of failure. This book is meant primarily for you, because I believe that you *can* learn if you give yourself a chance. I have wracked my brain to try to come up with ways to help unmotivated students. I finally decided to write this book because I could not bear seeing you feel so miserable. I will tell you about ways to make your education interesting and fun. Yes, it will be hard work. But it will also be satisfying, and you will feel a great sense of achievement for work well done.

Ask yourself the following questions to see if you are doing the best you can in school.

1. Do I listen to the teacher in class at all times?
2. Do I take notes while she talks?
3. Do I copy things she writes on the board?
4. Do I do the homework?
5. Do I study for quizzes and exams?
6. Do I not only ask the teacher for after-school help but also show up?

If you can answer *truthfully* that you do all of the above things but you still get D's and F's, no wonder you're discouraged. Don't give up, though. There are many things you can do to perform better and to get better grades, so read this book with an open mind. Be willing to try the suggestions and remember that you won't have overnight success. Gradually, you will experience an improvement as you put these suggestions into practice.

Why Bother?

Because you want to feel successful. Come on, admit it, aren't you tired of seeing certain classmates always get that A? Wouldn't you like to think of yourself as an A student instead of a D or F student? Of course you would. But the very act of admitting this desire means that you will then have to do something about it. I guess you noticed that I didn't mention C's. I didn't, because C stands for average. My goal is for you to do better than that. Don't be satisfied with C's unless you have done your very best. C's might be enough to keep your parents off your back, but don't get mired in mediocrity—always strive to do your best.

Because you want to get a decent job in the future so that you can have a comfortable life. If you don't work hard now, in later years you won't be able to afford that new car, take that exciting vacation, buy your favorite CDs, or help a worthy charitable cause that you feel passionate about. Instead, you will find yourself worrying about whether you can pay the electric bill before your power gets shut off.

GETTING MOTIVATED

Answer the following questions to discover why you cannot motivate yourself to do your schoolwork.

Do you have any specific action plan for what you want and need to do in school and in your life afterwards? Many teenagers do not have goals or a plan of action for their future. The *Goal Getter* section, which comes a bit later, will give you some tips on how to acheive more direction in your life.

Do you have good study habits? Read the *Study Skills* section to find out whether you are studying correctly and to get tips on how you can do better.

Are you lazy? Be honest when you answer this question, because it will make a big difference for your future. I believe that many kids who do not do well in school aren't really trying. They think there is too much work when, in reality, it's not all that hard. If you feel like I'm being harsh, I'm not. I simply want to get your attention. Many teenagers who do poorly need a wake-up call.

Do you take personal responsibility for the work you produce, or do you blame your mother, father, or teacher? It is important to remember that *you* are the one taking the tests and getting the grades, not your parents or the teacher.

Are you working too many hours at a part-time job so that when you get home you're too tired to study? I've had many students with this problem. I feel sorry for them because they are either in school, at work, or sleeping. They don't have time for anything else—including study. It may be time to

"Motivation toward school work is tough for us teenagers to maintain these days. There are so many social activities that it becomes easy to blow off school."

—Dan

Hey, Joe, is that you snoozing back there? Are we making too much noise for you?

change your life and work fewer hours, if you have the luxury. Your peace of mind should be more important to you than buying a car or new CDs.

Are you overextended in extracurricular activities? Are you on the student council, the track team, and in the band, too? Participation in all of these activities is lots of fun, but juggling all of them may unfortunately leave you no time to do your schoolwork or have downtime to relax. You may need to omit one or two activities. Both school and extracurricular activities are very important, so find your comfort zone; then you will be able to have balance in your life.

Do you participate in school activities? Many students simply go to school and leave right after, missing out on all of the opportunities for interacting with friends and becoming a member of the school community. I have seen students get involved in an extracurricular activity and witnessed their grades go up because they become more interested in school life in general. They are **awake.** You may be saying that there isn't a club that is devoted to your interests. If that's the case, then you can be the motivator for bringing a new club to your high school. Not everyone has the same interests, but if you have a special interest, talk to other students to get them to participate with you. It only takes two or three kids to start a club.

CLASSROOM SKILLS

It is important to know how to handle yourself in the classroom. Check out the following tips.

Listen carefully in class while the teacher is teaching. Analyze where he is going and why. Tune out any kids passing notes or acting goofy. Remember what your job is and do not be distracted. Above all, don't be the class clown who is creating the distraction! That will get you nowhere, except maybe the principal's office.

Copy the teacher's notes correctly from the board. Many times I've looked at students' notes and found that they did not correctly copy what I had written. If you have a speedy teacher who erases the board before you have a chance to copy the information down, ask her politely to slow down. And what about the teacher who is standing in the way while you're trying to get it all down? You can't tell her to get out of the way, but you could nicely tell her she is blocking your view. My students are always asking me to move out of the way. I know not to take it personally.

As soon as you can, go over what the teacher taught in class before you forget it. I know. After school you want to go out with your buddies to a fast food joint. Going over your notes is the last thing you want to do. Well, how about going over them at the end of the class when the teacher is taking care of permission slips and absence notices or during the first few minutes of the next class while the teacher is taking attendance?

Read your notes from class daily to see if you got all of the information. Supplement what you didn't get by consulting your textbook, another student, or asking your teacher right after class. There is an old saying, "A stitch in time saves nine." That means that if you cover all of the bases *now* instead of waiting until later, your life won't begin to unravel with the impossible amount of work you have to do.

Stay up to date on your classwork. When a teacher tells you to read a chapter for tomorrow, do it that very day so you don't get behind. If you put off doing your work, you will pay later by having too much material to learn for your test. Being caught up will make you successful. Getting behind will cause you great stress and may even cause you to get a D or an F. How can you get yourself pumped up, you ask? Try this: Imagine yourself in a footrace with the other students. Why not do yourself a favor and become the leader of the pack? It's much more fun to be ahead of the crowd than to try to catch up.

Write down your homework assignments every day in a special assignment book, with the date they are due. Date every day and scratch off each assignment when you complete it. It will give you a good feeling of accomplishment when you can scratch each one off. Why not do something radical to celebrate? How about playing a tune on your trumpet or singing a joyful song outside? Have fun.

Be friendly and courteous with your teacher. First of all, he is giving you your grade. If you are on the borderline between a B and a C, he is much more likely to boost you up if you are a considerate, courteous student who does the work. In addition, when you apply for admission to universities, to a tech school, or for a job, you may choose to ask him to write you a letter of recommendation. He may also be asked to recommend you for the cheerleading squad, the National Honor Society, or a special opportunity the following year. You want him on your side. Do not burn your bridges with any teacher.

When your teacher goes over a test that you just bombed, listen to the right answers. Ask yourself why you missed

Wake up! You'll never do any better if you don't pay attention to what is happening in class.

what you did. Did you study the wrong thing? Did you study the wrong way? Did you waste a lot of time preparing for something that wasn't on the test? In all of my years of teaching, I've seen many of the students who need to listen the most see their D or F grade, put their paper down, and start doing something else. They are the very ones who need to be listening. Wake up. You will never do any better if you don't pay attention to what is happening in class. Also, when you learn from your mistakes, you won't make them again.

STUDY SKILLS

Check out the following skills that will help you do a better job studying. Try making changes in how, where, and when you study until you find the right combination for *you*.

Find a quiet place in your house that is your very own. Create a nest where you can do your work most successfully—without interruption. Have good lighting and a work table or desk on which to write. Your special place will help you get the job done faster so that you will have more free time.

Study at your best time of day. Mine was always at night after my younger sisters and brothers went to bed. You might be most alert early in the morning. Find out when you are most alert and efficient in order to make the best use of your time.

Be a well-disciplined person. If you are extremely disciplined, you will be able to rest first, play basketball, take a nap, play with your dog, take a walk or whatever you like to do, and then do your homework. However, if you have a hard time getting started on your homework, do it as soon as you get home from school. Then you will have the rest of the evening to relax and do what you want.

Take responsibility for your own performance. When you tell yourself "I have to do this," you can put the need to work your hardest on your own shoulders, where it belongs. When you start to be in charge of your own education, instead of giving that job to your parents and your teachers, you will feel like a million dollars. Think of this as your way of gaining some independence from your parents. You are a capable person who does not need your parents and teachers to push you to do well. When they see that you are doing it on your own, they'll get off your back. Once you see how powerful and great this makes you feel, you'll do it in other areas of your life as well.

Pick your easiest assignment and do it first. This technique will help you if you have a hard time beginning your homework. Then you will be on a roll and emotionally able to take on the hard assignments. Okay, now that I've said that, you might be the kind of person who wants to do the exact opposite because you want to save your "dessert" for last—the easiest, sweetest part of your homework. That's okay also—you know what you need to do.

Analyze each homework assignment before you start your homework. Look over the entire task and figure out how it fits in with what your teacher taught you that day. Ask yourself what you are supposed to be practicing and learning. That's the reason teachers give you homework—to give you the practice you need to learn the material. I have seen students begin a homework assignment at the end of class by starting to fill in blanks without giving any thought to what they are doing. Step back from the assignment. See how it fits in with everything else you've learned so far in the class this year. By looking at the big picture, you will have a jump on preparing for your test and final exam.

Analyze where you are having problems in a class and concentrate on what you can do about it. Sometimes it's just a matter of stepping back to figure out what the problem is. Here are some possible reasons you might be doing poorly in a class:

- **Maybe you hate foreign languages** and are having a hard time studying your Spanish. There's so much to memorize and the verbs are driving you crazy. Find a way to get excited about learning it (or any other subject). Maybe you would like to take a trip to Mexico someday, so just imagine yourself being able to speak the language. Keep that thought in mind in class. It's a real thrill to be able to understand and communicate in a foreign language. Try it. You'll see it's fun.
- **You hate the teacher.** As I said in the section on getting along with teachers, you must let this one go and do your work. Don't hurt yourself. You're not going to like every teacher, just as you don't like every student. Get used to it. That's life.
- **You can see no reason for studying a subject such as geometry.** You may be saying, "When will I ever use it? It's a waste of my time." Geometry was my biggest nemesis in high school. I couldn't understand why I was studying it. On a beautiful May day, my teacher was describing how to prove a theorem as a bunch of us girls were looking out the window at some guys who were walking by. She saw us gazing longingly out the window and told us we were looking at the wrong

Complete your studying right away so you can RELAX. Most students procrastinate. Get your friends on the same schedule; that way you can hang out together after you've finished your work for school.

You'll hate school less when you start to succeed in your classes. It starts little by little. Don't give up. It's never too late to get back on track. Ya gotta believe, Baby.

angle. That was a funny moment in an otherwise tough class. And when I finally understood what I was supposed to be doing and how I could apply it to my own life, I felt proud about the grades I was finally able to achieve.

I can tell you one thing about my high school years: My hardest classes, where I had to really knock myself out to survive, were the ones that I remember the most. Ironically, the easy classes offered me no challenges and are just a blur in my memory. I learned the most in the tough classes with the hard teachers.

- **You truly have a difficult time reading.** If you find out in your junior year of high school that you are reading on a fourth grade level, of course you are going to be discouraged and humiliated. It takes guts to admit you have a problem, but you need to run, not walk, to your English teacher to ask him how you can get some extra help. If you are assertive and show teachers how much you care, they will make sure you get the help you need.

- **You're having trouble at home.** Maybe your parents are in the midst of divorce proceedings. But flunking your classes is not going to help. You might think that you are getting back at them for breaking up your family, or you may truly be depressed about the situation, but you really need to take good care of yourself—now more than ever. Your school counselor can suggest things you can do to help yourself, or you might talk to a teacher you like a lot. Sometimes just talking about how you feel helps. I am always glad when a student tells me what's going on in his life; then I am better able to help him with his problem. It's a win-win situation for everyone involved. The student feels better about his life and doesn't feel so alone, and the teacher gets him back on track so she can do her job.

- **You're having problems with a friend.** I have seen this many times in my years of teaching. It takes many forms: A friend tells a damaging lie about you; your friend is suicidal and is draining your energy so that you have no time for yourself; your friend caught you telling others about something she did that embarrasses her. Friends are important, but they should not interfere with your schoolwork. The two of you need to get your problems in perspective so that you can both do your schoolwork successfully. Try to work on your problems after school when both of you are not under so much stress from your classes.

- **You hate school.** I see this problem a lot. It makes me sad, because I know that if those kids were to get motivated and do their work, they would be carving out a better life for themselves and would feel great. Success builds on success. The more you achieve, the easier everything becomes—and the better you feel.

At the beginning of each school year, thumb through your books to see what's in them. Look at the different chapters to see what you are going to be studying in the class. It's like watching a preview before going to see a movie. Check out the appendices at the end of the book. They often contain useful information. Once, a boy in my advanced Spanish class went through the entire school year without looking in the back of his book. One day, at the end of May, he suddenly exclaimed, "Hey, the answers are in the back of the book." I heard him and was glad that he had not seen them before. Of course I ripped them out right then and there. I had already removed all of the other students' answers, but had missed his.

When reading and studying your new assignments, always look over what you are going to read. See how the chapter is organized. Look for main points and summaries. Check out all charts, pictures and their captions, and footnotes. You never know what might come in useful if you have to answer an essay question or your teacher decides to get sneaky and ask a question about a photo's caption.

Examine what you know, what you heard in class, and what you need to study. Focus on the information that gives you the greatest difficulty. Learn how to target the important stuff for study, and leave the rest behind.

Visualize each new concept you are supposed to learn. When studying something new, like a chapter on science, it is a good idea to visualize how each scientific principle works by seeing it work in your mind. Every subject will need a different approach to study. Ask your teacher for suggestions on how to study for a particular test. She will appreciate your interest and will probably have some good suggestions for you. Then everyone in the class can benefit. **Do not** sit there like a statue every day, giving no indication that you don't understand what's going on. **Speak up** and **do it now!** Why wait until it's too late?

Carefully read over the directions for each assignment. When doing your homework, read the entire assignment first, then answer the exercise questions. You won't learn as much

Be alert and listen to what your teacher says. Pay special attention to what she says at the beginning and end of class.

Don't drive yourself crazy doing your homework and studying. Use the skills listed to study smart and save yourself lots of time. That's what this book's for—to help you get the job done FAST and EASILY.

if you merely go looking for answers. Besides, there will be a lot of important information in the chapter that won't be questioned in the exercise. When it comes time for an exam, isn't it likely that your teacher will pick information that proves you read the entire chapter, not just that you found the answers to a couple of questions? Beware!

Do not study for any class more than 30 to 45 minutes at a time. Some students sit glued to a chair for three hours straight, but they don't really make any headway because they get burned out and zone out. They end up staring at what they're trying to study and are not really mentally present. Do yourself a favor and take a five- or ten-minute break. Get some exercise, scream a little, laugh a lot, wrestle with your younger brother, think about your spring vacation. Then COME BACK!

When studying something like foreign language verbs and vocabulary that you have to memorize, it is better to study in short bursts instead of sitting in a chair trying to hammer it out. Take your lists with you to study while waiting for a bus, for the dentist, or for your parent to pick you up at school. If you are studying foreign language words, it is also helpful to visualize what they mean instead of translating them into English. You will learn them much faster that way. Try it.

TRY THIS!

1. **In your journal write a short paragraph on how you feel about school.** Include why you feel that way. What experiences have you had in the past that make you feel that way? Did a teacher call you stupid? Did students laugh at you because you stuttered? Did you ever feel embarrassed about something?

2. **Again in your journal, write about how your past school experiences have affected your years in high school.** Do they make you want to do better in school, or have they turned you off to education? Do you feel like a loser because of these experiences? Is that a fair assessment of yourself?

3. **Write down the things you're good at.** Toot your own horn. You have a lot to offer the world. Just because you don't like math doesn't mean you can't succeed in school.

4. **If you have a negative view of school, write down reasons why it would help you to change your**

attitude and get to work again. Do you think this will be difficult for you? Why? Brainstorm ways to make this attitude adjustment less difficult for you.

5. **Write down some affirmations for you to say to get yourself fired up,** such as "I'm a smart person" and "I can do this schoolwork easily." Start saying them every day to get yourself back to work. Make all of your affirmations positive instead of saying such things as "I am not stupid."

BE A GOAL GETTER—HOW TO SET GOALS

The very idea of having to set goals and then carry them out seems overwhelming and pointless to many students. For them, it's like making a New Year's resolution that you never keep. Goals do not have to be false promises to yourself. Think of them a road map to where you're going. You wouldn't get in a car and start driving without thinking about where you were going, would you? It's the same way with school. Imagine yourself going on a trip that will last the rest of your life, because you will never stop learning new things. You can make plans for right now, for a month from now, and for a year from now. These are your goals.

A Sample Set of Goals

Your school goals might look like this:

Short-term goals: I will reread the chapters that are on the history test next Tuesday. I will make up a sample test composed of questions that I think the teacher will ask and will then take the test. I will listen to the teacher's review before the exam. I will overprepare for the exam so that I will do well.

Medium-term goals: I will improve my grade in history from a D to a B by changing my study habits. In all of my classes, I will motivate myself to do my best.

Long-term goals: I will improve my grades so much that I will be able to go on to college. I will start thinking about and seeing from now on how my high school classes are a preparation for my future.

It might be helpful to have goals for different areas in your life for things you want to achieve: for your school life outside of classes, for your personal everyday life, for your family life, and for the world you live in.

Other goals might include the following:

Imagine yourself driving along in your car with no idea where you're going. You're on automatic pilot. Suddenly, you look up and you're in the middle of a cornfield. How did that happen? Always know where you're going. Get your goals off the paper and into your daily actions.

Personal Goals: I will be a better friend to Shannon by listening to her instead of always trying to do the talking. I'm going to get to know Jim. I want to hang out with him.

Family Goals: I will spend more time with my parents, brothers, and sisters.

After-school Goals: I will join the biking club to get exercise and to be with friends who like to do what I do.

Goals For the World I Live In: I will get active in my town's new recycling program by getting my school involved.

Making up all of these goals will not mean a thing unless you can also write down *how* you plan to do them and how often. Then, you can assess how you're doing at different intervals. Check out your short-term goals once a week, your medium-term goals every month, and your long-term goals once a year. Have you been carrying them out? It is only by actually doing these things that you are going to improve and have a focus in your life for getting what you want and need.

Think of yourself as a Goal Getter and life will start to get easier and better for you. You will feel happier and more successful. Do not let yourself get lazy or discouraged—be persistent. Think of yourself as a prize fighter who is down for the count. Don't let the referee get to ten—pick yourself up off the mat and get back in the match before time's up. By the time the final round is over, you will be standing victorious because of your persistence!

Some caution for setting goals:

Do not make unrealistic goals for yourself such as: I am going to get all A's for the rest of my time in school. This could be impossible for you to do. There will always be a course or two that will trip you up even though you are doing your best.

You might find that your goals change as time passes. Be willing to revise them if they are no longer right for you. It's your life, after all, and you have a right to choose what you want it to be like.

Remember to work on your goals one day at a time and with persistence. You will get discouraged if you expect immediate success. Little by little you will start experiencing small successes. Celebrate these and never look back. From now on, you are moving forward. Enjoy the process. With each new success, you will enjoy it more and more.

TRY THIS!

1. **In your journal, write down what your life in school has been like up until now without setting goals.** Have

you felt adrift at sea or that your life in school lacked purpose? Write out your true feelings so that you can see how things really are for you. It is a good idea to write these things out so that some day you can go back and see where you used to be *before* you started setting goals.

2. **Write down your short-term, medium-term, and long-term goals for school.** Be sure to include how you're going to carry them out. Make a specific plan for checking the goals at regular intervals. You can mark a certain date every month on your calendar when you reassess where you're going. Remember, you're not a shipwrecked sailor. You are going someplace, and you have chosen that place yourself. You're a winner!

3. **Note the short-term accomplishments you have made at the end of each day.** These might include such things as:

    I did my science homework today.
    I studied for the history test tomorrow.
    I listened and took notes in all of my classes.
    I arrived on time to all of my classes.

    Give yourself credit for every minor accomplishment because these small victories turn into big ones. Celebrate every forward step you make.

4. **After six months, look at your goals and revise any you no longer feel you need to accomplish.** Reassess what you are doing and how it's working for you. Write these thoughts down also.

Nothing is set in stone, so don't be afraid to change your goals every now and then.

NOTE TAKING

Note taking can be a fairly simple process if you just do it. If you are totally bored in a class, it helps to take good notes because you will be mentally present to learn what the teacher is teaching. It requires a little discipline to take notes because you have to listen. Read the following tips on how to do it effectively.

Write your class notes on loose-leaf paper. Date each day's entries so that you will be able to find what you're looking for. To distinguish your class notes from your homework notes, you could put a *C* for class or *H* for home. You could also put all of your class notes on the left-hand side of the page and your homework notes on the right-hand side. Use headings for a change in topic so that you will have an easier time when you start studying. Find out what works best for you.

Copy the notes off the board EXACTLY as your teacher writes them. An x or y in the wrong place will cook you.

Have your papers organized so that you can find them easily. I have seen students rooting through tons of papers trying to find their notes or their homework. It's hilarious because I see myself in them. I'm not an organization freak either, but when you want to get something done, you should snap to attention and put things together logically so that you can SAVE TIME. Your goal is to learn and to take as many shortcuts as you can to get your work done so that you will have more free time. Try it. It works.

Find some way to identify important main points or likely test questions. I use an asterisk, but you can use a highlighter or a different colored pen. Decide what works best for you.

Write legibly so that you can read your own handwriting. Sounds funny, doesn't it? But I have had students tell me they can't understand what they wrote.

Find some shortcut abbreviations for common phrases such as "with" and "without." Many people write "w" and "w/o." Find your own way for other phrases, too, so you can avoid writer's cramp.

Write the notes from class discussions in your own words. Avoid simply writing verbatim what the teacher is saying. Think about what she's saying and what importance it has in the big picture. This is called "using your critical thinking skills." Analyze all aspects of an issue. It's an important part of your education to always ask why and how something has importance. Putting it in your own words makes you think.

SHORTCUT TO ACTION

1. Listen to the teacher in class at all times.
2. Take notes while your teacher talks.
3. Copy down the things your teacher writes on the board.
4. Do the homework.
5. Study for quizzes and exams.
6. Ask the teacher for help after school, and then make sure you show up.
7. Get involved in your school's activities. You'll have more fun and probably do better in your classes.
8. Heads up in class! LISTEN.
9. Have goals in all areas of your life—at school, at home, and in your personal life.
10. Celebrate when you do well.
11. Take good notes.
12. Copy from the board *exactly* what the teacher writes. Practice being precise.

CHAPTER 4

School Stuff Simplified

TESTING, TESTING—OH, NO, WE'RE GOING TO DIE!

There are two main parts to taking a test: The actual study time done at home and the taking of the test. We need to examine both parts of the process so that you will have a dynamite chance of being successful. While we're talking about tests, I want to tell you why you need to take them. One of the biggest reasons is that the vast majority of students would not study and master the material if there were no test at the end. It is human nature to procrastinate and to find a million other more fun things to do. This is just reality. Another reason for taking tests is so that your teacher can see if he is effectively teaching the subject. And tests enable the teacher to give you that Holy Grail of school—THE GRADE.

Tests are a fact of life that you must accept if you are to succeed in school. When you get fired up about them and start to experience some success, you will feel more challenged and try to do even better the next time. You might even beat out those oh-so-perfect honor students. Just think of the shock on their faces if you suddenly start to pass them by. It's fun to see students do it—they get so excited. While you aren't in competition with each other, if you are used to getting bad grades, you have a greater sense of satisfaction when you come out on top. Go for it. It's a fun game if you look at it that way. Find out what you can really do. You might surprise even yourself. Think of the reaction of your parents. I get excited for you just thinking about it.

Preparing for a Test

Preparing well for a test enables you to be calm and answer the questions. Otherwise, you might become a desperate person who resorts to cheating. Follow the guidelines given below to help you prepare for your tests.

Start studying as soon as your teacher presents new material in class. When you are first given new information in class, it would be a good idea to immediately start getting ready for your next test. Waiting until the night before a big exam to cram puts unnecessary stress on you can be avoided through consistent daily work in your classes.

Overprepare for a test. You cannot study for it too much. You will go in with lots of confidence and without being nervous. You will be able to enjoy the reward for your hard work. Bravo! Enjoy it with a great sense of satisfaction. You earned it.

Anticipate what your teacher will put on the test. Listen carefully to what he emphasizes in the day or two before the exam. Often, teachers completely review for an exam, and what they review gives you a huge clue as to what you need to concentrate on.

Ask your teacher for help immediately if you do not understand the new material. If you cannot get together because of scheduling conflicts, study with another classmate. It is often more fun to prepare for a test with someone else—preferably not with your boyfriend or girlfriend. You might be too easily distracted. Then again, I also remember lots of couples who studied together and did well on their exams, so only you can be the judge.

Beware of the multiple-choice, matching, and true-false tests. Students often think they don't have to study for these types of tests because they do not have to write in the correct answer. That is a bad assumption to make. Students who do not study for them usually get poor grades. It is no advantage to have these tests if you do not know the material being tested. They just become "multiple guess." The only advantage you have on these kinds of tests is that you do not have to memorize the material—you just have to recognize the right answer.

Try the bartering system with your friends. If you are an ace English student and your friend is a whiz in math, you might try a cooperative venture in which you help each other in your class specialty. Ask a friend if she would like to participate. It's more fun than going it alone. When I was a student, I tutored Latin in exchange for help in geometry. I always found that when I tutored Latin, I was always a far better student in the subject than if I studied it alone. Besides, it feels wonderful to help someone else get a better grade.

Get a good night's sleep. Because you have prepared for several days before an exam and don't have to cram, you will be able to go to bed at a decent hour and sleep well. Bravo for you!

Always eat a decent breakfast before you go to school. I had a hard time eating breakfast when I was in high school because my stomach was always nervous. Then my stomach

"Sometimes I wait until the night before to start studying for a test. Bad move. I always feel panicky or even go blank when I get the test. My advice is to start studying for a hard test several nights before."

—Jon

was always growling way before lunchtime. That is a distraction to you and other students. Eat pizza if you have to, but eat *something*.

Be sure you are physically comfortable when you take the test. Bring a jacket or sweater to put on if you get cold. If it is warm outside, dress in layers so you can take off a layer or put one on. Be sure and use the bathroom before the exam.

Avoid those panic-stricken, nervous students. They can make you nervous even though you feel calm and know your test material really well.

Don't listen to the A students who said they didn't study. Often, this is untrue. They probably did study but they simply want to look cool. Chances are they wouldn't do well if they didn't open their books. Remember to keep the focus on yourself while taking a test. Those *A* students may not have all of the answers. But *you* will.

Taking the Test

You've studied hard. Now it's time to talk about ways to operate while you're taking the test. Follow these guidelines to do a better job.

Look over the entire test before you start to answer any questions. Get a feel for what is included. Know the sections so you can budget your time.

Listen to your teacher give instructions for taking the test. Teachers often give important hints on taking the test. If you've already started taking the test and are not listening to him while he talks, you run the risk of missing many things because you were not paying attention.

Read the test directions carefully. I have had many students miss a whole section of a test because they did not read the directions. That's really sad, but it can be easily avoided.

Ask your teacher for help if you do not understand the directions. It is better to admit you don't understand something than to take the test and fail it. Be careful!

Look at each question carefully. Read what it actually says, not what you think it says. I have to admit that I have marked incorrect answers on answer sheets for some items because I *thought* it said one thing when it really said the exact opposite. Think about it; if your teacher can do it, you can, too! Slow down when taking a test.

Write down information you have studied, such as math formulas, on the actual exam. I think it's a good idea if it helps you get focused and in the test mode. Besides, you will have those formulas there while you're taking the test. Be sure your teacher says it's okay. Better to be safe than sorry.

Don't freak out when you first see a test. Stay calm, close your eyes, and breathe deeply.

Know how much time you have for the test. That way, you can budget your time effectively. Wear a watch to the test.

Skip over things you do not understand or know and come back to them later. Maybe something will jog your memory. While you're waiting for a breakthrough, you might as well be getting some easy points.

Do the sections that are worth the most points first. Spend your time strategically, gathering as many points as you can in as short a time as possible.

Work as fast as you can, but with accuracy. If you have a lot of time, then do the reverse. Work slowly. I watched one of my best students take exams. She did it slowly and methodically. She always scored a 99 or 100 percent. Usually the A students take the test as if there were a fire in the room and they have to get out as soon as possible. Find the approach that works for you.

After finishing the exam, do not turn it in. I always ask my students to put their heads down for a few minutes and to take an imaginary trip to the beach and then go over it again. They hate it when I make them do that, but they begrudgingly admit to me later that they did find silly mistakes. Hey, I'm not trying to win a popularity contest as a teacher. I'm just trying to do a good job.

Cross-reference all items in the exam. Sometimes an answer will appear in another question later. If you're alert, you'll see it right away. I've had students tell me that they forgot how to spell a Spanish word while all along it was there in another part of the test. Be alert for any gifts like that.

Do not give up during a test. Too many students throw in the towel before they have really tried to answer all of the questions. If you studied for the test, you will be able to do at least some of it correctly. Have confidence in yourself. If you tell yourself, "Math is hard for me and I can't do it," it will come true. You must tell yourself, "I can do it." Positive messages to yourself are very important.

Concentrate on each test item. I have seen students drifting away during an exam, so I know their exams will be terrible. They just check out, never to return. Do not lose your power of concentration. Give yourself a mental "ice-water bath." Go back to your test. After you finish, you will be grateful you did.

"Stay cool during your tests. I used to blank out as soon as I saw the test. I learned relaxation techniques and biofeedback."

—Laura

Open book tests. This is a deceptively hard kind of test to take—it is designed to be harder *because* you are allowed to use your book. If your teacher is giving an open book test, come to class having studied as hard as you would otherwise. The reason for studying is clear: You will know what is being tested, and you will know *where* to find supporting details in the book.

Write legibly and in big enough letters for your teacher to read. I hate to grade papers where the students write in itty-bitty letters. The older I get, the harder it is to read those papers. You might get a chuckle thinking about your teachers trying to decipher your handwriting, but some of them will be far less inclined to read your paper carefully if your writing is sloppy or hard to read. You want your teacher in as good a mood as possible when he's grading your work.

Do not cheat on an exam or help others cheat. Cheating is for losers and desperate people. If you do your work, you will never have to resort to this. It's a scary thought that any students puts their faith and trust in cheating. In my experience, cheaters never do well. They spend so much time trying to hide what they are doing that they waste precious test time. Trust your own brain and *use it!* Also, *do not* help others to cheat. If you give a friend an answer, you are just as guilty as he is. Don't let others use you.

For true/false questions, watch out for the words "never" and "always." Often this is a clue to you to mark the answer *false* because the words denote extreme statements. In addition, there are usually more false than true answers. Note that I said *usually.* Just be careful and give the right answer. Yeah, I know, easy for me to say since I'm not taking the test. Let's put it this way—I hope you get all of them right. I'm pulling for you 100 percent.

Multiple Choice Exams. On a multiple choice exam, look at the question and then think of the answer first without looking at the choices. Then, you will be focused on what you need to look for and won't be tempted by wrong answers. Often, an answer is close but is not the correct one. If you ask yourself the question first, you will be more likely to find the right answer. By the way, do not assume that you can't have *A* as your answer four times in a row. It doesn't happen often, but it has happened on some tests I have given in the past. Some "experts" tell you that the answer will probably only rarely be *A.* Maybe that's why I often have *A* as the answer—to outwit the experts! There is no substitute for knowing your stuff. Then, you won't have to deal with the law of averages—that's like buying a lottery ticket!

On an essay exam, be sure to answer what the question asks. Sometimes a student misunderstands what is being asked and writes about something completely wrong. If you do not understand the question at all, ask your teacher for clarification. He might give you a helpful hint. It's certainly worth a try. When answering an essay question, you will be asked to *think* and come up with an answer and supporting evidence. So don't try to b.s. your teacher. He will only get irritated having to read it.

Start with an outline before you begin to answer an essay question. The outline helps you organize your thoughts. Practice possible essay questions before your exam. Then step back and analzye your answers to see if you came up with truly penetrating responses that address the question. Use examples to prove your point. If your teacher has a pet theory relating to the question, be sure to include it. You can disagree with him in your own mind and maybe even at a later date. Or, you may opt to take a chance and offer an alternative argument. Just be sure to back up your argument with as many facts as you can. It's a risk to knowingly argue against what your teacher believes.

Multiple essay exams. If your teacher specifies that you are to answer three out of five essay questions, pick the ones you are most able to answer. Remember to answer only three of them because he will have to plough through tons of papers and will not appreciate your doing extra work. Similarly, if the instructions say you are to write 100 words for each question, *do not* write 200 words. You should write 100 words that are concise and to the point. You don't need the added verbiage anyway. It will just be fluff that will detract from the power of your answer.

Completing an essay question. Instead of writing too much, some students write too little. Be sure you cover all of the points asked in the question in as complete a manner as possible. Under-answering the question will get points taken off your grade. I have had students write two sentences for an essay question that should have had at least fifteen sentences. Again, a dry run a day or two before the exam can ensure you'll be more able to handle the pressure of answering the essay questions. When you study, think of possible essay questions and practice writing your responses. I enjoyed essay questions when I was in school, because I got to think instead of merely filling in blanks. It felt robotic to me to mark *a, b, c,* or *d.* In addition, I could be creative in my answers.

On an essay exam, don't just put down words on the paper. THINK before you write and make an outline. Use your mind well.

Take-home exams. Students always think take-home exams are so easy, but in reality you are expected to do much better on them than if you had taken the same exam in a class period. Be sure that you prepare each question carefully and that you back up all of your statements with accurate examples.

A PERSONAL NOTE

About ten years ago, I was tired of giving the same old kinds of tests on Spanish grammar and tried something new. I gave each student a take-home exam of sixteen pages and told them that they would have to explain why they wrote the answers they did. A group of four students divided up the pages equally. Each one was able to defend his answers on his part of the test, but when I questioned them on what the others prepared, they were not able to answer the questions satisfactorily. Needless to say, all four got terrible grades. Don't try to take shortcuts that will get you in trouble in the long run. Always think long-term instead of short-term. You will have more success that way.

Ignore distracting students. You know who they are: The gum poppers, the knuckle crackers, the sneezers, the coughers, the nail biters, the talk-to-themselfers, and the complainers. Tune them out. Think of them as white noise that after a while you won't hear because you will have gotten used to it. Your teacher will probably tell them to quiet down eventually. If she doesn't, and you're still bothered by them, ask her to do something about it. Don't let them make you lose your cool.

If you need more time to take a test, ask for it. Chances are, you are a slow test-taker. If you have some kind of learning disability that keeps you from finishing on time, always ask for more time. I have had some students ask me if they can stay longer. I believe, as their teacher, that they deserve more time when they are doing the best they can. They should not be penalized for needing more time. Note: This allowance does not include the students who know little but want more time. I always say to them, "You either know it or you don't." This may sound cruel, but it's true. If they had studied for the test, they would have finished as soon as the other students. They're the ones who sit there and wait for some divine inspiration.

Ask to see your exams. If a teacher never gives exams back, tell him you want to see them. I know some teachers don't give their students' tests back to them. Consequently, the kids cannot see their mistakes. I think this is incredibly stupid of teachers, because their students will just keep making the same mistakes. You have a right to see your tests. Exercise that right!

TRY THIS!

1. **If you have been doing poorly in a subject, listen carefully when your teacher goes over the test.** Analyze what you did wrong. Did you have a lot of careless errors? Did you study the wrong thing? Did you just not care or didn't try? Could you have done better?

2. **For the next week, listen carefully in all of your classes and take good notes.** Copy things off the board correctly. Pay attention to all of your teachers and write down their homework assignments as well as any hints they give you for studying for tests. If there's something you don't understand, ask your teacher. Study for the tests with a friend. When you take the tests, be mindful of all of the pointers I have given you.

3. **After you have finished this week, write how your test scores were.** Did doing all of the things from *Try This #2* make any difference? Why? Did it kill you to do all of those things or are you still in good health?

4. **Write down your goals for future tests and grades, saying what grades you want to get on them.** In order to get those grades, you have to back your goals up with some good, old-fashioned, hard work. Write down how you will feel when you get those good grades. Will you feel better about yourself?

"I used to not study much for exams, and so I got terrible grades. Another problem I had was being nervous, because I knew I didn't study enough. Now, I overprepare myself and am more relaxed when I take tests. I get better grades, too!"

—Caitlin

COOL TIPS TO CONQUER TIME

Time can be used to your advantage if you know how to maximize it. In this section you will learn how to make the best use of your available hours. This is a big thing for teenagers because so often, hours escape them, leaving them asking, "Where did the time go?" Your life is no longer like that of a little child who thought time would never pass until her birthday or Christmas. Now you can't stop it! It goes on without you if you're not careful. Read the following tips to conquer time and make it your ally.

First things first. To get all of your work done, you have to decide what are your most important assignments, and then you have to make sure that you do them first, especially if they are due the next day. If you have some long-term assignments that are due in two to three weeks, schedule time to start doing them A.S.A.P. so that you won't become hysterical or panicked on the night before the assignments are due. Plan ahead and you will be stress-free. You can have a checklist with your most important tasks on the top. As you finish each one, scratch it off the list with great flair. You might want to do a cheer and jump up and down to commemorate your mini-victory.

Do long-range planning. Carry a calendar with you for the year on which you mark down your future tests, term papers, and exams. When you see the big picture and all of the things you have to do, you will be better able to set up a schedule for the completion of all of the work.

Fight procrastination like a champion wrestler. PIN IT! You're the boss. Don't let it boss you. The longer you postpone doing something, the more trouble you get into with time. When it is time to get down to business, do you start lifting weights, painting your nails, or something else that does not have to be done right away just so you don't have to start studying? Examine how you manage time and you will learn a lot about what you need to do to change your system. If you still insist on procrastinating, go immediately to the section on stress in this book to get some help—you're going to need it. When I first started teaching, I jumped on exams to grade them immediately. But the longer I am in teaching, the harder it is for me to get started on grading them. Sometimes I begin with the hardest papers, but if I'm feeling super tired, I'll do the easier ones. Then, I'm usually in a groove and can take on the harder ones. I've even gone so far as to not allow myself to go to the bathroom until I finish a whole class's tests. There's an incentive for you! Make up some crazy rule of your own to follow so you can get your work done. Think of all of that extra free time you'll add up—it's like money in the bank.

Avoid watching TV until you get all of your work done. If you have a program you just have to watch, use it as a reward for getting some work done. Why not tape it and watch it on the weekend or some other day? Then you can fast-forward through the commercials and not waste so much time. I could say more about the bad influence of television, but you've probably heard it all from your parents.

Do one job at a time and finish it. Trying to do everything at once will drive you crazy and you'll probably get very little done. Focus on one thing at a time.

Watch the students in class who get the good grades. Study what they do to be successful. Is it that they listen attentively in class and take notes? Is it that they know how to cut out all of the less important information to get the main ideas? How do they manage their time? It always helps to watch successful people. They're doing something right, so why not copy them?

Reward yourself when you manage time well. Actually, your best reward will be lots more free time. Your friends will be procrastinating until the last minute and there you will be—guilt-free, wanting to go to a movie. Your trick will be to convert your friends to your new way of doing work so they will have time to be with you.

Take a ten-minute break every hour when doing your work so that you won't go crazy. Run around the block or take the dog for a walk.

Be flexible. Allow some extra time each day for unexpected things that come up. Students sometimes get the flu, a grandparent dies, or a parent has an operation. At these times, you will not be able to work as you usually do and you will realize the benefit of working ahead. In times of emergency, you won't be as stressed out by the schoolwork you're missing if you have been keeping up with all assignments.

Prioritize! This is a controversial suggestion. I'm sorry, but I told you I would be a realist and tell it like it is. There *are* students who cannot possibly get all of the things done that they have to do. They need to prioritize all of their tasks and concentrate on those subjects that give them the most difficulty. Maybe this means getting a B on a Spanish test instead of an A in order to study for a more difficult biology exam. You will have to make this decision for yourself—after all, it is your life.

Prepare yourself for life after high school by making yourself do your work. Don't count on Mom and Dad to be there to push you. They will give you more freedom when you perform well so you'll feel less like a baby. They'll also hassle you less because when you do your work, they are happy campers. Visualize what post-high school education will look like. Can you picture yourself getting it done by yourself or are you so attached to having Mom push you that you can't imagine having the motivation to get started on your own? Well, start right now—this very minute—and get on the ball. What you do now will make your life far easier after high school. Remember that doing your schoolwork is like going to a job—an unpaid job, for sure, but one that will ensure you

Sometimes you can't do everything you want to. You have to pick and choose what you need to study the most. Pace yourself and try to stay ahead of your assignments.

Put those phone calls on hold when you've got some serious studying to do.

have a comfortable life and are able to make a positive contribution to society. Also, you'll get your teachers off your back. You and your teacher might even become friends. Trust me, this can really happen!

Hold all calls. Your family will be happy to tell your friends that you are working on a paper and cannot be disturbed. Or, you can tell your friends that you only have five minutes to talk. If you know you're undisciplined, it's probably better not to take calls or you may end up talking to friends for 2 hours! Then you'll really be cooked.

Self-Talk for Time Management

If time is one of your big problems, say the following positive statements every day to keep yourself mindful of what you are doing to change things.

I control my own time.

I organize my time.

Time is my best ally.

I have more free time because I manage time so well.

I enjoy having my work done. It makes me feel successful.

My schoolwork is getting easier because I use time to my advantage.

TRY THIS!

1. **Write in your journal how you have been managing time to get your homework and studying done.** Has a constant lack of time frustrated you? Do you wait until the last minute to get things done? Do your parents get mad at you because you wait until the last minute to do big projects? Has the way you've been using your time been successful for you?

2. **Using the tips in the previous section for managing time, make a road map of goals for doing your work this coming week.** Make a week's calendar and write down everything you have to do on the appropriate due date. Then make up a schedule for getting it all done. Be sure to budget more time for a project than you think it will take. That will give you a big incentive to do it faster—but to also do it well. It will keep you focused on your job so that you can finish it earlier or still allow you to succeed and finish on time if something interrupts your work.

3. **Write in your journal how your concept of time has changed since you were a little kid.** Do your moments get more precious the older you get? If so, why? Are you bored because time just doesn't seem to move fast enough and time between weekends goes slower and slower? Why do think that is? Is it because you're *not* doing your homework, you're bored and unmotivated, and you're not involved in enough activities?

4. **Develop an action plan to address your problem with time.** Ask yourself how you can get all of your assignments turned in on time. What will you do differently to make sure you're not late to class? Would your life be less stressful if you did these things?

5. **Write a mini-essay about time and what it means to you.** Be philosophical. Is this a subject you hate to talk about? Why? Write how you can make time your ally.

6. **If you always postpone doing your assignments and projects until the last minute, write about the different crises you have created in your household because of your procrastination.** Did your parents, brothers, and sisters get drawn into these situations? How did that make them feel? How did it make you feel? Dig down deep and analyze why you created the crises in the first place.

7. **Write down some new, different, fun things you can do when you find yourself with all of this new free time.** Get crazy on this one. What can you do to make your life more interesting and fun? Have you always wanted to learn how to fence? Why not sign up for a course at a local junior college. One of my students did and he loved it. Treat yourself to something you've always wanted to do.

> *"To test my memory, I sometimes explain what is going to be on the test to a friend who is having trouble in the class. It helps me see what I don't know and what I need to remember better."*
>
> —Elizabeth

MAXING OUT YOUR MEMORY

Do you have a problem memorizing things? Check out the following tips for how to do a better job.

Tell yourself you can remember things. If you say you can't, then you won't. Listen to what you are telling yourself. You plan to fail before you even give yourself a chance to succeed. A doctor once told me, "Never say 'can't.'" I have tried all of my life not to say that word and it has helped me. Try it.

Memorize what you need to remember in small chunks. Then you can put the parts all together at the end. A warning:

Be sure you are memorizing correct information. Make sure you periodically review the stuff you need to know for a test or exam. Keep going over what you have studied from the beginning of the school year. Periodic review sessions every month or so will help you remember the material for a long time.

Play a concentration game to help you focus on remembering things. There are many shareware programs you can download from the Internet or America On Line to get the practice you need. If you don't have access to the Web, ask a friend to get some programs for you. There are have many different varieties for both the Mac and Windows platforms. This will give you good memory practice. It's just a matter of training your brain to do what you want it to. Exercise your brain to get it in shape.

Pay close attention in all of your classes. Write things down. When you write them down, you tend to remember them better. If you simply try to remember everything without writing it down, you are bound to forget a good percentage of the material. You will have your notes for reference later. Always focus on what your teacher is teaching. It will make your study time amazingly easy.

Repetition is good for languages and other classes. I tell my students to practice their Spanish verbs by repeating them over and over again as they do their physical exercises. Even though some of my students think I'm crazy, I sometimes do leglifts while I'm teaching. It's a great way for me to keep in shape! And while they wouldn't be caught dead doing it in front of others, some of my students have told me that they do it at home with lots of success. Imagine other ways you could practice things that you need to repeat over and over again to remember. How about dancing to wild and crazy music while you clean your room? You can kill *three* birds with one stone—memorize your stuff, get exercise, and clean your room. Be creative in how you solve your problems, but if music is going to play a part, make sure you don't listen to your favorite rock group. You might not be able to concentrate on your memorization if you hear lyrics that you know well. Your brain can't handle all of that at the same time. Quiet time would be better under the circumstances.

Work on memorizing things for 20-25 minutes at a time. Then get up and run in place, beat your pillow to vent your frustrations, scream a little, listen to a few tunes, check in with your parents to tell them how and what you're doing, or read a short story to your little brother.

Create a visual image of what you need to remember. If you are memorizing how to do a scientific experiment, visualize yourself doing it step by step, explaining each step as you go. In fact, you could pretend you're the teacher and practice teaching the material. It's fun and you may discover a new career you'd like to pursue. Hey, teaching's great, and the profession needs good people like you who understand what teenagers go through to learn.

Want to do it! If you don't care, nothing can get you going. One thing I always tell my students is to get mad at themselves. Learning is a matter of pride—you're out to show the world what you can do. Get yourself up off the floor and come back with lots of energy. You can do it.

Be creative in how you memorize the stuff you need to know. Once a boy came to see me after school for help with his Spanish verbs for a test the following day. He just couldn't remember them. I could see his body was there but his mind wasn't. He kept writing down a verb form as *venimos*. I finally decided to do something drastic and said, "No, it's *vinimos* with two *i's*," as I sent my two middle fingers flying in the air. At first he looked shocked that a teacher would flip him off, but I sure did get his attention. I started to laugh, and then so did he. The next day, when he got to that verb on the test, he started to laugh. The funny thing is that he never had another day's trouble with Spanish. He started to learn it because he was *mentally present.*

Have notes on small pieces of paper of the things you need to memorize. From time to time, study the information. Practicing several different times will help you memorize things rather than a marathon session where you sit there with an imaginary baseball bat over your head. No one likes the "jam it down your throat" approach!

Make relationships between something you already know and what you are currently learning. Always use the knowledge you have gained in the past to acquire new knowledge.

"For a real important test, I tape myself saying what I have to memorize. I listen to the tape on the way to and from work. It helps me get focused. I wish I didn't have to remember so much, but I guess there's no fighting it."

—Victor

A CALL TO TEENS

I've given you some crazy ideas that can help you memorize. Now, how about making up some of your own? In fact, I'd like to hear them and put them in the next edition of this book if they're crazy and creative enough to get kids pumped up to learn. You can reach me by e-mail at dueber@stlnet.com.

TRY THIS!

1. **Go get your favorite poem or speech and memorize it.** Do a dramatic reading of it first. Visualize what each line says so that you can remember it. Sing it in a dramatic tone or stretch out the dramatic parts. Practicing memorization on something you like will improve your ability when it comes time to memorize something less exciting—like math formulas or foreign language verbs.

2. **Take out something you have to memorize.** Turn it into a rap song and sing away. If you have a drum, beat on it rhythmically while you sing. Don't make this into too big a production or you will waste precious hours. It doesn't have to be a masterpiece, but if it is fantastic after only a short time of working at it, maybe you've developed a new career of song-writing. Now that sounds like fun.

3. **Come up with your own idea for memorizing stuff.** Use your imagination and creativity. The sky's the limit. You are the creator here.

BEEF UP YOUR VOCABULARY

A good vocabulary will serve you well in the future. Read the following tips on why and how to increase your vocabulary.

"Why should I increase my vocabulary?" you might ask. There are many reasons. When you read books of any kind, a good vocabulary helps you understand what you're reading. Also, because the SAT and ACT test vocabulary, you need to have a good command of words that often show up on those college entrance exams. Another more practical reason is that a good vocabulary shows that you are well educated and can open more doors for you in the job market. Using more than one or two syllable words in an interview will impress a potential employer. Simply put, you get more respect with a good vocabulary.

Read the following points on how to increase your vocabulary. Start using the suggestions in your studies.

Read books. One of the saddest things I see in my job is that many students do not want to read. They are almost proud of it. Reading increases your vocabulary by leaps and bounds and exercises your brain. When you get to college and have to read 100 pages a night, you won't want to be looking up word after word. If you learn as much as you can in high school, your job in college will be much easier. You will have an advantage over other students.

Look up new vocabulary words. When you have a reading assignment and run across a word you don't know, find out what it means. Passing by word after word without looking them up will catch up with you some day, so you might as well learn them now. The discipline you have now will pay off in the future. Enjoy words. They are what we use to communicate with others.

Go surfing. Get on the World Wide Web and do a search with the key words *English vocabulary.* I bet you come up with lots of sources for learning new words.

Learn about Latin and Greek prefixes and root words. Often, knowing them can help you figure out what a word means in English or another language. Let me give you an example. If you know the Latin root *fort* means *strong,* you will be able to figure out that the musical term *fortissimo* must mean that you play a piece forcefully or loud. The bibliography of this book lists books on vocabulary building that you can buy or pick up at your local library.

Write down the new vocabulary words you learn and put them in a sentence. Lots of students forget what they just looked up if they don't write it down. In fact, it would be a good idea to have a vocabulary notebook to enter words you have just learned.

Figure out what a word means by how it's used in the sentence. Often, students can understand what a word means without having to look it up, even if they have never seen it before. They use *context* clues. You can do this with practice. The more you read, the better you will become at fine-tuning this very important skill. And don't forget to write the word down in your new vocabulary notebook!

Get a good dictionary. A dictionary gives the following information about words, usually in this order:

- Origin of the word
- Pronunciation
- Part of speech (noun, pronoun, adjective, verb, conjunction, adverb, and interjection)
- Meaning
- Synonyms (similar words)
- Antonyms (opposite words)

Thumb through your dictionary. Get a good one such as the *American Heritage College Dictionary, Webster's New World College Dictionary,* or *Merriam Webster's Collegiate Dictionary.* You can use it for the rest of your life, so don't get the

Think of the dictionary as your friend. Learning new words will give you lots of WORD POWER. You'll be the Vocabulary Superman of your school.

See how many

funny-sounding

words you can find.

Then try to use them

when you talk and

write.

————————

cheapest one you can find. It will come in handy both now and in the future. Read the opening section of your dictionary for an explanation of the features it contains. It will have a pronunciation guide for new words as well as a list of the abbreviations used in the dictionary.

Fun New Words

Check out some of these new words. They may sound funny, but they are actually used in books all the time!

masticate	to chew
fractious	unruly—what students become when they are tired
bumptious	pushy in behavior
punctilious	precise, scrupulous
piffle	to talk or act in a feeble way
pusillanimous	cowardly
osculate	to kiss
ludicrous	laughable to the point of absurdity

The last word, *ludicrous,* appears in one of my favorite sayings in my classes: Life is ludicrous—and we must laugh at all of its absurdities. Saying that to myself and to my students makes life seem easier and I love hearing younger people use the word, like my nephew Danny, who once said that the long car trip he was going to have to take with his parents was ludicrous. It was neat to hear him say a word not often used.

Words are fun. Cultivate a new interest in learning them. You never know what crazy new word you'll pick up that will take the dullness out of your speech. It is NOT a crime to use big words.

IMPORTANT: Don't use big new words to impress your friends. Use them to make yourself a smarter, better person. Also, don't put too many of them in one sentence. You might intimidate people.

TRY THIS!

1. **With the next chapter you have to read for school, write down every word you don't know.** How many of those words were you able to figure out using context clues—how they were used in the sentence? I bet you understood quite a few of them. The hard part is being able to tell what a word means when it's pulled out of nowhere, like on the SAT and ACT.

2. **Make it your goal to learn five new vocabulary words a day.** Just think of how many new words you will be able to use by the end of the school year. You can make it into a game to see how many new words you can discover.

3. **Use your new vocabulary in conversations with other people.** Think of different words you can use to say the same thing. It can be fun if you make it a game.

READ TO TUNE UP YOUR BRAIN

Lots of kids groan when you tell them they need to read more. They see it as hard work. I maintain that you will never like to read unless you start to do it. I think reading is enjoyable. We read things for many reasons: to escape from our everyday activities, just for fun, for a class assignment, to broaden our horizons, and to learn to think better.

My advice to you is to read, read, read. The more you read, the better you get at it. You not only improve your reading skills, but also your vocabulary. As a reader, you advance by leaps and bounds in your ability to read quickly and effectively. If you hate to read, find books about things that interest you. I initially picked up Grateful Dead drummer Mickey Hart's book *Drumming at the Edge of Magic* because I was interested in drumming after I bought an African djembe. I wanted to know more about it and drumming in general. While I found the book fascinating for the information I learned about the subject, what I think was so neat about it is Hart's passion and excitement to learn all he can about drums and drumming. The key is to choose a book about something that will keep you hooked on it, that will make you want to turn the pages to find out more about the subject or to find out what happens next.

How to Read a Book More Effectively

Check out the different sections of the textbook you are starting to read. Learn how to use all of them. Always thumb through each one. You never know what helpful information you'll find.

Table of contents: It provides clues to the organization and topics in a book by indicating page numbers, chapter headings, and subheadings as well as gives you an overview of the material and provides the general location of topics. You can use the table of contents to see whether a book

Thumb through your new textbooks. Read the preface at the beginning of each book to see what the author's views are. Go to the back and see what's there. Maybe you'll find something you can use when studying for tests.

contains topics that are of interest to you. It gives more general information than the index, which is very detailed.

Glossaries: These are really small dictionaries often found in textbooks. They help you understand the unfamiliar words in the textbook. You can find new meanings for words you already know and learn new words you have never seen before.

Indexes: An index is an alphabetical directory of topics and names given in the text along with the page numbers where they can be found. It catalogs specific categories of information, enabling the reader to find important material quickly. Text indexes vary in complexity. For example, a history textbook might have a much more extensive index than a Spanish textbook.

Appendices: These give additional information on what you're studying. For example, in the appendix for a foreign language textbook, you'll find charts of regular and irregular verbs conjugated.

Reading School Assignments

Study and try out the following tips on how to read your school stuff without going crazy.

Read at a steady pace, concentrating as you go along. Do not take notes the first time.

Take notes the second time you read. What do you think the teacher will probably test you on? Write your notes in an easy to read, organized fashion.

IMPORTANT: If you don't have time to reread an assignment, at least read a whole section before you take notes. You must see the big picture to understand how the information you just read fits in with what you're supposed to be learning in the class.

Visualize and think about what you're reading in order to understand it. This takes concentration. Don't let your mind drift off to that cute guy in history class or to that beautiful girl in math class. You'll get finished reading a lot faster if you focus on your work.

Eliminate all distractions while reading. Tell your parents to take a message when friends call; you can call them back later. This is very important because you need to have 100 percent of your attention on what you're reading. You will also get the reading done faster. Then you can talk to your friends on the phone without feeling guilty.

After you have read all of your pages, stop and think about what you just read. Constantly ask yourself "What's the point here?" If you don't understand, take it one sentence at a time. How does it all fit in with what you are studying this year in the course and with what the teacher is currently teaching in class?

Read the chapter summary and the questions in the exercises at the end of the chapter before reading the chapter. This will tell you what you should look for in the chapter and will probably help you understand the reading better and with fewer hassles.

Realize when you read the same page seven times. If you're reading the same page over and over, stop what you're doing because you're not getting anywhere. Go do something else. Sometimes just getting away from the reading for a few minutes will help you focus better when you come back.

Read for context. Often you can figure out what a word means based on its use in the sentence. If that doesn't work, use your dictionary.

Read ahead of the lecture. If you are having trouble in a class, look ahead in the book to find out what the teacher will be teaching next. Then, you will at least have some familiarity with it. If your teacher knows you are doing this, he will be impressed with your zeal and far more likely to help you. Yes, this sounds like a real drag, but believe me, it's an incredibly smart thing to do. I've done it in the past for courses that were hard for me. Then I had a clue *before* the teacher started to teach the material.

When reading a textbook, always go to the end of the chapter and look at the questions. They'll tell you what you're supposed to be learning.

TRY THIS!

1. **On your next history assignment, read and visualize what you are reading.** Imagine the characters you are reading about and what they did. If reading about the Civil War, think about the impact of the war on peoples' lives. Look at the Civil War from Abraham Lincoln's, Robert E. Lee's, Jefferson Davis's, and a slave's perspectives. How are they different and why? Look at the economic and social impact of the war on ordinary people. Use your imagination to make history come alive.
2. **Turn off the stereo when you read.** Take no phone calls. See if your work goes faster. Sometimes one small change can make a huge difference.
3. **Remember how you practiced improving your memory skills?** Go back and review the techniques and use them while you read.

4. **Read actively.** Imagine yourself as the scientist doing research on what you're reading. What would be your next research study of the subject?

Reading for Your Future

To be a citizen of the world, you need to know what's going on. To depend solely on television for your information is not enough. Soon you will be voting in local, state, and presidential elections and will want to get as much information as possible from as many written sources as possible—magazines, newspapers, and books. Why is this important? Because everything you read or hear will have some element of truth, but not the whole truth. *You* are the person who will have to gather this information and make decisions on how to vote based on your own value system. Talk to people in countries who have just recently gained the freedom to vote, to gather together freely, to discuss political views. They are passionate about their views and about their new-found freedom. They can't stop talking about what they believe in. Our world gets more complicated every day. You have the chance to do something about it by getting involved. As an adult, I can't say I'm proud about what we have done to the business world, to the environment, and to the way we handle social problems. All of these problems will take *your* imagination and creativity to solve. Get involved and make a difference. Helping others makes your life much more worthwhile.

UPDATE: A few days ago, I went to a restaurant owned and operated by a former student of mine. I remember that he never wanted to read anything. He basically shuffled his way through school. Now he regrets it. He told me that every night he reads the paper so that he will know what is going on in the world and can talk to his customers. He feels at a disadvantage because he now realizes that if he had made more of an effort when he was in school, he would feel so much more confident running his business.

A CALL TO TEENS

For the next edition, I would like to know what books you have read that you both enjoyed and learned from. Please let me know why you liked the book, what you learned, and why you think other teenagers would like reading it. It will be fun to find out what your peers are reading in other parts of the country. My e-mail address is dueber@stlnet.com.

Library Skills

The Dewey Decimal System. The call numbers on books are based on the Dewey Decimal System, which is a cataloging process used in many school and community libraries for books, newspapers, and magazines. Check out the numbers below to get an idea of where you can find the kind of books you are looking for.

Classifications
000 General Works
100 Philosophy
200 Religion
300 Social Sciences
400 Languages
500 Pure Sciences
600 Applied Sciences
700 Art and Music
800 Literature
900 History

To give you an example, you will find that books on the American Revolution are classified under the number 973.3 and books on the Civil War are under 973.7. If you are looking for a specific book or for books on a specific aspect of one of these wars, you can look it up in the card catalogue to get an even more exact number. The card catalogue gives information like the title and author's name, the subject of the book, the number of pages, the city where it is published, the name of the publisher and the date of publication, and the catalog number—where to find the book. This is the call number and is in the upper left corner of the card.

IMPORTANT: Fiction books do not have numbers but are arranged according to the author's last name. Also, biographies are filed under *B* and alphabetized according to the person being written about. So, biographies of Abraham Lincoln are under the *L's* and biographies of Martin Luther King are under the *K's*. An *R* followed by the call number refers to reference books. These are books you must use in the library. You can't check them out; they are for reference only.

Reader's Guide to Periodical Literature. To find articles, students must use the *Readers' Guide to Periodical Literature,* which is published twice a month and can be found in the reference section of your library. You must know the topics that you want to look for in the *Readers' Guide,* because articles are indexed under subject. If you can't find it under

Don't let all those books overwhelm you. The library is organized to make it easy to find everything you need.

one name, brainstorm other names where the information you're seeking could be located.

Explore in your library. Take some time to explore the library. Just wandering around looking at things and their numbers will help you find stuff faster.

Take a library tour. Sometimes high school classes go to the library to learn how to use it. Pay attention! It will save you time later.

Ask your librarian for help. Librarians are paid to help you find books and information. They'll be glad you're making them do their job. It will make their time on the job more fulfilling. They're usually very helpful people.

Encyclopedias give general information, but they are not enough to use alone for research papers. Don't try to copy from them. That's dishonest and is called plagiarism. Teachers will usually know because the language used will not be in your usual writing style.

Interlibrary loans. Often, you can use the libraries of other high schools in your district. Sometimes high schools have a cooperative agreement with community and university libraries. Ask your school librarian for more information.

HOW TO WRITE A RESEARCH PAPER

Do you start to shake and shiver at the mere mention of writing a research paper? Most students do, especially if they saw their older sisters and brothers go through the experience. This is a natural reaction. The first time I had to write a paper, I thought I'd never make it through. There were so many things to do, so many details. I'd like to take away the emotional trauma so that you will see this as a fun experience. Here are some tips to help you through the rough spots.

Do it one step at a time. Instead of thinking about the paper as the end product, take it in small steps. Things tend to be less overwhelming when you take them one step at a time. Students often have trouble taking that first step, but once you do, the rest of the paper won't be so hard.

Try to think of your paper as an adventure. Think of this project as a fun journey. In most cases, students can pick their own topics. The part I always liked about writing papers was being able to explore ideas in the library. I enjoyed being responsible for learning new things, to not be spoon-fed information by the teacher. Look at your paper as if you were a dog being let off the leash, allowed to run free. You are being trusted to go off on your own and make things happen.

This paper is important for your education. Think of your first research paper as a giant leap forward in your education. You have crossed the magic threshold into a different world—a world in which you learn how to think for yourself. This is a journey where you are calling the shots. You get to stretch your mind and use you brain power to think critically. You don't need Mom or your teacher to hold you by the hand.

Remember your goal in writing the paper. Keep in mind that your teacher is asking you to write this research paper to prove you can do the following things: research, analyze, and organize all of the information you gather and write a coherent, thoughtful paper. What does "thoughtful" mean? It means you can take all of your research, write about it, and give your unique perspective on the information. This might be the hardest step for you to accomplish because often students just have to regurgitate information back to the teacher based on what has been taught and what is in the textbook. This may be the first time you have to think for yourself. Have courage. This is a very important step for you, not only for this paper, but for your life. You will be glad you did when you get to the other side and have the satisfaction of knowing that this is *your* creation. Enjoy the process.

Check out your attitude. Do you feel really negative about writing? Would you rather be boiled in oil than write this paper? Remember that 80 percent of researching and writing is attitude, and the rest is the work you will do. Shed that negative attitude like Superman sheds his street clothes. You are wasting your time, your energy, and your grade.

Meet all of your teacher's deadlines. He will probably ask you to do a series of tasks in stages. Each stage will be worth a certain number of points. If you miss any of those deadlines, you will lose points *before* you have even started to write the paper. Bad move. Too many students don't pay attention to the small details and find themselves stuck in a big hole.

Standard Research Paper Techniques

1. **Get your teacher's instructions about the number of pages required and deadlines for the different steps.** Yes, yes, I know I just told you that you would be on your own. You will be once you get through the initial stages of this paper, but it is important to know exactly what your teacher wants you to turn in and when. This is the mechanical phase of the paper, not the brainpower phase that you will be in charge of. If you are unsure of some of your teacher's instructions, be

What things interest you? What would you like to know more about? Brainstorm ideas for your research paper.

Have the attitude that learning new things is fun. Don't waste your energy dreading something. Jump in and make it fun!

sure and ask lots of questions. You will save yourself many headaches down the road. Get all of the little details out of the way so that you can strut your stuff.

2. **What should I write about?** Now, for the fun part. Start thinking about possible topics. If you are writing this paper for a history class, flip through your textbook looking for things that interest you. Write down each of the topics that you enjoyed reading about. If you didn't enjoy reading anything in the book, figure out which period of history that you studied interested you the most. With that information in mind, go to the library. See what you can find on that period of history. If you are having trouble finding something, ask the librarian for help. She will probably have some good advice for you. And remember, if you treat her courteously, she will be happy to help you. Most people go out of their way to help teenagers who are courteous and kind.

If you feel overwhelmed by this paper and are finding it hard to take this first step, ask someone to help you focus. Once I helped a teenager get started on his paper. He was very frustrated and didn't know where to begin. He was fascinated about pirates and wanted to make this his topic. I asked him what he knew about pirates. He told me all he knew and then we brainstormed how he could get this into a historical theme. We finally focused on the historical impact the pirates had on the countries of England and Spain. Once he got started, he was able to do it. He was very proud of the B he got on the paper, and rightly so! So often, taking that first step is the hardest part of all.

3. **You next step is to start doing the research in the library.** Often you can get information on the Internet too, but do not use this as your only source of information. Books should be the source of most of your research. Back to the pirate example. Since the student was interested in pirates and their historical impact on countries, he had to see if he could get enough information on his topic. The student found out everything he could and was then able to find a common theme in all of his information. If he found more information on the economic impact of pirates instead of their political impact, then he knew he must head in that direction.

4. **What kind of information do you need for this paper?** Once you have narrowed down your topic you can be more focused on the type of information you need to

get for your paper. While doing the research, be sure you identify each new source in as complete a fashion as possible. Write down the name of the book you are using, its author, the publisher, and the publication date. When you copy something directly from a book, use quotation marks so that you will know this is a direct quote. Use the page number where you found the information. Keeping complete records will enable you to give credit to other authors.

Always present your ideas in a clear and logical way.

5. **After you get your research done, sit back and relax.** Read over all of your information and try to get a sense of what you want to say about the subject. What is your opinion about all of this? Being able to put your unique perspective on what you have learned will help you write a better paper. Simply repeating what you have discovered is not enough. You must approach all of this information from your own critical perspective. What conclusions can you draw from all of this? After you have done this, you are ready for the next step.

6. **Write your thesis statement.** My student saw that the pirates' sacking of Spanish ships had a devastating impact on Spain's economy and that this was one of the most important reasons for Spain's eventual decline. So his thesis statement became, "The pirates' continual sacking of Spain's ships was one of the most important reasons for Spain's eventual fall from world domination."

7. **Write an outline giving all of the ideas you want to include in the paper.** Be sure your ideas are presented in a logical order, leading the reader to reach the inescapable conclusion that yes, your thesis statement has merit.

8. **Now, write your paper!** Your job now is to start to write the paper, always keeping in mind that you are presenting information to prove the thesis statement. This is where your research comes in. You will include all of your sources that show how your thesis makes sense. You will include your unique perspective on all of this information. Try not to get sidetracked. Keep asking yourself if what you are writing supports your thesis.

Caveats (Warnings)

Be sure you meet all of your teacher's deadlines. He sets these deadlines for your protection so you won't wait until the last minute to research and write this paper. I can't

Be sure and give credit to an author when you use his ideas and conclusions.

mention this warning too many times. Too often, students do not meet the deadlines and lose important points on the total score of their papers. They also make their families miserable because they are hysterically trying to get the paper done in one day, asking Mom or Dad for help. This is not the way to treat your family or yourself.

Do not copy anything from books and pretend that you wrote it. This is called plagiarism. You must give credit to the proper source. Besides, your teacher will probably know you did not write what you plagiarized. Teachers have a sixth sense about this. They know your writing style and the sophistication of your writing. You run the risk of getting an *F* when you copy someone else's work. Paraphrasing—putting ideas you find in books into your own words—is okay as long as you credit sources where appropriate. So stay out of trouble and do your paper honestly.

Get a variety of sources for the paper. Use books, magazines, and newspapers. Do not use articles from the encyclopedia except for general knowledge about your subject. When taking notes on a specific source, write your own interpretation immediately. Then, when you start to write the paper, you won't have to spend a lot of time trying to figure out why you took those notes. It's easy to forget why that information caught your attention.

Keep all of your notes in a safe place, such as an envelope or a file folder. If you keep your notes and your bibliographic information in one place, you won't lose important data and will be able to write your paper more easily.

Do all of your paragraphs support your thesis statement? Go back through your paper after you write it and delete any information that does not help prove your thesis statement. Your goal is to write only things that will back up what you are saying.

Keep your teacher informed about what you are doing. That way you will get her expert advice and know immediately if you are on the right track. Remember, she's the one giving you the grade. Play the game—her game.

Step back from your paper. After you have finished writing the paper, set it aside for a day. Then come back to it and look at it with a more critical eye. Did you express yourself well? Are you confident that your readers will see things as you do because you have stated your ideas so effectively or do you see where you can shore up parts of the paper? Your job in this stage is to rewrite sections you feel are weak.

Mechanics. After your final draft is completed, do the following things. If you don't, it won't matter how good the ideas in your paper are—*your grade will suffer.*

- **Check your spelling.** If unsure of a word, go look it up. Use your word processor's spell checker. Ask your mother or father to proofread the paper for you.
- **Check your punctuation.** Did you use quotation marks for all quotes?
- **Check out your paragraphs.** Are they cohesive? Are some of them too long or too short? Can you separate some of them or add to others? Do you have good transitions between paragraphs that let the reader move easily from one paragraph to another. If there is an abrupt change of ideas in the next paragraph, this will have a jarring effect on the reader. Make sure all of the paragraphs flow. A good technique here would be to read the paper out loud. You will then know if it sounds good.
- **Check the clarity of your wording.** Should you substitute words that will make your sentences clearer? Have you used slang in the paper, like "King Philip II was really ticked off"? If so, take it out because you are not speaking to your audience, you are writing to them. Research papers are considered formal writing.
- **Check out your bibliography.** Is it exactly in the format your teacher wants you to use? If not, change it. Doing your own thing here is not advisable. Your teacher has asked for the information in this way for good reasons. Don't try to reinvent the wheel, thinking you know a better way. It's just not a smart thing to do.
- **Check for typos.** Be sure your work is neat. Your teacher will be able to devote all of her time reading what you wrote and will not be distracted by sloppiness. Think of this as getting yourself an insurance policy.

USING THE COMPUTER

Here are some things you should know about computers:

Computers have taken over the world. It is impossible to imagine our modern world without them. Virtually everything is computerized. You must adapt to computers and accept their importance or you will get left behind. Many mistakenly believe that only people working as computer programmers

After you finish writing the paper, set it aside for a day. Then go back and pretend to be the teacher. Check to see if you have logical sentences, good punctuation and spelling, and logical ideas.

Computers are a time-saving invention. They help you do things faster. Use them as much as you can.

and keyboarders are affected by this constantly changing revolution of computer use. The fact is that computers are used in just about every field imaginable. Even police officers have computers in their patrol cars so that they can check a license plate and get a criminal record on someone they stop on the road. Many office workers now work at home and stay in contact with the workplace via e-mail and the Internet. You might some day be able to save yourself a lot of time and money for gas by working in a home office.

Things used to be a lot simpler. Students prepared for a certain job and then worked for the same company all of their working lives. Now companies are downsizing, and there is very little loyalty to the workers in most corporations. Because of this new trend in business, the more skills you have, the more indispensable you will be to the company you work for. Knowledge of how to use computers is extremely important. Even if you choose to start your own business, you will need a good, well-rounded education, including business, people, and computer skills. Many start-up businesses fail because the people have no clue how to run the business. They might have a good product, but if they don't know how to manufacture it and market it with the latest technology, they will not make it.

Computers are much easier to use than typewriters. With a computer, you don't have to worry about mechanics, centering the page, and erasures like you do with a typewriter. Instead of retyping the entire page, you can instantly make changes on your computer, which leaves you with more time to be creative and to solve other problems.

Knowledge of computer technology has become an educational necessity. School districts all over the country are scrambling to catch up to changes in the computer world. Changes happen so fast that equipment is quickly surpassed by newer, faster machines. When you go to college, you might find yourself having to connect with professors via the Internet. You will be able to find assignments, get feedback from your teachers, and even take exams online. When you become computer proficient and are connected to the World Wide Web, you can communicate with others via e-mail and get, evaluate, and sort through information on the Web.

The best way to learn computers is to learn by doing. Jump in and start to experiment and explore. Software companies have made it amazingly easy to figure out how to use their programs, with the entire user's manual built into the program or offer online help so you can get assistance while you work. The more computer literate you are, the more attractive you will look to companies hiring new employees. It's always a good idea to develop and improve your skills in as many areas as possible.

Facts About the Internet

The Internet is a worldwide network of computers connected by means of satellite links. Universities and other large organizations such as corporations have their computers permanently linked to each other via millions of connections, like a jellyfish with many tentacles. Home computer users connect to the Internet by dialing via a modem (a device which enables computers to communicate through the telephone lines) to a server on the network. The server you connect to is provided by an Internet Service Provider (ISP) such as America Online (AOL). AOL is the largest ISP provider and is very popular because it provides local phone numbers in the medium-sized and large cities that enable you to keep in contact with family, friends, and your business via the Internet.

By using the Internet to connect to other computers, you can become friends with other people and share information on an incredible number of subjects. One of the most common uses of the Internet is to send and receive e-mail. You may also have group discussions with people from all over the world at one time or surf the World Wide Web.

The World Wide Web is the most popular and easiest way to access and exchange information. This is because all you have to do to move from one part of the Web to another is point your mouse at certain words or pictures and click. These special words or pictures are called links.

Most educational institutions are establishing a presence on the World Wide Web. To keep up with the competition, all kinds of businesses are feeling obligated to get on the Web because it is becoming a way for many of them to provide information about their services or their products. If you want to know about a college, check the Web for information. You can save yourself a lot of time by researching online.

Surfing the Web is a safe way to surf without crashing on shore. You'll lose track of time while you explore, so leave the surfing until after your work is done.

SHORTCUT TO ACTION

1. Start studying several days before a test. Then, you won't get stressed out.
2. Listen carefully to your teacher's explanations and descriptions of what's on the test.
3. Listen to EVERYTHING the teacher says when he hands out the test. He will give you important instructions and information.
4. Listen when your teacher goes over already graded exams. Some of the things you messed up might show up on the final exam.
5. Do your most important assignments and those due the soonest first.
6. Relax when studying. Don't drive yourself crazy.
7. Memorize things in small chunks. Take frequent breaks.
8. Repeat what you're memorizing over and over again at different times of the day and in different places.
9. Learn as many new words as you can in high school. The more you learn now, the easier college will be for you.
10. Read, read, read. It keeps your brain active.
11. Learn how to use your library as soon as you get to high school. Good library skills come in handy when you have to write a research paper.
12. Learn how to use a computer and surf the Web. Both can help you get a better education.

CHAPTER 5

GRINDING OUT THE GRADES

GRADE STUFF SIMPLIFIED

I saved the discussion of grades for the last topic on school skills because I think too many students think of grades as the *only* thing in high school. I like to think of it as an aid for you to see how you're doing in school. Your grades can help you assess whether you are doing your job well or whether you have to make some changes.

One thing I want to make clear before we go on with this discussion of grades is that your self-worth is *not* based on your grades. Just because you got an F in history does not mean you are a bad person. Failure in a class is an *event,* not a person. Remember that distinction so you keep all of this in perspective.

Study the following points about grades. It is always good to step back from something to get a different perspective.

Learning is not just about grades. You learn in order to improve your critical thinking skills (your ability to THINK) and your vocabulary. You are preparing for a future in which everything you have learned will help you cope with all of the demands that will be made on you just to pay your bills, raise a family, adapt to inevitable change, and live fully. Even though you may never make use of your geometry skills, you will have exercised and used your mind in a different way so that you will be able to solve other kinds of problems in the future. A well-exercised mind allows you to deal flexibly with your life.

Some students do not see why they need to do any school work. One boy told me he just wanted to be an auto mechanic. I told him that was great—we need good, well-educated mechanics. He will be able to deal with people and to solve problems in his work *because of his education*. I love to talk to mechanics and people who work with their hands but who are also thinkers—seeing their points of view helps me learn a lot.

Grades are important. You need to pay attention to them. Unfortunately, they often determine how a student feels about himself. I have seen kids feel like failures and go into a downward spiral because of their grades. But you *can* do something about what is happening to you in school. You need to step back from the situation and have a talk with yourself. I always tell my students they can do better, but they have to believe it. There is no greater joy for me than when a student gets back on track. It is what has kept me in teaching all of these years. I sure haven't stayed because I love grading papers!

Know what determines your grade. Be sure and ask each teacher what his grades are based on. Sometimes students in my class don't do their homework, which is a significant percentage of the grade. By looking at homework points as an insurance policy, you will see how those points help pad your grade if you fail a test. You won't be completely lost if you have gotten all of your homework points. Don't hurt yourself by not doing this simple task. Besides, homework helps you learn your material. That's the reason teachers ask you to do it in the first place.

Constantly update your grade in each class. From time to time, take a minute after class to talk with your teacher about your grade. Do not just sit there and wait for that dreaded progress report. The teacher is only your coach. You're the one out there playing the game. Take charge now.

Be active in class, not passive. Look at your posture in class. Do you automatically sit in the back row and slouch in your seat? Do you look like you're half asleep? When you sit up straight, you are more attentive, do better, and feel better about yourself.

How much time do you spend doing homework? Many students have told me that they only study 30 minutes a day. That is not enough. You should probably study at least two hours every night. If you find you can get everything done in half an hour, you're taking classes that are too easy for you. You might want to look into getting a few harder classes in your schedule next year so you won't be so bored in school.

Do your very best. Be proud and satisfied with what you have produced. Don't beat yourself up if you have done all you can and a C is the grade you got. To get a C in a demanding class, such as calculus or English, when you've worked especially hard can be a reason to celebrate.Ask yourself the following questions to determine if you should be proud about your grade.

1. Did I pay attention to the teacher and take notes in class?
2. Did I copy information correctly from the board?
3. Did I participate in class discussions?
4. Did I do all of my homework and hand it in on time?

When you improve your grade in a hard class, jump up and down and CELEBRATE. You have accomplished something good. You're on your way!

5. Did I study for quizzes, tests, and exams?
6. Did I get help from the teacher if I didn't understand something?

If you can answer that you did all of these six things, then you did the best you can and no one can tell you otherwise. Search your conscience on this one, though. It's important to be totally honest with yourself so that you can make needed changes. For some students, not handing in the homework is what does them in. Where are you not doing the best you can?

The following poem was written by my mother, Dorothy Carpenter, in 1926, when she was in high school.

My English Lesson

I sat alone at evening time,
A hard school day had reached its close;
My brain tried long to find a rhyme
My English lesson to compose.

But I was weary with the task
And gladly would have gone to bed,
But knew Miss Callahan would ask
Me why I didn't write instead.

Thus, in a situation bad,
I tried my best to find a way,
And used what little brain I had
Preparing for the next school day.

I do not like to thus complain,
But, truly, I was much afraid
To enter class without this strain
To bolster up my poor, poor grade.

My English may not stand the test,
But you should know, Miss Callahan,
Though this may seem a silly jest,
I still have done the best I can.

Even back then, students had to sweat out their school assignments and worried about doing a good job—you're not alone!

Class rank. Try to get in the top half of your graduating class. It will ensure your entrance into more postsecondary schools and training programs. Remember that good grades are the outside world's way of judging you. If you get fairly good grades, employers and colleges will see you as a person who is responsible and dependable. If you get bad grades, you may be viewed as irresponsible and not a hard worker.

You may be seen as a risky investment. That's just the way it is. Accept it now. Get the best grades you can.

Be proud of your good grades. An outstanding student got the school's highest athletic award at a school assembly but didn't want her GPA announced to the whole school. She had nearly all A's. It's sad that we let others determine how we're going to feel about ourselves. The student should not have felt she had to hide how smart she was. I have only seen this happen in academics—never in speech meets or basketball games. The girl who scores the winning basket is the hero of the day, but if she appears too smart, she is not highly regarded by some students. It's easier to make fun of someone with good grades than to get them yourself. People who use their brains to succeed in school spend their energies pulling themselves up, not putting others down. Don't put others down because you're not working hard enough to get decent grades. Be honest with yourself. It is absolutely essential for your future.

When good grades become an obsession. Some students can become so obsessed with getting perfect grades that they cannot accept a mere B. Marsha got perfect grades in high school and felt on top of the world until she went away to college. She went to a very competitive college where she was a small fish in a big pond. There, she did not get all A's. She had some B's and C's. She could not deal with what seemed to her proof that she was worthless as a human being. She had to be perfect all of the time. When she could not attain perfection, she became depressed and returned to her home town feeling like a loser. She lay around the house for several days and finally committed suicide because she simply could not face life. For her, there was no way out. If you ever find yourself in a situation like this, please get help. You are NOT worthless. You are simply human. It is not possible for anyone to be perfect. Accept that what is you have done in school is your best work. Do not set high standards for yourself that you can never reach. You are bound to be unhappy if you do. Give yourself a break. Remember, grades do not determine your self-worth. The student who gets all A's is not worth more than the student who gets average grades. Your grades are what you *do,* not who you are.

Look at the so-called nerds who get good grades. A lot of them are going to be the ones who bring home the big bucks. They'll be the ones you envy some day.

A TALE OF TWO STUDENTS

Sean gets B's and C's in school, but he has to struggle to get them. His classmate Jim gets A's and B's with very little effort. Who do you think is going to be more prepared to join the job market and do good work—Sean or Jim? The truth is that

*Do you have to work
to get good grades?
Despair not. You are
preparing yourself
for a career as a
good, productive
worker.*

_____

Sean will be the more prepared because he has had to use his tenacity to get through his courses. He knows how to work hard. Jim, however, because he has always had an easy school life, is the one who will have a harder time coping the first time something difficult comes his way. If you are a student who gets all A's and B's without any effort, you need to get into harder classes to give you the challenge you need to learn how to work hard. Don't avoid taking the harder class because you probably won't get an A. The extra work you have to do will help you become a better student and a more determined person.

Is it ever too late to get better grades? No! If you decide in your junior year that you need to get better grades, it is *not* too late. You may not get into Harvard or Yale, but then, not many people do. Many colleges will cut you some slack when they see that you started getting serious in school. They will give more weight to your latest grades and will be more likely to take a chance on you because they feel you have matured and are on your way to bigger and better things.

Can I coast through my last semester of high school? You'd better not try this one. Many seniors contract the disease they call "senioritis" and coast through their last semester, getting wretched grades. I have always advised my seniors not to do this because colleges want to see your second semester grades. Yes, you might have already been admitted to the college of your choice, but you don't want your GPA to fall too much. I have had students who were put on academic probation because their senior grades were terrible. They're in trouble before they even get to college. I've even known of cases where students lost their scholarships and their admission to a school. *Be careful, seniors!*

"None of this will help me. This is all a lot of bull." I know some of you are saying this while reading this chapter. I don't blame you for feeling that way. You have had a rough time in school. The only thing I can tell you is that you won't know what you can do until you try a different way. You know what you have been doing doesn't work. Ask your teachers how you can learn better. Ask your best friend for help in a hard subject. Don't suffer in silence. Sometimes we just have to admit we *don't* know what to do to change things. You will find your niche, a good place in this world, if you become aware of what you need to do to change things. Hang in there.

What is a GPA?

GPA stands for grade point average. Your GPA is the standard measure of your success in high school. They are used to determine your rank in class and they factor into college admission decisions, athletic and academic scholarships, qualification for special programs, and work opportunities. Please note that your GPA follows you each year—it is the average of all of your grades from freshman year on.

How to calculate your GPA:

Generally schools use the following point system:

A 4 points
B 3 points
C 2 points
D 1 point
F 0 points

IMPORTANT: Generally, the highest GPA you can have is a 4.0 in most schools. Some schools, however, have honors courses that have a higher value, so that an A might be calculated at 4.5 points. Be sure and check your school's grade point policy before you try to calculate your GPA. Here's an example of Rick's grades:

English	B	3 points
History	B	3 points
Art	A	4 points
Math	D	1 point
Spanish	C	2 points
Physical Education	B	3 points

Add up the points Rick gained in each class and then divide by the total number of classes. The 16 points (total points) divided by 6 (the number of classes he took), gives Rick a GPA of 2.66.

TRY THIS!

1. **Look at a class or classes where you want to improve your grade.** Using all of the information you have learned from this book, write up a game plan (a goal) for improving your grades. What are you going to do differently in each class? Make up a schedule for assessing this. How are you going to celebrate when you get a better grade? Get your parents involved in this.

2. **Write in your journal why grades should be important to you.** If you are not trying, include why you refuse to try to do better. Write down all of your feelings on this one. After you have finished writing, go for a walk and think about what you just wrote. Can you do something differently? What? What's the payoff

What kinds of activities will you do to learn new things when you're an adult? Will you set a good example for your kids when they start school? Will they learn from you that learning is fun?

Don't just sit there when you're failing a class.

Do something!

for you in the future? What happens if you don't do well? Are you just used to feeling like a failure so that it feels comfortable to you? Is it easier to blame someone else, such as your parents, for your bad grades, so that you won't have to take responsibility for them? Really go deep into this issue to figure it out. It's important and will help you make changes.

ATTENTION, STUDENTS: YOU WILL BE LIFELONG LEARNERS!

Cultivate a curiosity and interest in new things. Resolve to keep up on current affairs, new scientific discoveries, and the latest technology. Read, read, read. You will stay young at heart if you do not get stale and stuck in your ways. Open up to new things and enjoy learning for learning's sake. Why, you ask? You never know when your new-found knowledge will help you in some part of your life. With education, you give yourself the following things:

Empowerment to have the tools to do what you want with your life.
Freedom to make decisions about what you want to do in the future.
Independence to make changes when you want to improve your life.
Knowledge to explore different areas until you find your life's work.

THINGS TO DO IF YOU'RE IN AN IMPOSSIBLE CLASS

Check Over Your Schedule. As soon as you get your schedule in the summer, look at it. Were any mistakes made on the schedule? Did you get put into an advanced science class even though you barely passed last year? Did you fail Spanish 1 but are now signed up for Spanish 2?

Talk to your guidance counselor. You need to talk to your counselor as soon as possible *before* school starts. If you go to school before the first day of classes, you will have a better chance of seeing your counselor and getting things straightened out. Often counselors come back to school two to four weeks before anyone else. If you wait until the first day of school, your counselor will be overwhelmed with students trying to get out of a class because they don't like the teacher or because their friends eat in a different lunch period. She will be much less likely to be able to help you.

What do I do if the class is harder than I expected? If you're in a class and don't understand anything that's going on, you should ask yourself whether you are really trying hard enough. If you have given the class all of the energy and time you have and have seen the teacher for help, do the following. STEP 1: Talk to your teacher about solutions. STEP 2: Talk to your parents. STEP 3: Talk to your counselor. Your counselor checks your placement and can work with you, your teacher, and your parents to resolve the problem. I don't believe there's a teacher alive who wants a student to stay in a class if he has tried everything and is still feeling overwhelmed and totally lost.

However, too often students give up without even trying. This is very bad for your future. To admit defeat automatically when you have not even tried to do the class work is not good. You must have a more combative attitude—combat your negative image of yourself. Go to the teacher for help. Ask questions. Get your friends to help you. We spend so much time in life pretending we're okay when we're not. Admit you have a problem; then you can do something about it. Don't just accept an *F* without fighting back. If you are working to the best of your ability, then you may need to try to transfer to a less difficult class. Sometimes a student is put in the wrong class. It is not fair to have to stay in an impossible class. Talk to your teacher, parents, and counselor for help.

Check out these charts. You can see what kinds of jobs pay good salaries. Notice that the jobs in List 2 require specialized training but do not require a college degree. And, they pay a decent salary. Do the kind of job that will make you happiest.

DROPPING OUT—WHY NOT?

Do you want to flip burgers the rest of your life? You will not be using your mind as well as you could if you stayed in school and got your education. Plus, by flipping burgers, you're constantly standing on your feet. Feet need a rest too. Give them a break. Stay in school and sit a spell.

High School dropouts earn much less than high school and college graduates. Check out the average hourly wage and annual salary of the following professions.

Profession	Hourly Wage	Annual Wage*	Training Required
1			
Cashier	$6.96	$14,480	None
Waitress	$5.87	$12,200	None
Cook (fast food)	$6.11	$12,700	None
Baggage porter/ bellhop	$6.92	$14,400	None
Parking lot attendant	$7.06	$14,680	None

Profession	Hourly Wage	Annual Wage*	Training Required
2			
Heating, air conditioning and refrigeration mechanic	$14.48	$30,120	High school diploma or associate's degree
Fire inspector	$20.36	$42,340	High school diploma or associate's degree
Aircraft mechanic	$17.65	$36,710	High school diploma or associate's degree
3			
Financial manager	$27.43	$57,060	High school diploma
General manager	$29.31	$60,960	4-year college
Education administrator	$26.87	$55,900	Some graduate work
Management analyst	$25.05	$52,110	Some graduate work

Information gathered from the Bureau of Labor Statistics of the U.S. Department of Labor, 1997, the latest figures available when this book went to press.

*To figure out an annual income or salary from an hourly wage, multiply the hourly wage by 2080 (the average number of working hours in a year—52 weeks x 40 hours per week).

List 1 includes the type of jobs for which high school dropouts qualify. These are the jobs you will be doing if you do not finish high school.

List 2 includes jobs you can do with a high school diploma and additional training, either through trade school or an employer training program. No employer will consider training you for a career if you don't have that high school degree.

List 3 includes jobs for which you must have a college degree.

Notice the huge salary difference when you get a college degree. It makes a big difference to get more education. It pays to hang in there and keep on going. Some day you will be very glad you did.

Fast food jobs are survival-only jobs. You will have to work overtime hours to pay all of your bills. Minimum wage jobs are dead-end jobs. If you are thinking of dropping out of high school, consider the consequences.

Higher education pays off big time. With your high school education and training after high school, you will be able to take better care of your future family. You will have enough extra money to travel and do the things you enjoy. You don't want to have to live with your parents because you can't afford to live on your own, do you? You need to graduate from high school, then get some training or a college education. That's just a fact of life.

You want some self-respect. If you drop out now, you will always regret it when you're older. People will not treat you with as much respect as they do people with more education. I have talked to numerous people who did not continue their education after high school and they all regret not going on to trade school or college.

70 to 80 percent of criminals are high school dropouts. Because they are having a hard time paying their bills, they turn to crime to feed themselves and their families. Don't become a part of this tragic statistic.

High school graduates, on the average, earn $6415 more per year than high school dropouts. Information gathered from the Bureau of the Census, 1994, the latest figures available when this book went to press.

Students from low-income families are 2.4 times more likely to drop out of school than are children from middle-income families, and 10.5 times more likely than students from high-income families. Information gathered from the U.S. Department of Commerce, Economics and Statistics Administration, 1993, the latest figures available when this book went to press.

OTHER OPTIONS BESIDES YOUR HIGH SCHOOL

Some of you will have a hard time surviving in a regular public high school. When you think that there is no way for you to be successful, you might turn to cutting classes, doing drugs, or just drop out. If you find yourself in this situation and you have truly tried your hardest to do well but you just seem to keep getting into trouble, talk to your counselor about other options. Here are some of the things you can do instead of attending your regular public high school:

Some larger districts have magnet schools. If you live in a large school district that has magnet schools, call up the administrative office to check out what the requirements are

If you hate your regular school and have done every-thing possible to do well, talk to your counselor about other ways you can get the classes you need to graduate.

Students who drop out of high school can go back and get a GED in order to be eligible for college or training programs. It's never too late!

for admission. Often, these schools have special schools for the arts, music, or technology. They can be a great option for students who are unhappy with their public high school.

Many districts have alternative schools for students who fail to succeed in the regular public high school. Ask your counselor if you can transfer. She will help you if she feels you need to make a change.

Summer school helps you get back on track. If you fail some classes and are hopelessly behind, you can catch up by taking summer school classes. It should help you to catch up with the classmates you started high school with. Do you want to be in classes with freshmen and sophomores when you should be a junior or senior?

Correspondence courses are another option. Some high schools allow you to take correspondence courses associated with your state university for credit. You have to be very motivated to work on your own, do the classwork, send it in, and take the tests. No one will be demanding that you take tests at a certain time. You alone will determine whether you pass the class.

The General Educational Development (GED) test. If you don't finish high school, you can take a test that certifies you have a high school–level knowledge of reading and writing skills and know English grammar. In addition, passing the test will show that you know as much math, social studies, and science as the typical high school graduate. When you pass the test, you will get a certificate known as the GED.

Students take the GED for many reasons. Some may be very bright and feel that high school is a waste of their time. Others take it because they had problems with drugs and alcohol in high school and either dropped out or failed. Most students who pass the GED go on to a community college. Another option is to get a job with an employer who will train you for a profession. Many companies are willing to give a GED-certified student a chance if he shows lots of promise and ambition. In addition, some four-year colleges accept GED students. One university I know of even has a scholarship for high-scoring GED students.

You must never give up hope, even if you flunk several classes or drop out of high school. I know a boy who handcuffed himself to his bed so that he wouldn't have to go to school. He dropped out of high school, but later got his GED. He is making a good living now and has gone on to get a college degree. His grades were good, but he just hated high school. There are many routes to success and no student should *ever* feel that his life is hopeless. Never give up hope.

If you are hopelessly bored in high school and are a senior, often you can graduate a semester early. If your school won't let you leave a semester early, you can explore the option of taking high school courses in the morning and college courses in the afternoon. My nephew took a junior college English composition course and felt that it made him more prepared for writing papers in college. In addition, he felt he was more psychologically prepared to start college. Talk to your counselor about dual enrollment options.

Ask your counselor about dual enrollment—you can take college-level courses while you're still in high school.

More Facts on the GED

- **The current GED consists of five tests** in the areas of writing skills, social studies, science, literature and the arts, and math. Each part of the test requires you to use general knowledge and thinking skills to answer questions.
- **The test itself is composed of the following sections:**
  Writing Skills, Part I (55 questions, 75 minutes)
    35% sentence structure
    35% usage
    30% spelling, punctuation, and capitalization
  Writing Skills, Part II (essay, 45 minutes)
  Social Studies (64 questions, 85 minutes)
    25% history
    20% economics
    20% political science
    15% geography
    20% behavioral sciences
  Science (66 questions, 95 minutes)
    50% life science
    50% physical science
  Interpreting Literature and the Arts (45 questions, 65 minutes)
    50% popular literature
    25% classical literature
    25% commentary on literature and the arts
  Mathematics (56 questions, 90 minutes)
    50% arithmetic
    30% algebra
    20% geometry
- **How to prepare for the test.** Many school districts and colleges have adult education programs that provide you with the instruction you need to take the test and can counsel you on your weakest areas. In addition,

cable television and public television stations sometimes carry a television series to prepare for the GED. Also, many bookstores and libraries have specific books that help you practice for all sections of the GED. Ask your librarian or bookstore for help. Finally, student classes to prepare for the GED take an average of 3–6 months; some students are ready sooner and some students need longer to study. For more information, call 800-62-MYGED.

YOUR SCHOOL GUIDANCE COUNSELOR

Your counselor:

- Monitors your grades and reviews your progress toward earning enough credits to graduate.
- Helps you explore different career options and college choices.
- Writes letters of recommendation to colleges and employers on your behalf.
- Is your advocate if you have trouble with friends, teachers, or with family members. He or she helps you sort through your feelings and come up with some possible solutions to your problems.
- Helps you straighten out scheduling conflicts. The counselor's job is to advise you how to take care of problems.
- Helps you choose courses that are appropriate for you based on your future career choice and your ability. He knows the requirements well and can tell you if a certain class fulfills a requirement such as practical arts or fine arts.

Students often don't go to the counselor because they think counselors are too busy to see them. Yes, counselors are very busy, but if you have a valid need, you have every right to take up his or her time.

Things Your Counselor Doesn't Want You to Do

I asked several counselors the kinds of things kids do that bug them. Here are some of the things they said.

Don't procrastinate. Give your recommendation letters to your counselor *at least* two weeks before he has to mail them. Four weeks would be even better. He has a lot of letters to write for other seniors. Understand that he can only do so much. In addition, give him pre-addressed stamped envelopes so that he can simply drop the recommendations in the mail. Writing a thank-you note afterwards would be a nice gesture.

Don't lie. Be honest. Don't tell him only the partial truth, leaving out important details. This will cause both of you a lot of trouble later on.

Don't beg him not to tell your parents if it's about something that involves your safety or the safety of others.

Don't blame him for your placement in the wrong class. You should know where you belong. Let me give you an example. A student signed up for Spanish 2 in March but then failed Spanish 1 in June. He knew he should not go on to Spanish 2 if he didn't even know the Spanish 1 material, so he went to his counselor and switched his fall class. Like I said before, you must take control of your destiny by keeping close track of your classes.

Don't say you'll do something and then not do it. If you are not going to do something, then don't say you will.

Don't fall apart without letting your counselor know first! Ask lots of questions. Ask for help when you need it. Don't wait until you are in a terrible situation; early intervention is best.

College and Career Center

Many schools have a college and career center where you can find information on:

- careers and occupations
- four-year colleges and universities and two-year schools
- financial aid and scholarships
- students with special needs
- technical, business, and nursing schools and career training programs

Do the research necessary to plan your future.

SHORTCUT TO ACTION

1. Your grades are very important. Just as a baseball pitcher is judged on his ERA and a hitter on his RBI's, your grades tell how well you are doing your job.
2. Spend at least two hours on homework every night. If you finish your written work, study your foreign language or math, for example.
3. When you're failing a class, ask your teacher for help. Don't be proud while you go down in flames. It doesn't pay.
4. If you feel totally lost in a class, ask the teacher if you should be in a different class. She might have a strategy you can use to catch up with the other students.
5. Stay in school. You'll make more money for the rest of your life. Drop out and your only option will be minimum wage jobs.

PART 2

PERSONAL SKILLS

CHAPTER 6

Getting Along With Important People

HOW TO GET ALONG WITH YOUR PARENTS

Since teenagers often complain about the problems they have with their parents, let's take a look at what to do to make this important relationship better. We will examine what students like you have said you need from your parents and at what your parents need from you. I hope you will then be able to look at the situation from both points of view, and get some perspective on the age-old struggle between teens and parents.

What You Need From Your Parents

Respect. Every teenager needs to feel he is a worthy person who deserves respect. In your interactions with your parents, you must be trustworthy and honest in order to be respected.

Independence. No teenager wants to be tied to his mother's apron strings, but putting some distance between yourself and your parents when you love them and depend on them is tricky. Some tips will follow.

Privacy. You would like to keep your personal belongings, such as greeting cards, letters, and your journal, away from a parent's prying eyes. Many teenagers have told me that parents read their letters "just because." You have a right to your privacy, but this becomes a sticky issue if your parents feel you are endangering your life with drugs or alcohol or are suicidal. Then the rules go out the window because their primary job is to protect you. They love you and do not want to see you destroy yourself. So always be open and communicative with your parents. If you tell them what's going on in your life, they won't feel they need to pry. If you have nothing to hide, this should not be a problem.

To be heard. You would like to feel that your opinion carries a lot of value in your family. Communication works both ways. Parents need to listen to their teens and teens need to listen to their parents.

What Your Parents Need From You

To be heard. Many parents get frustrated when their teenagers refuse to listen and become defensive toward them. Both sides need to chill out and start over. Keep a calm tone of voice and be rational when you talk to your parents. Speak to them in a logical manner.

Respect. Parents want you to value their viewpoint. After all, they have been through a lot more than you have and have more experience. They also do not want you to make fun of what they believe in and what they do. Lots of teenagers think parents (as well as anyone over 25) are hopelessly old-fashioned and out of touch. You don't like it when they treat you like a dumb teenager, do you? They don't like being treated like old fossils either.

Privacy. Parents also need privacy. Do you always give your opinion on everything they do, or do you respect them and trust that they know what they're doing? Do you leave them alone while they grapple with life's everyday problems, such as paying the mortgage and managing hectic schedules, or are you always telling them what they should do as if they were too dumb to figure it out for themselves?

Responsibility. Your parents want to see that you have a sense of responsibility. Do you do what you say you're going to do? Do you tell the truth? Do you do your schoolwork like you're supposed to? Can they count on you?

Communication. Parents want to know how you are doing. If you let them know what is going on in your life, they will be less fearful about what *could* happen to you when they see you coping with your problems on your own.

Sense of family. It is important to value your place in the family. One thing to remember is that your family will most likely be there for you even if you do something they are not proud of. The bond between family members is very strong. Do your part to make your family a happy and healthy one.

Why Your Parents Act Like They Do

They love you and they're afraid you'll get hurt. They read the newspapers and listen to the news and get scared hearing of all of the terrible things happening around them. They have to worry about you getting date raped, robbed, or hurt in an accident, no matter how unlikely it is that such an event will actually happen. Wherever you're concerned, your parents will always worry about you. It's normal for them. They can't help it. It's the parent thing to do. You might as well get used to it and accept it. It won't go away.

Do you storm away enraged at your parents and use every bad word you can think of? Bad idea. There are better ways to get what you need.

You want to get your parents off your back, right? Do things in a nice way. Remember, you can catch more flies with honey than vinegar.

They are afraid for you. They can still remember the things they used to do in high school when they were your age, and that gets their imaginations running wild. Many of them are thinking, "Gosh, I hope she doesn't do the kind of stuff that I did." They survived whatever they might have done, but they know there's a chance you may not. Parents have very active imaginations. You will probably be the same way when you have kids.

They want you to have the best life has to offer, and they think that by worrying and monitoring you closely, you have a better chance of being successful. Many times they treat you like this because of their own experiences while they were in high school. They remember some very painful things that happened to them, and again, they want to protect you. They don't want you to make the same mistakes as they did. If you communicate with them, maybe they'll relax and give you a little more breathing room.

How To Get What You Need From Your Parents

Respect. You must show yourself to be worthy of respect. Do *you* respect your parents because they are older than you and they are your parents, or do you refuse to do anything with them because you think they are "over the hill?" This works both ways. Parents need to respect you, too, but sometimes both sides get entrenched in a battle against each other because they can't see what the other needs. It is always a good idea to look at your parents when they speak to you and to avoid calling them names or leave the room swearing. Try to stay with them and listen to what they say, no matter how hard it may be. You probably need to "train them" in how you would like to be treated. You have a better chance of pulling this off if you don't start shouting and getting angry.

Independence. This is an easy thing to obtain if you show that you are responsible. Do your homework. Get decent grades in school. Drive with care and avoid accidents. Do your fair share of chores around the house. Be an all-around good person. The more they trust you, the more freedom your parents will give you. Try it. It works!

Privacy. Along with everything you've already read, if you show no signs of using drugs or alcohol or of having serious emotional problems, your parents should never need to invade your privacy.

To be heard. If you speak respectfully when talking to your parents and have logical reasons for what you want to do and how you feel, your parents should be able to hear you. If you try everything and nothing works, see the next section for ideas that can help.

Unreasonable Parents and Other Problems

I hope that you won't have to read this section, but if you have serious problems with your parents, *please read it carefully.* I know that the majority of parents are very conscientious about how they treat and relate to their children. Sometimes, however, you may find yourself in a bad situation. Check out some of the following tips for what to do when you don't feel you are to blame for the poor teenager-parent relationship.

Your parents are never satisfied with what you do. You always feel as though you aren't good enough. I hear this from teenagers a lot. In fact, I can remember that I worked really hard to please my parents by getting good grades. One day, in my sophomore year, I brought home my report card. All of my grades were either 98 or 99 percent. But my father laughed and asked, "Why didn't you get a 100?" I know today that he was just joking, but I was furious and vowed from that moment on never to go after high grades. The only problem was that I shot myself in the foot because I was not eligible for scholarships when I got out of high school. I had to work for my tuition, because I was one of eight children and my parents could not afford to send me to school. Do not hurt yourself because a parent makes you angry. Be good to yourself and know that you are OK as you are. The vast majority of teenagers start out by doing the best they can and get discouraged when they get all A's and one B. Some parents will focus on the B instead of realizing that the kid had to knock himself out to get all of those A's.

If your parents are alcoholics or drug users. This happens more often than our society cares to admit. We are in major denial about the bad effect drugs and alcohol have on the users and the people they come into contact with. As a teenager, you have your own problems trying to figure out what kind of person you want to become; you shouldn't have to deal with parents who are users. Fortunately, there is help for you. Look up Alcoholics Anonymous in your phone book and call them to ask where an Alateen meeting is being held near you. At Alateen you can talk with other teens who have the same problems you do—whose parents use drugs or alcohol. You will be able to separate yourself from your parents' problems more effectively. You can learn that what they do is not your problem. You cannot change them. Please

Sometimes parents upset you. These suggestions can help you figure out what to do about it.

Talking to a counselor or teacher can help a lot if your parents get divorced.

also realize that if your parents are substance abusers, you are more likely to be one. Be careful out there. Don't start and you will be okay. Don't forget: your counselor is another contact you can use for support.

If your parents are getting a divorce. Many teenagers go through a trauma as severe as their divorcing parents. Often, Mom will pit the teen against Dad or vice versa. You are often embroiled in their problems and feel like you're stuck in the middle. You need to extricate yourself as soon as possible. You did *not* create their marital problems, nor can you solve them. Try to stay detached from their battles and take care of yourself. That is the most important thing you can do—keep yourself stable and above water. Many kids talk to a teacher they trust or to a counselor or minister to get some distance from the situation in order to be able to see things more clearly. If your grades are suffering, or you are very depressed because of what is happening to your parents, tell them that you would like to go to counseling. Many students who have gone to a therapist have told me that they were able to learn good coping skills so that they could take care of themselves while crazy things were going on in their house. For more information on this painful subject, see Chapter 9 on teenage traumas and read Susan's story to see how she hurt herself and how much she regrets it today.

SUSAN WANTS YOU TO KNOW

In the seventh grade, my dad just walked out one day. My mom said, "Go after him, he'll come back if you ask." He didn't.

In eighth grade, my parents divorced. It was the beginning of my life as a pawn. I was shuffled between them, the recipient of angry, hateful comments about the other. My job as the oldest was to be Mom's listener, companion, and commiserator. I was responsible for my siblings, the keeper of my parents' secrets, their messenger, and the ideal teen.

I started high school in a new city. I didn't know anyone, and my siblings were in different schools. I didn't eat lunch for the first two years—the cafeteria was too intimidating.

My parents were always on edge. Mom was either angry and yelling or crying. Dad was jovial and happy with his new life and family. I learned to become as quiet and invisible as I could be. If no one noticed me, they couldn't hurt me. Mom and her family were always telling us Dad left *us,* Dad didn't love *us,* Dad was just staying in touch with us to hurt Mom. Dad was always saying Mom was lazy, crazy, mean, grasping, vindictive, foolish, stupid, a witch.

I survived because I stopped participating in life. I stopped feeling and caring about my parents and myself. Enough people were telling me how to act, what I could and couldn't say, what to wear, and where to live. My life became about passive aggression. Dad expected good grades, so I got C's. Mom wanted me to "look good," so I only wore jeans and kept my hair hanging in my face. Dad wanted me to have a vision and strive for success, so I started smoking cigarettes, slouched, and didn't clean my room. Every decision or non-decision I made was about them and how to disappoint them. None of my decisions considered what I really wanted or what would be good for me.

What I didn't realize was that the most important person in my world was me. I let high school fly by without participating. I have no memories or experiences from band, or sports, or dances, no dating, no chorus, no plays, or science projects.

I was in my late 20's when I looked around and actually saw the missed opportunities. I had only done just enough to get by in school, skimmed through the easiest college programs, and stumbled into low paying, unfulfilling jobs. My dating life was either nonexistent or with men who were not kind, loving, or fulfilling to me. The survival methods of my high school days were beginning to destroy the adult I had become.

Videotape your parents talking about their lives. You'll probably understand them better after you do.

TRY THIS!

1. **Remember the quote about honey and vinegar?** For a week, treat your parents as you want to be treated. Respect them, speak to them, spend some time with them. Listen to what they say. Try to see things from their perspective. Put yourself in their place. Notice if you see a change in their behavior toward you.
2. **Ask your parents about what their lives were like when they were teenagers.** Ask them about their classes, dating, teachers, and anything else you can think of. Did you learn anything interesting from them? Do you think that because their lives were so different, you have a hard time understanding each other?
3. **Videotape or audiotape your parents talking about their lives.** It will show them how much you care about them. Ask them about their parents and about their own past. Ask them how they feel about a lot of important issues and why. How did your parents feel when you interviewed them? Were they pleased? A future benefit will be that you can listen and watch the tapes of your parents with your own children some day. Your kids will appreciate learning more about their grandparents.

Parents Are Only Human

I have seen many teenagers struggle with their parents. Your teen years are a hard time for you and them because your parents are used to treating you like a kid when you want to be treated as an adult. It's an awkward time. Hang in there and try to be as mature as possible. Try to see things from their perspective. Often, they have good reasons for feeling the way they do. Try to find out just why they have so many rules or why they won't let you do certain things.

Most parents are doing the best they can. Just remember, your complete independence from Mom and Dad will come sooner than you can imagine. It just seems like an eternity right now. When you move out of the house, you will see that they made your life easier by taking care of lots of things for you. Now, you will have to do those things for yourself.

HOW TO GET ALONG WITH FRIENDS

Friendship can be a tricky proposition, but there is nothing more satisfying than having friends you can love and who love you. To have friends, you must be a friend. Read how Michael, a fourth grader at Stony Mountain Elementary School in Manitoba, Canada, described a friend:

> *My friend is*
> *like water*
> *that never drips from a tap.*
> *My friend is*
> *like the covers on my bed*
> *that keep me warm at night.*
> *My friend is*
> *like a cloud*
> *that never rains on me.*
> *My friend is*
> *like a puddle*
> *that never drains away.*
> *My friend likes me and I like him.*

When we are younger, we love others unconditionally. The older we get, the more requirements we have for friends and the more demanding we become. Often, we are more cautious in approaching friendship because someone hurt us in the past. We also become less accepting of ourselves because we realize that we too may have hurt a friend when we were younger. Study how basic being a friend is to Michael. He does not complicate life by having unreal expectations of his friends. For him, friendship is so simple. It can be simple for you, too, if you try.

What Friends Are

Friends come in many varieties—short, tall, talkative, and quiet—but they all have common characteristics.

They can be trusted. If you tell your friends your deepest secrets, you know they will not tell anyone else. This is a tough one for teenagers, because some of you do not know how to keep secrets. Many times I have heard stories of how a student confided in another only to find out that his trust was betrayed. Are you the kind of friend who hears something from one friend that was supposed to be kept secret, and then you go out and tell a mutual friend, "Did you hear that Foxy Freda spent the night with Steve Studman?" In high school, news travels like a wildfire that is impossible to put out. The result is usually that a friendship is broken forever. Stand by your friends, don't bad-mouth them behind their backs. Be direct with them. Tell them how what they are doing makes *you* feel. Be willing to listen to what they say to you also.

"I like to go out with my friends. We talk about what's going on in our lives. They always make me feel good."

—Erica

AMY WANTS YOU TO KNOW

I told my friend Monica that I had an abortion. She told my friends about it. Then everyone started talking about it in school. Students I didn't even know were calling me a slut. I was so mad that I told her off, and now we aren't friends any more. She really hurt me.

They are patient and forgive your mistakes and faults. Yes, we all have our faults and our dark sides. We are not perfect—but we try to do the best we can. Friends are going to accept us in our imperfect condition and still love us. What Foxy Freda did with Steve Studman is her problem. You cannot change her, but you can tell her how you feel about what she is doing—that she is putting her reputation and future in danger, is in danger of contracting a sexual disease, that you are afraid for her as a friend, and that you really care about her. Sometimes being a friend means that you are courageous and honest in order to stand up for what you believe in. This is very hard for people of all ages.

True friends are willing to support your dreams for the future. They listen to you and hear what you want to accomplish and may even have some helpful suggestions for how you can get there. They don't trash everything you have dreamed of or tell you all of the pitfalls you'll encounter. In short, they believe in you.

They are there when you most need them—in good times and bad. When you are having problems with a friend, your parents, or a teacher, they listen to you and understand why you feel the way you do. They do not give you advice unless you ask for it. They just listen.

Give your friends a break. Don't ask them to jump through hoops for you.

They have a good sense of humor and like to have fun. They do the things with you that you both enjoy. They are not always studying or watching TV. They have time for you.

They are interesting to talk to. They have more than one or two subjects they can talk about. After you have been with them, you feel that you have really been fortunate to have learned something about them, about yourself, and about the world.

And the bottom line: You feel good when you are with them. You don't leave their company feeling bad about yourself or ashamed because you've done something that they think is horrible. They don't criticize who and what you are. They love you no matter what.

How You Can Be a Friend

Answer the following questions to see whether or not you are a good friend to others as well as to see what you need to do to make yourself a better friend. This is something everyone can always get better at it. Even I am still learning how to be a better friend. It just goes to show that your education will never stop. You will always be learning new things.

Can you be trusted? If a good friend tells you a secret, do you guard it closely or do you go out and blab to another friend, who will probably go out and tell others? Trustworthiness is very important if you truly want to share your deepest self with others.

Are you patient with your friends? Do you forgive them when they make mistakes that hurt you? If you are unable to forgive others, the person you are really hurting is yourself. To forgive is to permit yourself to accept what has happened and move on. Try not to take on other people's problems. If you protect yourself, you will feel better and can be the loving person you want to be.

Are you supportive of a friend's ideas? Or do you immediately start raising objections to what she wants to do? This can be a tough area in which to improve yourself because it is hard to keep quiet when you think a friend has a crazy, impossible idea. However, sometimes we need to make our own mistakes in order to learn from them. The only thing that you, as a friend, should be doing is making sure that you are there for her and that you accept and support her.

Are you there when a friend needs you? I know a student whose mother left the family for another man she met in an Internet chatroom. Would you be able to talk about something like this to your friend? Would you be afraid you wouldn't know what to do or say? When a friend is having family problems, do you act disinterested and only want to talk about your own problems? Think about this. Friendship should work for both parties. Remember, all your friend really wants you to do is listen and understand how he feels.

Do you like to go out with friends, laugh, and have fun, or are you a stick-in-the-mud who doesn't want to do anything because it's too "boring?" When you think something sounds boring, try to use your imagination. Get those brain cells whirring to come up with exciting ideas for Saturday night. They can be crazy and fun. Who says you have to be "normal" and always go to a movie or the mall? *That's boring!*

Are you an interesting person to talk to, or do you simply answer yes or no and not much more? A way to be a more interesting person is to read newspapers and books in order to have things to talk about. Reading books can give you a lot of ideas about life's deepest questions that you can discuss with your friends. Who says you have to talk only about sex, drugs, and rock and roll?

Are you easy to be with, or are you always complaining about something? I used to be angry and too self-centered to see anyone else's problems other than my own. I couldn't see how my attitude affected other people. It is important to ask yourself how you relate to others. Are you a positive person who loves life or are you always complaining? No one wants to be with someone who is always upset about something.

Now that you have taken the time to ask yourself these seven questions, ask yourself if you are the kind of person you would want to be friends with and if your friends are the kind that you want in your life. The biggest question you can ask yourself is whether or not it is worthwhile for you to continue being a friend to others who are not there for you. Do you think these friends will come out of their self-absorption soon and see things more clearly? If so, then continuing the friendship is a smart thing to do. If this is a permanent condition, you must not allow yourself to be a victim and to be abused. You have a life of your own. You need to concentrate on developing yourself. Become what *you* want to be.

Things NOT to Do to a Friend

Don't compare. It doesn't pay to compare yourself to your friends. Value your own talents and promise. Do your personal best. Don't use others' talents, skills, choices, and lives as a benchmark for yourself. We are all different. Let me give you an example: Your friend may be a great football

Who says you have to do the same thing every week? See who can come up with the most creative idea for Saturday night. Your weekends don't have to be boring!

*What kind of
reputation do you
have? Is it a good
one? Do you think
your reputation is
important? Why?*

player, but you may be a better basketball player. Your school might support the football team more than the basketball team, so you might wish that you got the same attention as he does. That's part of life, but I truly believe that things will even out. What's important today will be unimportant in a few years. At any rate, accept your friend as he is and hope that he will do the same for you.

Don't be a fair-weather friend. Do you sit by and let others trash your friend? Are they saying things you know are not true? Don't be afraid to stand up and set them straight. Be honest and loyal.

Don't abandon your friend when things get rough. If your friend Jessica's mother has cancer and is dying, can you stay friends with her and help her through a very difficult time? Are you afraid of saying the wrong thing to her? The truth is, all you have to do is just be there. Your friend will understand that all of this is new to you. Just show your love. You don't need to say a thing.

Don't get in the middle of a dispute between two other friends. I've seen this mistake happen many times in my high school. When others get involved in the problems of two friends, it can escalate into a bad scene, with people taking sides. You won't be helping the original players when you put your two cents in. Often, both sides just get madder and no one wins. Learn not to interfere with other people's problems. You have enough of your own, don't you?

Your Reputation

Talking about reputations is important for teenagers because you are going through a period of intense feelings, trying to figure out who you are and who you want to be. You do not need to have people spreading bad rumors about you throughout the school. Let me give you an example of how important one's reputation is. Once I saw a group of boys laughing, so I asked them what was so funny. They told me that one of the girls in their class had slept with five different guys while on spring break. I told them I didn't think it was very funny and felt very sad for her. When I saw her mother later, she told me she couldn't understand why her daughter had not been invited to the Prom. The girl has since recovered from her bad reputation and has a nice boyfriend in college. She went through some bad times while still in high school. But you *can* survive a bad reputation in high school. Just do your best to always do the right thing, and hopefully your reputation will remain unstained.

If some of your "friends" are spreading false rumors about you, hold your head up high. You know what the truth is, and those people who believe you are your true friends. The others are gossipmongers who you don't need in your life. You deserve the best friends possible.

When Your Friends Are Bad for You

Usually your friends are good for you and help make you a better person. However, that is not always the case. Ask yourself the following questions:

- Are you a smart student who hangs around with kids who don't do their homework, get bad grades, and who are not interested in school?
- Are your friends drug users or big drinkers?
- Is it getting increasingly hard for you to say no when offered drugs or alcohol?
- Are you a user yourself?

If you answered yes to any of these questions, you might consider taking a look at whether these friends are good for you. Even more important, ask yourself why you hang around with them. Is it because you don't feel good enough to be friends with kids who get good grades and who do the right thing? Are you afraid that you won't be seen as "cool" if you do hang out with them?

An important part of being friends with others is periodically assessing whether a friendship is good for you. Often students will continue to hang around with friends who have no motivation to do well in school or who are doing drugs. There are many reasons; for some, it may become a habit or they may want to please their friends. Others fear being bad-mouthed if they stop hanging out with those kinds of kids.

"I used to think I had to go along with whatever my friends wanted to do. It got me into a lot of trouble—drugs and alcohol. My parents didn't trust me anymore. I felt miserable. Luckily, I went through drug treatment. I'm doing okay now, one day at a time, with God's help and my AA program."

—Stan

TOM WANTS YOU TO KNOW

I used to hang out with friends who had no ambition. We'd sit around smoking marijuana, not doing our schoolwork, going nowhere. In my junior year, I decided I'd better start studying. I'm in college now and much happier with my life. I'm on my own and I have to make my own life work. I'm glad my mom kept on me to do my schoolwork. Now, when I come back home and see my old friends, I can see that they're never going to change. It's too bad, but I feel uncomfortable around most of them now. The friends I'm making in college have plans for their future and are going someplace. So am I.

Check out the

messages you give

yourself. Do you call

yourself terrible

names? Could you

change those

messages into good

ones?

HOW TO GET ALONG WITH YOURSELF

One of the things I've noticed in all of my years of teaching is how many kids beat themselves up because they don't think they're "good enough." When I was in high school, I didn't feel like I measured up to my classmates. I conquered that and now no longer feel as though I won't get a passing grade from people I come in contact with. There are many things you can do to feel better about yourself. You may be saying, "Hey, wait a minute, I feel great about myself," but it is a rare teenager who is totally comfortable with himself. Read on for some ideas for things you can do to feel like you can take on the world.

TRY THIS!

Try doing the following things to make your life happier and calm.

1. **You can use the following self-talk every day.** Say these affirmations in the morning before you go to school (and even on weekends) and at night before you go to bed. If you don't like the ones I give you, you can make up your own. Make this one of your most important projects and remind yourself of these affirmations throughout your day. If you feel you are a worthwhile person who has something to give to the world, you will have incredible power to be successful in whatever you decide to do.

   I am a worthwhile person.
   I am a loving person.
   I am peaceful and calm.
   I am positive and upbeat.
   I can do it.
   I'm a nice person.
   I'm a winner.
   I will succeed.

2. **Write in a journal either before or after school about how your day went.** Spill. Tell it like it is. Get all of your angry, negative feelings out on paper. You will feel better if you get in the habit of doing this writing. By the way, if you have a nosy brother or sister who might try to read your private thoughts, you can always write them on the computer and get a shareware program to encrypt your journal or save it with a password or under a phony name, like "English homework." If you

don't have a computer, how about writing your entries in the foreign language you're studying? Not only will they be protected from snooping eyes, but you'll also get great practice in using your new language. I'm sure this sounds a bit paranoid, but I know this was a concern for me when I was your age.

3. **In your journal, write the things you're grateful for.** Do this every day. Sometimes we tend to get wrapped up in what's wrong with our lives, or we get upset with our parents, teachers, and friends. It helps to think about people who are less fortunate than you so that you don't take your own good fortune for granted. And don't forget to thank your parents for the nice things they do for you!

4. **Live with integrity.** That's a big word, but I will explain what it means by using a few examples. If you break a clock in a classroom while the teacher is out, tell the teacher you were the one who did it. If you get stopped by the police and they discover beer in your car, tell your parents what happened and accept the consequences. If you didn't study for a test, admit it to your parents and the teacher. See what all of these examples have in common? They show a teen taking responsibility, being honorable, and telling the truth—living with integrity. People will always prefer to deal with you the rest of your life and they will naturally want to be with you because they will trust you. Earn their trust. Be an upright, decent person. This doesn't mean that you have to be a doormat and do whatever others want. You are the only person who can take care of yourself. And it's your job to do just that. Don't let anyone else bring you down.

You are a special person with special talents. Each one of us has something valuable to contribute to the world. Believe in yourself!

SHORTCUT TO ACTION

1. You need your parents to give you respect, independence, and privacy. You will get what you want when you live responsibly, courteously, and with integrity.
2. Your parents need you to listen to them and to show them respect. They want you to be a part of the family. Spending quality time with them is important.
3. Your parents are your first teachers. They want you to learn important life lessons before you leave the nest.
4. When you and your family continue to have problems, do not be afraid to ask to see a therapist. He can help you see how you can do your part to de-escalate the problems.
5. Your parents are no more perfect than you are. Cut them some slack. They want what is best for you and are doing the best they can.
6. Choose your friends carefully. Believe in yourself: You can be a good friend and you can have good friends.
7. Don't gossip. You don't want to tarnish someone else's reputation.
8. Be there for your friends in good times and in bad times. The mark of a true friend is one who doesn't take off when times get bad. Be loyal and faithful.
9. Stay out of other friends' disputes. If you get involved, you will only complicate the situation.
10. Watch your self-talk. Always say positive things to yourself. Sometimes we can be our own worst enemies.

CHAPTER 7

CHILL OUT— HANDLE STRESS LIKE A CHAMPION

Do you sometimes feel like your nerves are hanging out all over your body? Do you get nervous when you have to play in a big game? Do your hands start to sweat when you begin taking an exam? Do you dread facing your parents after finding out you failed your English class? You are suffering from stress—a tension of the mind and body. At your age, stress usually doesn't take the same physical toll as it does on people who have lived with it for 30 years or more. However, it's a good thing to stop it now because the longer you let it go on, the more likely you are to have high blood pressure or a heart attack when you're in your 40s, 50s, and 60s.

I want to emphasize here that many teenagers are under severe stress. Maria might have a mother dying of cancer, Joe might be having girlfriend troubles, Anne might be dealing with depression, Hank may be wondering if he's gay, and Elizabeth might be trying to decide where to go to college. Whatever the cause of your stress, it is important to deal with it now before you let it control you.

SIGNS OF STRESS

Read the following signs to see if you are stressed out. Then you can read examples of how to reduce your stress in *healthy ways*.

You have trouble sleeping at night because your brain just won't shut down. Maybe you are worrying about taking an exam, getting a term paper done, surviving your foreign language course, or wondering what you're going to do with your life when you graduate. Any number of situations could be causing your stress.

You start drinking alcohol or taking drugs to "relax" because life seems too hard. I have asked many students why they drink alcohol. They almost invariably say it is to relax. Using drugs or alcohol to de-stress your life is very dangerous. You will hear more about this in Chapter 12.

You've lost that carefree feeling and feel downtrodden, worrying constantly. To worry about things you cannot change is to make yourself miserable and will only cause more problems.

You have frequent headaches, a nervous stomach, an ugly skin rash, or acne. Physical symptoms are often caused by stress.

You think too much. You are so busy analyzing your problems that you become mentally paralyzed and find yourself unable to do anything else.

We cause ourselves more stress by obsessing about things. What you worry about today will probably seem unimportant next week.

STRESS RELIEVERS

Try some of the following ideas to eliminate stress from your life. I'm sure that you can come up with some ideas of your own, too.

Plan ahead for potential situations in your life. Get that term paper done a day or two early in case something happens. You never know when something might pop up that would keep you from your work, like an illness in the family.

Keep a calendar to write down important assignments and dates, including your work schedule. Check the calendar every day to ensure that you are keeping up with everything. Plan how you will get everything done with the least amount of stress.

Eliminate caffeine from your diet. If you drink caffeinated coffee or lots of soda, cut back and see if you become less nervous. Eliminating caffeine really helped me. My students told me I drank too much coffee, so I took their advice and cut back. I drink only decaffeinated beverages now, and I'm much calmer.

Pack up your school papers the night before. Put all of your assignments for tomorrow in your backpack tonight. Check to make sure you have everything. Go through your assignments in your assignment book. Knowing you are well organized and that all you have to do in the morning is grab the bag and run will help you sleep better. Who wants to run around helter-skelter early in the morning? Rushing to get ready can be nerve-wracking.

Leave ten minutes earlier for school every day. Even though traffic is always terrible ten to fifteen minutes before

Think ahead. What do you have to get accomplished? Do the most important things first. You can redecorate your room some other day!

school starts, teachers still do not like students coming in late every day. Tardiness causes you and the teacher unneeded stress.

Be able to say "no." Some students always agree to joining committees, meetings, workshops, and retreats or to working overtime regardless of how much they have to do. Learn how to say no—it's an important part of your education. If people find out you'll say yes to everything, word will get around. Pretty soon, everyone will be asking you to serve on a new committee or volunteer project. Make it clear that you aren't *always* available.

Allow yourself to be imperfect. It's okay when you don't do everything perfectly. If you make a mistake, accept it, forgive yourself, learn from it, and move on. Don't obsess about something you can't change.

If you have a tough task to do, try to get it out of the way first. Then all other assignments will be simple for you to finish. You'll gain a real sense of accomplishment.

Don't overestimate how much you can do in one day. Remember, you only have a few hours of free time, so do the best you can. If you can't get everything done for school that you need to do, is there a club or activity you can cut out of your schedule?

Be sure your study area is neat and clean. Usually if your work space is a disaster area, it will be harder for you to get down to business and concentrate. Organize your papers by putting them in places where you can find them. Organizing your work area helps organize your thoughts.

Be sure to schedule fun activities every day or you will burn out and hate school. Go out with your friends on weekends.

Keep your worry to a minimum. Many of the things we worry about never happen. Learn not to worry so much—it won't do any good and it's a big creator of stress. If you do your work to the best of your ability, relax. You will survive.

Stay away from negative people. When you're around someone who complains all of the time, he'll steal your energy. You will be unable to get all of your work done because you are feeling low.

Laugh a lot. Watch funny programs on TV. See the humorous side of life. There's a lot to laugh about. Whenever I say, "Life is ludicrous," it is always said with a sense of humor. Laugh, laugh, laugh, and then go and laugh some more. Laughter is one of the best stress relievers. Once I stepped outside of my classroom to talk to another teacher for a few minutes. While I was gone, the students changed the whole room around, moving everything from the front to the back. They even moved my purse, desk, and briefcase in that short period of time. When I walked in, I couldn't believe what they had done. But instead of getting angry, I laughed at what they had been able to accomplish. It was good for us to laugh together, and they actually worked harder at their Spanish after that. It's truly amazing what laughter will do for you.

Live each moment with joy. The past is behind you and the future hasn't happened yet. The only moment we have is this very one we are living, so enjoy it! Life is beautiful. Look around you at the flowers, the stars, the sky, and trees. Smell that fresh air. Watch and listen to the wind whistling through the trees. Otherwise, you will be miserable and stressed throughout your life.

Get out in nature and enjoy the beauty. You don't have to hike ten miles. Just sit there, dream, and relax. Take a friend along to get away from the nonsense of society and to heal any problems that might exist between the two of you. Let nature do her thing.

Be sure you get a good night's sleep. I've seen countless students stressed out because they're doing too much— they're taking hard classes, they're involved with several student activities, and they have an afterschool job. And they wonder why they're stressed out! There just isn't enough time in the day to do everything and to make sure you're well rested. You must get your sleep—that's a basic physical need.

Wear a favorite bracelet or ring every day that will remind you to chill out. If you associate it with relaxation, you will be mindful of how you are reacting to life's daily stresses. Try it and see if it works for you.

A Special Stress Reliever

In order to de-stress your life, you can turn the negative messages you give yourself, which cause undue stress, into positive messages. Study the following examples to see how you can become more positive and stop stressing yourself out.

- **Negative Message:** I will never finish writing this term paper on time.
  Positive Message: I'll get this paper done on time if I do it gradually, one step at a time. I will keep at it until it is finished. I am calm.
- **Negative Message:** I can't believe I only got a 75 on the English exam. I'm so stupid.
  Positive Message: I will do better on the next exam. It's okay once in a while to get a C. I'm only human.

Remember, you're only one person. You can't do everything, so just do what you can to the best of your abilities. That's all anyone can ask of you.

Listen to your favorite music. Close your eyes and take a deep breath. Let your mind wander for a half hour. Chill!

- **Negative Message:** My friend Jennifer didn't speak to me this morning. She is probably mad at me for something I did.
  Positive Message: Jennifer must be having a bad day. I'll have to go out of my way to be friendly to her.
- **Negative Message:** I'm not as good in math as my friends.
  Positive Message: I'm good at other subjects. It's okay if I'm not good at everything.
- **Negative Message:** I have to get the best grade in biology class to be okay.
  Positive Message: No matter what grade I get in class, I am still okay. My grade does not define who I am.
- **Negative Message:** I dropped the ball in the end zone. The touchdown would have won the game for our school. Kids are disappointed in me. I let them down.
  Positive Message: Even the pros drop the ball from time to time. I have learned what to do next time. Everyone makes mistakes.

Physical Stress Relievers

Take five deep breaths with your eyes closed. Breathe in slowly through your nose and exhale through your mouth. Relax and think of nothing else.

Do a relaxation exercise. Close your eyes, sag your shoulders down, and slowly roll your head around in a complete circle first in one direction and then in the other. Do this exercise several times.

Try progressive relaxation. Sit or lie down in a comfortable, quiet place—not in the middle of the student cafeteria. Start from your head and work your way down to your toes. Tense up each part of your body and hold it for about five seconds, then relax. Remember to just be in the moment, concentrating only on tensing and relaxing your body. Shut out the rest of the world. Enjoy the feeling of release as you let go of each part of your body's muscle tension.

Take a mental break from a stressful situation. Imagine yourself in your favorite place. Is it a beach or a favorite tree in the park? For 30 seconds, close your eyes and visualize yourself there.

Get some exercise. Take a bicycle ride or a brisk walk around the neighborhood. Moving around helps loosen up your muscles and your mind.

Get away from your desk and go outside. If you're studying for a big exam and just can't take it anymore, get up and walk around. Go look at the moon and stars.

If you are angry and stressed out, try punching a punching bag to get all of your anger out. If you're angry at someone, punching a bag first will allow you to be rational and calm when you talk to that person later. Explosive anger will only cause you more problems. Get it out in a healthy way.

TRY THIS!

1. **Every day do something thoughtful for someone else.** Set aside your stressful feelings so that you can feel better about yourself. You will see that there's more to life than just grades, classes, and exams. Have you talked to your grandparents recently or done something nice for a friend? Just as ignoring your schoolwork can be a disaster, so, too, can obsessing about grades and exams. Make it your goal to have a balanced life.

2. **Sit next to a shy student who doesn't seem to have many friends.** Find out something about him. Resolve to be nice to all kids instead of just to your good friends. It helps to spread good feelings and you feel less stress when you are doing kind things for others.

3. **Instead of fearing that an exam will be terrible, calmly prepare for the test in advance,** methodically learning and memorizing the material one chunk at a time. Tell yourself that you have done a good job preparing, that you are ready for the exam, and that you're even looking forward to it. These kinds of messages promote good stress—the kind that pumps you up to do neat things.

Remember to breathe deeply when you feel stress. Simply becoming aware of your breathing will help you feel better.

SHORTCUT TO ACTION

1. Signs of stress include trouble sleeping at night, taking drugs or drinking alcohol "to relax," worrying constantly, having constant headaches or stomachaches, and analyzing too much.
2. To relieve stress, plan ahead, eliminate caffeine from your diet, learn how to say no, laugh a lot, and get a good night's sleep.
3. Breathe deeply when you feel stressed out.
4. Go for a walk or to a park to take a mental break from a stressful situation.
5. Get lots of exercise. Ride your bike, start jogging, or take brisk walks.
6. Visit with friends—get in the habit of giving each other hugs.
7. Get rid of your tension and anger by punching a punching bag.
8. Overprepare for an exam so you won't be nervous.
9. Help others to get your mind off your own problems and stresses.
10. Do something completely different to relax. Go to a bookstore and browse. Go to a museum and wander around just for fun. Go fly a kite. Go ride your bike.

CHAPTER 8

LIVE SUCCESSFULLY WITH JOY AND FUN

I think this is one of the most important chapters in the book because how you handle yourself now determines how successful you will be later in life. Read and start doing the things mentioned here and your life will get better.

FEELING GOOD ABOUT YOUR LIFE

Do the right thing. When you are honorable and have integrity, you feel better about yourself. Here's an example: You are in a store and the clerk undercharges you. Do you tell her she undercharged you or do you walk out without saying a word? If you tell her, she'll be grateful to you because her register won't come up short at the end of the day. When we cheat somebody, even if it is their mistake, we may not immediately feel guilty. But a lifetime of cheating adds up to a poor self-image. Hold your head high, be honorable, and always do what you know is right. You'll feel good about yourself.

Greet and treat others in your life pleasantly. It doesn't cost a thing to smile at others. Smiling helps make their day and yours better. Love begets love.

Emphasize the good in your life. It's easy to fall into a downward spiral when you think about the negative things in your life. Sometimes it's just a matter of changing your focus. Be thankful for what you have and try to be a more positive person. Whenever you start to feel negative, start thinking about the good things are happening for you and be philosophical about the bad. They shall pass with time.

You don't always have to be right. Each person has his own point of view, and each view has its own merits. You aren't the only one who has opinions, so don't always try to prove you "know it all." Ask yourself, "Would I rather be right or happy?" Sometimes trying to make others believe and live like we want them to is an impossible task. Ease up on this and accept that we are all different.

Increase your energy level. There are many ways to boost your energy level. One good way is to exercise vigorously several times a week. It helps clear the brain, allowing you to think better and to be more positive. Exercise also motivates you to get your work done without a lot of procrastination.

Look at the messages you give yourself. I used to call myself an idiot when I did something stupid. Now, I always catch myself and realize that I cannot achieve perfection. It's an impossible goal that can make your life miserable. Don't be your own worst enemy—cut yourself some slack and watch what you say to yourself!

On a sheet of paper make two lists: your good qualities and your bad qualities. Which list is longer? If the list of bad qualities is longer, take action. Talk to a friend you really trust. Ask her if she sees you the same way you see yourself. You might be very surprised that she does not see you in such a negative way. Then you can change how you feel by taking some more time to focus on creating a longer list of good qualities.

Express your love for the people in your life. Don't wait to tell your loved ones how you feel about them—tell them now! My friend's father told her he loved her for the first time a week before he died. Imagine how happy she would have been if she had heard it a lot sooner. Your goal is to be a loving, good person and to do what you feel is right. Doing it now will give you an incredible power for the rest of your life.

Read biographies of famous people to get inspiration for your own life. A quality that many well-known people share is that they had a dream, persistence, and a belief in themselves. Drawing inspiration from these people will enable you to keep going back to what you want to accomplish until you succeed. Thomas Edison's teachers called him "too stupid to learn," and he had 3,000 failed experiments before he invented the light bulb. So don't ever give up!

Be forceful, not a wimp. Do you say things such as "I'll do it," "Yes, I'll be there," and "I can do that," or do you say things like "I'll try," "maybe," and "I hope so?" Which phrases sound more forceful? If you have trouble committing yourself to doing things for other, ask yourself why. Take what you learn from yourself and make an effort to eradicate future wimpy behavior.

Listen to others to understand what they are trying to say. Seeing and understanding their points of view is an important skill. Check out the special section entitled *Listening Skills.*

When you fail at something, think of it as a good lesson. Move on and keep challenging yourself. The more you learn, the less you will fail.

Emphasize the strengths of other people in your life instead of judging and being critical of them. Ask yourself if those things you are critical of are really all that important, or are the people you care about good, loving people who are truly there for you? That's what should count, not how they dress, walk, or talk.

Stop being so self-absorbed and take a real interest in other people's lives. When you can care about others and accept them unconditionally, you have discovered how to truly love. This is something that you really have to work at before you get it right. Just remember that you're not perfect, so you shouldn't expect perfection of others.

Say thanks when someone does something nice for you. Expressions of gratitude make both you and the recipient feel good. Take no one for granted. It's important to live each day with gratitude for the *good people* you have in your life.

Help your parents. If you see that your parents are stressed out because they have too many things to do, help them out. Mow the lawn, wash the kitchen floor, give the dog a bath. Your parents will appreciate it.

In your journal, write down all of the good things you do. You will be surprised at how many things you discover. When you see yourself as successful, you become so. Think positive!

Feel good about your personal appearance. Are you neat and clean or do you dress like a slob? Try wearing clothes that don't say, "Kick me. I'm no good." However, don't automatically judge others by how they dress. I've taught many students who have strange hairstyles or who wear bizarre clothes. Oftentimes, these are creative people expressing their individuality who should be given the benefit of the doubt. The point is that if you are proud of your own appearance, others will see your self-confidence.

Listen to your inner voice (your gut feeling). When I was a kid, I went sledding with some friends on a nearby hill. But the hill looked slick, and there wasn't anyone else sledding on it. My gut feeling told me, "Julie, don't do it, it's too dangerous," but I went ahead down the hill to please my friends. That was a wrong move because, sure enough, I couldn't steer the sled and ran into a big icy snow pile, fell, and broke my hand. Don't be afraid of the messages you receive from your inner voice. One thing I always tell my students is that if your gut feeling tells you not to do something, listen to it. It's usually right when it comes to decisions about hanging out with friends who aren't good for you, drinking alcohol or smoking marijuana, or doing something that your instincts tell you is wrong.

Find someone you respect and admire who could be a role model to you. This could be a teacher, a family friend, a senior in your high school, or your boss at work. Watch what he does to be successful. How does he relate to other people? Talk to him and find out about the experiences he had to get him where he is today. If you learn from his example, you will garner some useful tips that will last you the rest of your life.

Be able to learn from others. Be open and realize that you don't know everything. Other people can offer you new ideas and information that will enhance your life.

Be your own best friend. Spend some time alone in a quiet place. Ask yourself where you're going and how you're doing to make changes in your life.

TRY THIS!

1. **In your journal write as much as you want about the following topic: "I am happiest when . . ."** Writing will give you some clarity about who you are, what your interests are, and what you like to do in life.
2. **Think about the things you do to validate yourself and to reward yourself.** Then consider what you do to validate others and to express appreciation for them.
3. **What achievements have you had that give meaning to your life?** How have they changed your life? Do you want more of the same achievements or do you want to change the focus of your life to achieve other things?
4. **Write down three things you can do to better yourself.** It's important to be honest about this in order to make any real changes in your life. There isn't a person on the planet who can say he doesn't need to make any changes to be a better person. We all can improve ourselves.
5. **In your journal, write down the negative messages you give yourself.** Think of ways you can make them positive messages. Then actually do it in your everyday life.
6. **Each week try doing something you have always told yourself you could never do.** I'm not saying to go bungee jumping in the Grand Canyon. Make it something simple and start conquering your fears about it. Always be proactive in your life, not reactive. Don't wait for bad things to happen to you. Go out and make good things happen so that you can be in charge of your life.

7. **Think back to the times when your inner voice spoke to you.** Write down when you listened to it. Did you save yourself from some very bad situations? Also write down when you did *not* listen to it. Did you get into a lot of trouble? How can you honor this helpful voice? What will it take to get you to listen to it?

8. **Talk to your Mom or Dad about their concept of the inner voice.** Ask them if they ever did things it told them not to and how they learned to listen to the voice. Talk to them about their past experiences and what happened to them. They will feel flattered that you care enough to ask and that you value their opinions.

9. **Pick out someone you know to be a good person whom you feel is very successful.** Ask her how she got to where she is today and what sacrifices she had to make. Ask her what tough personal changes she had to make to be the person she is today. Although it might be hard, ask her for some advice—you show great strength and humility when you admit that you need to make improvements in your own life. She will be impressed with your candor and insight.

MANAGE YOUR MONEY WITH SKILL

Just as grades do not determine your worthiness as a person, neither does money. Talking about money can be a touchy subject because some people have more of it than others. A big part of this section will discuss how to budget your money and stretch your dollars. You don't have to come from a rich family to live comfortably as long as you're careful about how you spend your money.

Managing your expenses now will help you prepare for your future. Good habits acquired while you're still in high school will serve you well when you get a job or go to college. Smart money management is an art that is acquired through lots of practice and patience in your early adult years. Check out the following tips that will help you get a handle on a very important skill.

Start an early savings plan. You can save part of the money you get as gifts from relatives and from your salary. If you budget a certain percentage that you will always put in the bank, you will get into the habit of saving early on. Many Americans do not know how to save. As a result, millions are in serious debt because they spend too much. It's always good to have a cushion to fall back on in case of emergencies.

Start keeping track of what you spend. Write down what you spend your money on, then periodically go back and review your list. Were all of your expenses absolutely necessary? Think about where you could cut your costs. Instead of buying lunch at school, consider packing a healthy lunch. Or you could consider making tapes of each your friends' CDs instead of buying your own.

Get your own checking account. With the money you have saved, open your own checking account. Ask your parents to teach you how to write checks and keep the checkbook balanced. Understanding how to keep a checkbook is a basic financial skill you will utilize the rest of your life. I know a woman who has never balanced her checkbook. Because she had no idea as to what kind of money she was spending, she never placed any in savings. Now she will have to work many more years than most people because she can't afford to retire. Don't make that mistake. Keep your checkbook balanced every month and don't forget to write down your ATM withdrawals. It might seem tedious at first, but record keeping is really not that hard once you get used to it.

IMPORTANT: Always know your bank balance. When you write a check for more than what's left in your account, the bank charges you at least a $25 service fee. Always try to avoid late fees, service charges, and bounced checks. Many students get into trouble when they don't keep a running record of the bank balance in their checking account. Learn from their mistakes.

Fight peer pressure. Many students have told me that they feel they have to spend as much money as their friends because they don't want to be called cheap. I have a friend who used to laugh at me because I was thrifty and cut out coupons. Today, she wishes she had done the same thing because her financial situation is not what she would like it to be. No matter what others say, stick to your money management program and remember that you are on your way to fiscal freedom.

Live responsibly. Too many people just assume Social Security will be waiting to take care of them when they retire. The fact is, however, that Social Security money is not enough to live on. Plan ahead for your own financial security, saving a certain percentage every pay period for your own retirement. When you reach retirement age, you will be glad you did because you will have more financial freedom to do the things you want to do.

Don't demand too much from your parents. Remember that they have many expenses, such as mortgage payments

Having good money habits when you're young will pay off in the future.

No, you don't have to have or spend as much money as your friends to have a good time.

and gas, electric, phone, sewer, trash, water, medical, and dental bills. They are probably also saving up for your college education. Because of their financial burdens, your view of what you need and your parents' view may be at opposite poles. What do you do in that case? *Compromise!* When you show your parents that you can be reasonable about money and understand their financial problems, they will do the best they can to give you what you truly need.

IMPORTANT: Don't accuse your parents of being tightwads, of not caring about you, of just thinking of themselves, or of being selfish. When you talk to them like that, they will be even more entrenched in their view of money and will not be willing to bend. Plus, you'll hurt their feelings. Be reasonable and listen to what they say. Where can both sides compromise? Reevaluate your expenses and your projected needs for money. Can you find any place where you could trim down what you spend and need? If you can, your parents will be very grateful to you.

Stomp out your need for instant gratification. The vast majority of people need to work on this. The truth is, though, that advertisers encourage us to buy through their commercials and ads. We are trained when we are little kids to use the "right" kind of cereal, the "right" toys, and the "right" clothes. Watch and listen to commercials, read the ads in the newspapers, and look at how you, your friends, and your parents spend money. You have your own mind and should try to make your own spending decisions. Try not to let someone else tell you what you can't do without.

Don't Make Excuses

Anne doesn't want you to have the difficult time she has had with money. She didn't learn how to manage her financial affairs until she was well into her adult years. Her story is intended to be a wake-up call for you if you never give money a second thought.

ANNE WANTS YOU TO KNOW

I could blame it on my parents.

After all, they thought that a girl from a "nice" family shouldn't hold a paying job in high school. It just wouldn't look right and would indicate that her father wasn't a good provider. I could always ask for what I wanted or needed, and I'd usually get it. I didn't even have any money when I had to buy birthday gifts for my parents—they'd give me the money. That should have been my first clue that something wasn't right.

I lived at home while I went to college, and Mom and Dad paid for just about everything. Going to college and getting a degree was considered a good job for a girl in my family. My parents real goal in sending me to college, though, wasn't so I could study to become a nurse or teacher, but so that I could find a man to marry. Then, I could stay home, keep house, cook, and have kids—the old version of the American Dream.

Or I could blame it on my ex-husband.

I never had a checking account before we married because I never thought I needed one. After the wedding, we opened joint savings and checking accounts. I took care of the bills for a short while, but when I made mistakes in balancing the checkbook, he took over. I thought that was great; after all, what did I know about money? Besides, it was a whole lot easier. We even used to joke that he made the money while I spent it. What I'm getting at here is that money management wasn't never a priority for me. I wasn't even aware that it needed to be.

We divorced when I was in my 40s, and I still didn't have the money management skills I needed. For the first time in my life I had to pay the bills, watch what I spent money on, budget, and save. I was totally unprepared. And sad. And depressed. And overwhelmed. And bewildered.

But why assess blame in the first place? It's just the way things were when I was in training to be an adult. There were things I needed to learn, but I didn't learn them until much later than other people did.

Who was right? Who was wrong? Who cares? The point is that I had to do lots of learning quickly. I had friends who were in the financial field and asked them for advice. I asked my father what he thought I should do. He wanted to take care of me again, but I knew that I'd never learn if I let him. I made some financial blunders, some bigger than others. I also made some very wise investments and other financial decisions, too. Some of those are still paying off.

The lesson I finally learned wasn't just about money. That's not what this is all about. **It's about preparing myself for life, to take care of myself in all ways, not just financially.** It is a lesson about I need to do to take care of myself when it comes to my emotional, physical, and spiritual health as well as having joy and fun, loving myself and others, and protecting myself. The list could go on and on. But, it boils down to this:

If you don't learn the basics when you're young, you will need to learn them when you are an adult. Then, it takes longer, is more difficult, and is very embarrassing. It's playing catch-up, and it is *not fun*.

Don't make excuses for not taking care of yourself and your money—that's your responsibility.

USING CREDIT CARDS

Credit cards are useful for three reasons:

They are convenient. When you have to buy something, you don't need to have cash on you. In addition, you pay only once every month.

They help you establish a credit history. When the time comes to buy a home or a car, a good credit history built up using credit cards will show you are responsible in paying your bills.

They're great in emergencies. Sometimes you don't have the cash to pay for emergency car repairs on the road. Then, your credit card can be a godsend.

Pay off your credit card balance every month—not just the minimum balance. You'll stay out of trouble that way.

Use of Credit Cards Can Shovel You Under

Credit card companies make their money from people who *don't* pay off their entire bill every month. The customers who pay the entire amount at the end of the month are not their favorite people. Read the following information about credit cards so that you can avoid their traps later on in your life. *Forewarned is forearmed.*

Do not buy anything you cannot pay for at the end of the month. That may not always be possible, especially if you need to pay for such things as your newborn baby's medical expenses or your college tuition. However, always ask yourself if you truly need something before you charge it on a credit card. Can you pay for it at the end of the month? If you can't, you probably shouldn't buy it. This rule has always worked for me, and I've never found myself owing a credit card company any interest. Make sure you can pay off those credit cards every month!

If you can't pay the full balance, pay off as much as you can beyond the minimum payment. The trick is to get all of your debt paid off. Carrying over unpaid charges from month to month causes you to pay an incredible amount on interest. It just keeps multiplying and multiplying.

Watch Out for the Following Things:

- **Read the fine print.** Many credit card companies charge an annual fee. Yes, you may be earning frequent flyer miles, but at what cost? You'd have to charge a lot of money on your credit card to make up that annual fee of $35. Also, don't forget to read those little flyers they stick in your bill every once in a while. Sometimes they're telling you that the interest rates are going up or that there is now an annual fee to use the card.
- **Watch out for late fees** if your check doesn't arrive to the company on the due date, you might have to pay a late fee as well as the interest charges. That hurts, especially when you're on a budget and don't have much money. Be careful!
- **Check what the grace period is.** When you receive the bill, how much time do you have to pay it? Most credit card companies give you at least two weeks to pay, but some are more strict.
- **Beware of cash advances on your credit cards.** You start paying interest on the money as soon as you get it. If you have an emergency and must get cash this way, pay the bill off as soon as possible.

- **Beware of changing interest rates.** Sometimes the credit card company has a low interest rate to get you hooked. After a year or two, they raise the interest rate. Be sure to read the fine print.

Don't let your boss pressure you into working more hours than you want to.

JUGGLING A JOB AND SCHOOL

Many students have jobs during the school year. We'll look at how you can do your best job working and still survive and thrive in school. It is not an impossible task but you must be very careful how you play the game. Remember, school's very important for your future.

Work only 10–12 hours per week, preferably on weekends. The students who work 20–25 hours per week always have trouble getting their schoolwork done. Invariably, they come into school sleepy and too tired to function at their normal ability. One of my students told me recently that she was exhausted because her boss pressured her to do inventory at the store. She didn't get home until 1 a.m. She was a zombie and had a hard time keeping her eyes open in my class.

Be sure your boss knows school is your top priority. Employers are duty bound to honor the fact that you are a student by not asking you to stay past 9 or 10 p.m. Any employer who asks you to close a fast food restaurant is asking too much. Also, depending on your age there might be laws that prohibit you from working beyond a certain hour. Know your rights!

Is school your top priority? I know that some of my students have agreed to work long hours because they want the extra cash. They're anxious to make that car payment and have money for expenses. You may be able to work more hours, but if your grades are suffering, you're shortchanging yourself. Consider whether or not your short-term gains are worth your long-term losses. You might have a terrible attendance and academic school record. You might skip classes because you're too tired to go. If you're not in class, you won't learn. If you don't learn, you won't get that high school diploma. If you don't get that high school diploma, you will not be eligible for college, companies' training programs, or trade school. And if you don't get that post-high school training, you will be stuck doing the same kind of job you're doing right now, like closing a fast food restaurant.

Try to get a job where you can use your skills. For example, if you love animals, maybe you could work for a veterinarian or an animal hospital. The more experience you

Find an interesting job that will give you new, important skills.

get in the field you want to enter, the better your future job prospects will look. It's not too early to investigate different places where you can find a job. Meet lots of new people; ask them questions; see if there's a need you can fill, using your special talents and interests. If you don't ask, you'll never know. Yes, you will get turned down by lots of people, but they may know someone who could use your services. Getting to know as many people as you can will help you in the future. You'll be remembered when you come back with a college degree or training from a tech school.

Think about starting your own business. Maybe you could start a lawn mowing business. I've known students who make $6000 a summer doing that. They are their own bosses whose only task is to do a good job mowing lawns, at certain time intervals. Maybe you could start an informal camp for small pre-school children. You would get to use your creativity to invent new games for them to play and new projects to do. Look around and see what kind of needs your neighbors and family members have, then see if there's a way you can fill those needs while making some money.

Show that you have a good work ethic. If you will be starting your own business, you will need references— recommendation letters from your customers or phone numbers that people can call to talk to your past employers or customers. Maybe you could get a few of your favorite teachers to write letters for you, stating that you are a reliable worker and a good and honest person.

Keep your eyes open when looking for a job. Be alert for any opportunity. Many stores place Help Wanted signs in the window, and your school counselor may have a bulletin board of part-time job opportunities for you to check out.

Start looking for a summer job in March. The better jobs usually get snapped up before you even start thinking about getting a summer job. Remember the old proverb, "The early bird catches the worm."

A job is good preparation for post-high school training. Never underestimate the skills you acquire in an afternoon or summer job. Whether you go to college or trade school or get training from a company, the social skills you gain from working with other people will benefit you later in life.

Have fun while you work. I've seen kids having a blast at their jobs, while others complain about everything—and you should hear them complain! If you find yourself working with negative people, *get out.* Any job will be fun if you approach it with the right attitude.

Be courteous. Good things happen to people who do a good job in a polite manner. Whenever I see a teenager who's doing a terrific job, I tell his boss because when it comes time to handing out raises, an employer will remember that this kid's been complimented by customers. So, no matter how crabby or nasty a customer has been to you, don't let it get to you. Treat others as you would wish to be treated and not only will you succeed in your job, but you will also keep yourself centered and happy.

When your boss asks you to do a harder job, DO IT. You'll be getting more experience and more confidence in yourself. Never underestimate the value of stretching beyond what you think you can do. It's a real growth experience.

You can do a good job. Have confidence in yourself. I worked for a doctor in my first job, running his office while he saw patients. I was really scared at first, but after a few days, I gained confidence. It was a fun job because I got to do things I had never done.

Thank the people who have helped you. It always pays to thank anyone who has made your path smoother in your job. Thank that woman who recommended you to your boss. Thank your boss for giving you more responsibility and having confidence in you. Never underestimate their importance in your life.

Do not work full-time during spring break. Students who don't take a vacation during spring break are usually worn out all the time. *You deserve a vacation.* Take it!

If you're having a bad day, turn it around with a smile.

A SOUND MIND IN A SOUND BODY

We all like to eat junk—it just tastes so good. But let's examine some facts about food and our eating habits. Too many people today aren't eating healthy foods and aren't getting enough exercise. If you do, great! You've been following the counsel of the ancient Greeks, keeping a "sound mind in a sound body." But if you don't, read on. Maybe you will see some things you could change in your life.

Eventually, junk food will land on your gut, your waist, or your hips. Most teenagers can eat anything and not gain a pound. I was like that, too. My friends used to call me a *bag of bones*. Well, not anymore. I've spread out since those days. For the majority of adults, keeping that weight from creeping up each year becomes a constant battle. Be careful.

Junk food tastes great, but too much of it will land on your hips and waist. Learn how to push yourself away from the table before you eat too much.

Junk food is okay if you don't gorge on it. Try to limit your intake of chips, sodas, and candy. If you can push yourself away from the table when you are no longer hungry, you will be better off.

Don't inhale your food. Eat slowly, let your food digest. When you eat fast, you tend to eat more. Carry on a conversation while eating to slow yourself down—but make sure you talk only in between bites. No one wants to see a mouthful of partially chewed food!

Read a book on nutrition. Lots of books give you game plans for avoiding foods with high fat content and can even give you suggestions on what items won't pack on the pounds at fast food restaurants.

Don't drink diet drinks, then turn around and pig out. Yes, diet drinks will save a few calories, but if the rest of your meal is high in fat, sugar, and calories, you really don't save that much. Look at the whole meal.

Don't reward yourself with junk food. Let's say you get an *A* on a calculus exam. You'll want to go out and celebrate with your friends. Instead of getting a pizza with pepperoni or sausage you could try something a bit more healthy, such as a salad with dressing on the side. If you're careful where you go to celebrate, you have a better chance of eating healthy foods. Many restaurants can even provide you with the fat content and calories of the dishes they offer.

Become aware of nutrition information—your life depends on it. For example, many teenagers hate milk and refuse to drink it. That's a *big* mistake! They're setting themselves up for a lot of problems when they're older. Many elderly people, especially women, have bones that become extremely fragile because they have not gotten the necessary calcium. They often suffer hip fractures and have to go into nursing homes. Get that calcium, guys and girls, to build strong bones. The more milk you drink, the better. Three or four glasses a day is not too much for any of you.

Don't diet. People who diet often get discouraged, give up, and consume more food because they have felt deprived. However, the experts say it is better to be careful about what you eat rather than trying extreme diets that are unrealistic.

Exercise. Getting exercise is important for both your physical and mental health. I am never happier than after I take a 20 mile bike ride. I come home energized and feel more able to do my daily tasks that are hard or boring.

Drink at least 8 glasses of water a day. Not soda! Water is good for your skin, helps tame your appetite, and keeps your body balanced. Of course, you will have more trips to the bathroom. Just think of it as flushing out your system. I knew a student who used to drink milk for breakfast and then soda for the rest of the day. She became so dehydrated that she fainted at school. She had to be hospitalized until her fluids were back to normal.

If you have a weight problem, write down everything you eat. Do this for two weeks and then analyze it. You'd be surprised about what you really eat. Where can you cut back without starving to death or depriving yourself of important nutrients? What could you substitute for those chips or candy bar? Could you learn to like fruit and vegetables more? You won't know until you try. Experiment until you find a vegetable you like to munch on. When you get that urge to pig out, reach for a glass of water and a fistful of vegetables. Crunch and munch to your heart's content.

Live by this plan: Eat only when you're hungry, eat what you want, and stop when you are no longer hungry. Let your stomach give you the signal it has had enough. Chew your food slowly and *enjoy every bite!*

Your bone density is determined during your teenage years, so drink milk every day. If you can't drink milk, ask your doctor about calcium supplements.

GET A LIFE—A SOCIAL LIFE

It is important to take vacations and have breaks. These are the times when you get together with your friends and have fun. Check out some tips for having a good social life. It's important for your mental well being!

Having a social life in high school will make you a happier person. There are friends out there for you—people you can hang out with. You just have to find them.

See that girl over there eating lunch alone? You could do a very nice thing and go over and ask her to eat with you. Everyone needs a friend, and it's always a good thing to reach out and befriend others. You might find out that she's a fascinating person once you get to know her.

Brainstorm ways to improve your social life. One way is to get involved in clubs or extracurricular activities. How about working on a play? Try your hand at acting, or if that thought horrifies you, there are many other things you can do to be a part of a group that has lots of fun. You can be a makeup artist, work the lights, design and build the stage scenery, sew costumes, sell tickets, be an assistant director, or be an usher. Ask around to find out how you can get involved.

Be open to new experiences. Do you hate sports because you can't play at a varsity level? Check out intramural teams

Have a lousy social life? It will never get better unless you start doing something differently. Go to football games and cheer with the students or work in the concession stand. Get out there and get involved!

in your school. Do you love to play chess, but there's no chess club in your school? Start one yourself! When you like to do something passionately, share your love with other students. You'll have more fun doing it and you'll have friends to hang out with on vacation and on weekends.

Volunteer. A lot of my students have made new friends while working to help others. They have built homes for the poor with Habitat for Humanity and gone to Central America to help build churches, ballfields, and schools. Helping others gives you a good feeling, makes the world a better place, and helps you meet other like-minded kids.

Go on school-sponsored trips. When you share an experience such as travel you have an immediate bond. I've taken students on trips to Spain and have seen them develop lifelong friendships. Besides, school trips help you become a more mature person. I know of one boy who went to Spain with me who was a "mama's boy." By the time we got home, he had grown up and become a totally different person. He even went back to visit his host family and encouraged his parents to host a Spanish student for a school year. He now has friendships in Spain with kids he would have never known if he had not gone on the trip.

Make friends with people you're comfortable with. You probably don't want to hang out with kids who have different value systems than you or who won't accept you as you are. Always be true to yourself.

DATING AND THE OPPOSITE SEX

Having a special guy or girl in your life can make you feel more energized and complete as a person. Things can seem a lot easier to handle when you have someone who truly cares about you. Not all teens, however, want to date one person exclusively. Some prefer to go out in groups first so that they can get to know a person well from a different perspective before becoming involved in a serious relationship. Check out these tips on dating to help you make the most of this important and fun part of teen life.

Get to know that guy or girl you're interested in first as a friend. Don't be in a rush to get serious with someone before you get to know one another. Have fun and relax.

Don't ask a potential boyfriend/girlfriend to jump through hoops for you. No one is duty bound to wait on you, to tell you you're wonderful all of the time, or to do everything *you* want to do. If a potential girlfriend or boyfriend treats you that way, run for your freedom as fast as you can.

Don't be sexually aggressive. This doesn't just go for the guys anymore. Boys have told me they have gone out with girls who have literally attacked them. Many teens have told me that they had a sexual relationship before they were ready. It is much better to have a good friendship before you even start thinking about sex and to be sure that you are mature enough to handle all of the responsibilities that come along with it.

Don't come on too strong. This has nothing to do with sex. Some kids start dating each other and either one or both begin to take over the other's life to make plans for the future. Give each other some breathing space—dating is supposed to be fun!

Watch the small talk. If you're the kind of person who needs to talk constantly, you're probably just nervous. Relax. Breath deeply and believe in yourself. You are likeable just the way you are, and some quiet moments together can be good for both of you. Give your voice a rest. See what happens.

Don't expect your new boyfriend or girlfriend to be perfect. No one can live up to that, so just have a good time.

Demand respect from your friend. Don't let yourself be treated like a doormat, a sex object, or as a punching bag. No human being should accept that kind of disrespectful treatment from anyone.

Cheap Dates

Check out some of the things you can do together for little or no money.

- Take a hike in a nearby park.
- Have a picnic in the park.
- Go ice or in-line skating.
- Rent a video and pop some popcorn.
- Play Scrabble or Monopoly together. Invite some other friends to play with you.
- Study together at the library. Take occasional breaks to talk.
- Play miniature golf.
- See a matinee movie.
- Go to your local art museum.
- Go to a coffeehouse for good conversation.
- Take a bike ride.

Get to know him or her as a friend before you start dating. You will have more respect for each other and will treat each other better.

- Meet up with friends for a soccer game.
- Cheer on your high school sports teams.
- Check your local newspaper for ideas, like lectures, book signings and readings, or parades.

You don't have to go to expensive restaurants to have a good time, and if your girlfriend or boyfriend thinks otherwise, find someone else to date. Being able to do a variety of things together will keep your relationship fun and will encourage you both to explore the world around you. Have a good time.

PERSONAL SAFETY

This section will give you tips on how to avoid being the victim of a crime. Many of these tips might sound kind of alarmist, but file them away in your memory bank. They'll come in handy in the future. Being aware of potential risks will help you be prepared to avoid them.

Walk with confidence. When you move with assertiveness and purpose, you don't look like a victim. Criminals like to attack people who look uncertain. If you look like you know what you're doing and where you're going, they will think twice before they go after you.

Protect your possessions. Keep your purse or wallet with you at all times, carrying it under your arm or deep in your pocket. Always zip up the outer opening of your purse. Don't give a thief an open invitation to rob you.

Always tell someone where you're going and when you'll be back. Many teenagers don't want to tell their parents where they're going because they don't think it is any of their business. This is a big mistake from a personal safety standpoint. You should always let someone else know your whereabouts, and besides, do you really want your parents to worry about you?

When walking or jogging, don't wear headphones. You'll never hear if someone comes up behind you. And while we're at it, it's always better to go with someone else. Attackers look for a victim who's alone and vulnerable.

Always be aware of your surroundings and stay away from high-risk areas. It is always a good idea to check out the scene around you. If you're parking your car at a shopping center, do you see any people hanging around and acting suspiciously? If so, go to the other end of the mall and park. And remember that your chances of running into trouble are much greater in places with a history of crime. If you must go through these areas, stay alert. One thing I do to avoid being carjacked or robbed at a traffic light is approach the red light slowly. When the light changes to green, I proceed through without ever having actually stopped.

When traveling by car, keep your doors locked and windows up. Ten years ago, this was not a safety concern, but today you should always be on the alert for carjackers. If someone should try to get into your car at a traffic light, they can't if your doors are locked. Yes, this will probably never happen to you, but why take that chance. You never know when you're going to be in the wrong place at the wrong time.

Be sure your car is in good operating condition. Are your tires in good shape? When was the last time you checked them? Do you get your oil changed every 3,000 miles? Do you have enough gas? Do you have money with you in case of a car emergency? If you drive an old clunker, keep it in good condition and take care of repairs immediately.

Have your car key ready to open the door. Don't get to your car and then have to fumble around to find your key. You don't want to be an easy target. And always check to see if anyone in on the backseat or on the floor of your parked car *before* you get in.

Trust your intuition. If you see someone standing around when you get to your destination and your inner voice tells you he doesn't look right, leave the area immediately. My motto is, "Better safe than sorry." Don't take unnecessary chances.

If you think someone is following you, drive to the nearest open business. This happened to me once at night. No matter which way I turned, he was always behind me, following closely. Luckily, the stores were still open. I went into a store and asked a salesman to call the police. By the time the patrol car got there, he had left. It was an upsetting incident that has always stayed with me.

Avoid deserted parking lots and public places. If you work in a building late at night, ask someone to accompany you to your car. People are always glad to help. You shouldn't have to feel unsafe.

If someone tries to get into your car, drive away. If you can't drive away, lean on your horn to get people's attention.

If you drive home alone from work late at night, carry a cellular phone. Keep a cell phone in your car at all times. You never know when you're going to need to call for help or how far the next pay phone may be.

Don't allow yourself to be a victim. Plan ahead and avoid dangerous areas of town.

SCHOOL VIOLENCE

Since the school shooting at Columbine High School in Colorado, protecting kids from school violence has become an important issue for everyone to discuss. The following tips will help you if you are afraid that someone in your school might become violent toward you, your classmates, or your teachers.

If you hear someone threaten another student, REPORT IT! Many students feel that it's wrong to snitch on others. Which is worse—getting a student to stop his threats or seeing him carry them out? You may be saving someone's life.

Do not taunt other students. If you can't say something nice to another student, don't say anything at all. The idea that "that's just the way high school kids act" is absurd. Why *should* they act that way? When I ask students to give me good reasons for doing this, they cannot come up with even one. Let's make the world a better place. Start by keeping verbal violence out of your school. Be kind to others.

If you know students are buying guns and bringing them to school, REPORT THEM. Even though those students may not intend to use them against anyone, guns and other weapons do not belong in school at any time. Help create a safe learning environment.

Report students who are making bombs and making threats. Take them seriously. Many of my students have said they have heard threats, but they don't believe the students who said them meant it. That's the same thing the kids at Columbine said about the two teenaged gunmen who killed twelve students and a teacher. It's always better to protect your safety and that of others by reporting what you know to principals, counselors, or teachers. Be strong and do the right thing for yourself and all of your fellow classmates.

It is not normal to be subjected to abuse of any kind in school, whether it be verbal, physical, or sexual. Report any abuse to school authorities. If they do not do anything about it, have your parents call the school to insist something be done to stop it. **You have a right to feel safe in school.**

DRIVING TIPS

Did you know that car crashes are the number one cause of death for 15- to 20-year-olds? Keep this fact in mind when you first start to drive because everything is new to you. It helps to keep the following points in mind to avoid accidents and traffic tickets.

When you first start to drive, stick close to home. Get your experience on roads you know. You can build your confidence on familiar streets before you try more dangerous situations.

Slow down on rainslick roads or highways. You cannot stop as fast or safely on wet surfaces, so you run the risk of losing control of your car when you start to slide. Even if other people are driving like maniacs, slow down, drive carefully, and use good judgment.

Slow down on snow or ice. These conditions are even worse than when it's raining. It is always better not to go out in bad weather if you don't absolutely have to. If you do have to get someplace, you have a better chance of getting there if you don't try to go too fast. Always watch the other cars—people drive incredibly fast under these conditions and cause many accidents. Avoid those drivers if you can.

Drive defensively. Don't listen to the radio too loudly or put on makeup while you're driving. Always stay alert to what other cars are doing. Some people out there are drunk, hopped up on drugs, or drive too dangerously. Most people are safe drivers, but there are enough bad drivers out there to be a real problem.

Practice your driving skills. Don't throw out your driver's manual as soon as you get your license. Put into practice all of its suggestions. Learn how to use both side mirrors. They are lifesavers. If you don't feel you are seeing everything to the left of you, lean forward a bit to bring in the whole area. Always use your turn signals to change lanes.

Observe the speed limit. There are many people who don't obey the limit, but why risk the chance of getting a ticket? Obey the law, and you'll stay out of trouble. Speeding tickets are expensive, and besides, if you get rack up too many points on your license, your insurance company will find out and hike up your rates.

Do not use obscene gestures when driving. You'll just incite the other driver. When someone is driving as if possessed by a demon, slow down and let him get around you. I'd rather have an insane person in front of me, where I can see him, than behind me, so I can keep my distance.

Don't be a hotdog driver. Some people like to show off by driving like a mad fool. The truth is that you put yourself, the occupants of your car, and people in other cars in danger if you cannot control your car. Save your car racing for the racetrack.

Do not drink and drive or get in the car with anyone who has been drinking. This is a big one for teenagers. People

When it is raining or snowing, the roads will be more dangerous. Slow down and avoid stopping too suddenly. Stay farther behind cars than you usually do. Let faster drivers pass you.

who have been drinking are *not* safe drivers. You may have seen your parents drive after they have been drinking, but that does not make it all right. Use common sense here. More than 21 percent of teen traffic fatalities are caused by the driver's drinking.

Do not use your car as a weapon. Some people take their anger out on the road—they're the road rage–aholics. Nothing is worth cutting people off the road, tailgating, or purposely running into other cars. You are *not* playing bumper cars. The stakes are higher and can be deadly. *Think before you react!*

Fasten your safety belt. Surveys have shown that as many as 25 percent of teenagers do not fasten their seat belts. Be sure your friends buckle up also. Don't be lazy and think, "Oh, I'm only going a few miles down the road." Most accidents happen close to home.

Don't loan your car to a friend. He will be unfamiliar with your car, he may not be covered by your car insurance, or he may be a really bad driver. Don't take chances. You are responsible for getting your car home safely.

Tell yourself, "I will not have an accident." Too many students are casual about their driving. According to the National Safety Council, more than 35 percent of young drivers have an accident reported to the police in their first year of driving. Always be aware of how you drive. Be careful each time you drive. Pay attention to your driving at all times. Drive defensively.

PHONE POWER

How you talk on the phone says a lot about how you manage yourself in school, at home, and at work. Prospective employers, college admissions officers, and others will learn a lot about you by how you speak on the phone. Teach yourself good phone manners so the person on the other end of the line will have a good impression of you.

Answer the phone with a nice voice. Avoid sounding bored or talking in a monotone.

Don't ask, "Who is this?" An abrupt question is jarring to the person on the line. It is more polite to say, "May I ask who's calling?"

Write messages down carefully. When someone calls a family member who is not home, take the message carefully, writing down everything accurately. Remember that your family members' calls are just as important as yours.

Make your excuses. If you can't talk because you're working on a school project or doing homework, tell your friend you'll call back later when you finish.

Don't talk to the same friend every night for hours. Some kids want to talk for hours on the phone because they are not focused on school. They may be getting bad grades. Avoid the kind of friends who never do homework. They might drag you down with them.

If you accidentally dial the wrong number, don't just hang up. Say, "I'm sorry, I have the wrong number."

BANISH BOREDOM FROM YOUR LIFE

I wish I had a dollar for all the teenagers who have told me they were bored. Check out the following ideas of things to do to fight boredom.

Do volunteer work. Helping others will give you a new lease on life. You will see that there are others less fortunate than you, you'll feel good about helping others, and you'll meet people who will enrich your life. Teenagers are an incredibly powerful group in our society, capable of contributing so much to make the world a better place. And who knows, maybe someday you will need help, too. Someone like you will step forward to contribute volunteer hours.

Check out summer school enrichment classes. Many school districts are now offering courses on a wide variety of interesting topics. Summer school is no longer only for kids who failed their classes.

Become a tutor in a subject you know well. You'll get good practice while you teach and you'll feel good, too.

Check out international travel programs. Many students go to other countries to practice the foreign language they're studying.

Get a summer job. If you only want to work during the summer, check out seasonal jobs, such as at day camps, swimming pools, outdoor ice cream stands, or amusement parks.

Get involved in a school activity. Some students have built houses for Habitat for Humanity, taken trips with school groups, signed up for sports teams, or worked to make Homecoming a great experience for everyone. Do something; don't stay at home and complain that life is so boring when there are many things you could do.

Take up a hobby. Collect the new quarters that are coming out every couple of months. Read some books on how to take

Use good manners when you speak on the phone. You never know who's on the other end of the line. It could be a prospective employer or a college admissions officer.

Check out the

National Endow-

ment for the

Humanities' sug-

gested reading list.

_____

better photographs. Practice photographing your family and friends. I started taking photos while I was in high school. We have some hilarious family pictures from that period in my life.

Read some good books for fun and to get ready for the next school year. Look over the following list of books to read, published by the National Endowment for the Humanities for grades 7 through 12. Read the ones that sound good to you. You can never read too much.

Grades 7-8

Alcott, Louisa May	*Little Men*
Bagnold, Enid	*National Velvet*
Blackmore, Richard D.	*Lorna Doone*
Boulle, Pierre	*Bridge Over the River Kwai*
Bradbury, Ray	*Dandelion Wine; Fahrenheit 451; The Illustrated Man; The Martian Chronicles*
Buchan, John	*The Thirty-Nine Steps*
Bunyan, John	*The Pilgrim's Progress*
Carroll, Lewis	*Alice's Adventures in Wonderland; Through the Looking Glass*
Clark, Walter	*The Ox-Bow Incident*
Cooper, James Fenimore	*The Deerslayer; The Last of the Mohicans*
Curie, Eve	*Madame Curie: A Biography*
Dana, Richard Henry	*Two Years Before the Mast*
Day, Clarence	*Life with Father*
Defoe, Daniel	*Robinson Crusoe*
Dickens, Charles	*A Christmas Carol*
Douglas, Lloyd C.	*The Robe*
Doyle, Arthur Conan	*Adventures of Sherlock Holmes*
Dumas, Alexandre	*The Count of Monte Cristo; The Three Musketeers*
Du Maurier, Daphne	*Rebecca*
Edmonds, Walter D.	*Drums Along the Mohawk*
Ferber, Edna	*Cimarron*
Forbes, Esther	*Johnny Tremaine*
Forester, C. S.	*The African Queen;* The *Hornblower* series
Frank, Anne	*The Diary of a Young Girl*
Frost, Robert	*Poems*
Gallico, Paul	*The Snow Goose*
Gunther, John	*Death Be Not Proud*
Guthrie, A. B.	*The Big Sky*

Haggard, H. Rider	*King Solomon's Mines*
Hansberry, Lorraine	*A Raisin in the Sun*
Hemingway, Ernest	*The Old Man and the Sea*
Hersey, John	*A Bell for Adano; Hiroshima; The Wall*
Heyerdahl, Thor	*Kon-Tiki*
Hilton, James	*Goodbye, Mr. Chips; The Lost Horizon*
Hudson, W. H.	*Green Mansions*
Hughes, Richard	*A High Wind in Jamaica*
Hugo, Victor	*The Hunchback of Notre Dame*
Irving, Washington	*The Legend of Sleepy Hollow*
Keller, Helen	*The Story of My Life*
Kennedy, John F.	*Profiles in Courage*
Kipling, Rudyard	*Kim*
Knowles, John	*A Separate Peace*
Lee, Harper	*To Kill a Mockingbird*
London, Jack	*The Sea Wolf*
Lord, Walter	*A Night to Remember*
Malory, Sir Thomas	*Le Morte d'Arthur*
Maxwell, Gavin	*Ring of Bright Water*
McCullers, Carson	*The Member of the Wedding*
Michener, James	*The Bridges at Toko-ri*
Mitchell, Margaret	*Gone with the Wind*
Nordhoff, Charles, and J. N. Hall	*Mutiny on the Bounty*
O'Dell, Scott	*Island of the Blue Dolphins*
Orczy, Baroness Emma	*The Scarlet Pimpernel*
Paton, Alan	*Cry, the Beloved Country*
Pyle, Howard	*Men of Iron*
Rawlings, Marjorie Kinnan	*The Yearling*
Renault, Mary	*The King Must Die*
Roberts, Kenneth	*Northwest Passage*
Saint-Exupery, Antoine de	*The Little Prince; Wind, Sand and Stars*
Saki	*Stories*
Schaefer, Jack	*Shane*
Scott, Sir Walter	*Ivanhoe*
Shelley, Mary	*Frankenstein*
Smith, Betty	*A Tree Grows in Brooklyn*
Steinbeck, John	*The Pearl; Tortilla Flat*
Stevenson, Robert Louis	*The Black Arrow; The Strange Case of Dr. Jekyll and Mr. Hyde*
Stoker, Bram	*Dracula*
Thurber, James	*The Thurber Carnival*
Tolkien, J. R. R.	*The Hobbit; The Lord of the Rings*

Books can open up new worlds for you. Go ahead—jump in!

Twain, Mark	*The Adventures of Huckleberry Finn; The Adventures of Tom Sawyer; A Connecticut Yankee in King Arthur's Court; The Innocents Abroad; Life on the Mississippi; The Prince and the Pauper*
Verne, Jules	*Around the World in Eighty Days; Journey to the Center of the Earth; The Mysterious Island; 20,000 Leagues Under the Sea*
Wallace, Lewis	*Ben-Hur*
Washington, Booker T.	*Up from Slavery*
Wells, H. G.	*The Time Machine; War of the Worlds*
Wharton, Edith	*Ethan Frome*
Wilder, Thornton	*The Bridge of San Luis Rey*
Wister, Owen	*The Virginian*
Yates, Elizabeth	*Amos Fortune, Free Man*

Grades 9–12

Agee, James	*A Death in the Family*
Anderson, Sherwood	*Winesburg, Ohio*
Austen, Jane	*Emma; Northanger Abbey; Pride and Prejudice; Sense and Sensibility*
Baldwin, James	*Go Tell It on the Mountain*
Balzac, Honore de	*Pere Goriot*
Beckett, Samuel	*Waiting for Godot*
The Bible	*Old Testament; New Testament*
Bolt, Robert	*A Man for All Seasons*
Brontë, Charlotte	*Jane Eyre*
Brontë, Emily	*Wuthering Heights*
Browning, Robert	*Poems*
Buck, Pearl	*The Good Earth*
Butler, Samuel	*The Way of All Flesh*
Camus, Albert	*The Plague; The Stranger*
Cather, Willa	*Death Comes for the Archbishop; My Antonia*
Cervantes, Miguel	*Don Quixote*
Chaucer, Geoffrey	*The Canterbury Tales*
Chekhov, Anton	*The Cherry Orchard*
Chopin, Kate	*The Awakening*
Collins, Wilkie	*The Moonstone*
Conrad, Joseph	*Heart of Darkness; Lord Jim; The Secret Sharer; Victory*
Crane, Stephen	*The Red Badge of Courage*

Dante	*The Divine Comedy*
Defoe, Daniel	*Moll Flanders*
Dickens, Charles	*Bleak House; David Copperfield; Great Expectations; Hard Times; Oliver Twist; A Tale of Two Cities*
Dickinson, Emily	*Poems*
Dinesen, Isak	*Out of Africa*
Dostoyevsky, Fyodor	*The Brothers Karamazov; Crime and Punishment*
Dreiser, Theodore	*An American Tragedy; Sister Carrie*
Eliot, George	*Adam Bede; Middlemarch; Mill on the Floss; Silas Marner*
Eliot, T. S.	*Murder in the Cathedral*
Ellison, Ralph	*The Invisible Man*
Emerson, Ralph Waldo	*Essays*
Faulkner, William	*Absalom, Absalom!; As I Lay Dying; Intruder in the Dust; Light in August; The Sound and the Fury*
Fielding, Henry	*Joseph Andrews; Tom Jones*
Fitzgerald, F. Scott	*The Great Gatsby; Tender is the Night*
Flaubert, Gustave	*Madame Bovary*
Forster, E. M.	*A Passage to India; A Room with a View*
Franklin, Benjamin	*The Autobiography of Benjamin Franklin*
Galsworthy, John	*The Forsyte Saga*
Golding, William	*Lord of the Flies*
Goldsmith, Oliver	*She Stoops to Conquer*
Graves, Robert	*I, Claudius*
Greene, Graham	*The Heart of the Matter; The Power and the Glory*
Hamilton, Edith	*Mythology*
Hardy, Thomas	*Far From the Madding Crowd; Jude the Obscure; The Mayor of Casterbridge; The Return of the Native; Tess of the D'Urbervilles*
Hawthorne, Nathaniel	*The House of the Seven Gables; The Scarlet Letter*
Hemingway, Ernest	*A Farewell to Arms; For Whom the Bell Tolls; The Sun Also Rises*
Henry, O.	*Stories*
Hersey, John	*A Single Pebble*
Hesse, Hermann	*Demian; Siddhartha; Steppenwolf*
Homer	*The Iliad; The Odyssey*
Hughes, Langston	*Poems*
Hugo, Victor	*Les Miserables*

Reading doesn't just entertain, it also gives you the skills you need to learn faster and better.

Huxley, Aldous	*Brave New World*
Ibsen, Henrik	*A Doll's House; An Enemy of the People; Ghosts; Hedda Gabler; The Master Builder; The Wild Duck*
James, Henry	*The American; Daisy Miller; The Portrait of a Lady; The Turn of the Screw*
Joyce, James	*A Portrait of the Artist as a Young Man; Dubliners*
Kafka, Franz	*The Castle; Metamorphosis; The Trial*
Keats, John	*Poems*
Kerouac, Jack	*On the Road*
Koestler, Arthur	*Darkness at Noon*
Lawrence, D. H.	*Sons and Lovers*
Lawrence, Jerome, and Robert E. Lee	*Inherit the Wind*
Lewis, Sinclair	*Arrowsmith; Babbitt; Main Street*
Llewellyn, Richard	*How Green Was My Valley*
Machiavelli	*The Prince*
MacLeish, Archibald	*J. B.*
Mann, Thomas	*Buddenbrooks; The Magic Mountain*
Marlowe, Christopher	*Dr. Faustus*
Maugham, Somerset	*Of Human Bondage*
McCullers, Carson	*The Heart Is a Lonely Hunter*
Melville, Herman	*Billy Budd; Moby-Dick; Typee*
Miller, Arthur	*The Crucible; Death of a Salesman*
Monsarrat, Nicholas	*The Cruel Sea*
O'Neill, Eugene	*The Emperor Jones; Long Day's Journey into Night; Mourning Becomes Electra*
Orwell, George	*Animal Farm; 1984*
Pasternak, Boris	*Doctor Zhivago*
Poe, Edgar Allan	Short stories
Remarque, Erich	*All Quiet on the Western Front*
Rölvaag, O. E.	*Giants in the Earth*
Rostand, Edmond	*Cyrano de Bergerac*
Salinger, J. D.	*The Catcher in the Rye*
Sandburg, Carl	*Abraham Lincoln: The Prairie Years; Abraham Lincoln: The War Years*
Saroyan, William	*The Human Comedy*
Sayers, Dorothy	*The Nine Tailors*
Shakespeare, William	Plays and sonnets
Shaw, George Bernard	*Arms and the Man; Major Barbara; Pygmalion; Saint Joan*

Sheridan, Richard B.	*The School for Scandal*	
Shute, Nevil	*On the Beach*	
Sinclair, Upton	*The Jungle*	
Sophocles	*Antigone; Oedipus Rex*	
Steinbeck, John	*East of Eden; The Grapes of Wrath; Of Mice and Men*	
Stowe, Harriet Beecher	*Uncle Tom's Cabin*	
Swift, Jonathan	*Gulliver's Travels*	
Thackeray, William M.	*Vanity Fair*	
Thoreau, Henry David	*Walden*	
Tolstoy, Leo	*Anna Karenina; War and Peace*	
Trollope, Anthony	*Barchester Towers*	
Turgenev, Ivan	*Fathers and Sons*	
Twain, Mark	*Pudd'nhead Wilson*	
Updike, John	*Rabbit, Run*	
Vergil	*The Aeneid*	
Voltaire	*Candide*	
Warren, Robert Penn	*All the King's Men*	
Waugh, Evelyn	*Brideshead Revisited; A Handful of Dust*	
Wharton, Edith	*The Age of Innocence*	
White, T. H.	*The Once and Future King; The Sword in the Stone*	
Wilde, Oscar	*The Importance of Being Earnest; The Picture of Dorian Gray*	
Wilder, Thornton	*Our Town*	
Williams, Tennessee	*The Glass Menagerie; A Streetcar Named Desire*	
Wolfe, Thomas	*Look Homeward, Angel*	
Woolf, Virginia	*Mrs. Dalloway; To the Lighthouse*	
Wouk, Herman	*The Caine Mutiny*	
Wright, Richard	*Black Boy; Native Son*	

Don't just sit there.

Get up and DO

something!

_____

SHORTCUT TO ACTION

1. A good personal appearance will make you feel better about yourself.
2. Learn how to save money at an early age.
3. Keep track of what you spend.
4. Use credit cards wisely and sparingly.
5. When you have a job, work only 10–12 hours per week. Make schoolwork your top priority.
6. Have some fun in school. Get involved in extracurricular activities.
7. Try new things—you will be a more interesting person.
8. Eat food that is good for you. Don't forget that calcium.
9. Drink eight glasses of water a day.
10. Learn how to save money on dates. You're not a millionaire.
11. Always keep your personal safety in mind. Keep your eyes open at all times—especially when you are going places alone.
12. Drive carefully and defensively at all times. That other driver can cause you to be in a terrible accident.
13. Remember, speed kills on the road. Slow down.
14. Your phone manners tell what kind of a person you are. Always speak courteously. You will be preparing yourself for the job market.
15. To fight boredom, do volunteer work, read some good books, or get a summer job.

CHAPTER 9

Teenage Traumas

SHYNESS—A BIG HURDLE TO JUMP

I have always felt a special kinship with shy kids, because I used to be shy. I was afraid of my own shadow and wanted to go unnoticed. Now, I know now that I lacked confidence in myself and thought that people didn't care how I felt. As a result, I tended to fade into the woodwork.

While thinking about this typical teenage problem, I thought back to my school years and how I dealt with overcoming my shyness. You, too, can gain lots of personal power, have more confidence in yourself, and, as a result, have more friends. It takes courage and determination, but it is worth the effort. Check out these ideas on what you can do to become more outgoing.

Make a mental image of yourself doing neat things. Put as many details as possible in your imaginary scenario. Do research on the things you're interested in. Then make a plan of action for starting little by little to do things you've always wanted to do.

Practice what you are going to do either by yourself or with a friend. When I was a student, I spent two months at a summer school in Mexico with a friend. We and several other students lived with a Mexican family. One of the other Americans was fluent in Spanish and totally dominated the conversation at the dinner table. After a few days, we decided to spend the time before dinner looking up vocabulary words to be able to talk about what we were interested in—our town, our school, our families, and our friends. **Never give up!**

Practice conversing with yourself in a full-length mirror. See how your way of talking and your body language can improve. These practice sessions can give you the confidence you need to speak up and be seen and heard. Keep quiet and no one will ever take you seriously.

TRY THIS!

1. **Take one new risk a day.** Write in your journal every day what happened. Someone might react badly to

your new risk, but that's okay. You'll have more victories than defeats. In fact, don't think of them as defeats. Think of them as learning experiences. They are often painful, but they will help you progress much more rapidly.

2. **Practice how you will talk to a person you would like to get to know in your school.** Then go to school and try it out. Think about what happened and figure out why it did or didn't work. How can you change what you did for the next time?

3. **Write about recent encounters that didn't turn out well.** Did you learn something from them? Were they painful to you? If painful, did they kill you or are you still alive? Can you see that your life did not end when the events occurred? Ask yourself how important any of these things will be five or ten years from now. You won't even remember them. Get a perspective on things.

4. **Remember that your relationships in school will not determine what your future will be like.** I have met many people who were considered nerds and geeks in high school who later became very successful after they learned and perfected the life skills explained in this book. Think of high school as preparation for bigger and better things down the road. Your whole life won't be spent here!

5. **Make a list of your goals for overcoming shyness.** Make up short-term, mid-term, and long-term goals. Reassess them periodically in your journal. In fact, it might be good to have a special goal-getter book to read and write in from time to time.

Get together with another shy friend and brainstorm ways you can be more assertive and less afraid of speaking out.

PHYSICAL DISABILITIES

When you see someone with a disability, do you cringe because you don't know how to react? Do you taunt the person? It is easy to learn how to handle yourself when in the company of someone who is disabled. And if you are disabled, read the tips for how to feel good about yourself, how to present yourself to the public, and how to be a successful person.

How to Treat the Physically Disabled

The best way to treat someone with a disability is to remember that she is a human being, with feelings, dreams, and ideas, just like you. As long as you practice the skills I

No two people are alike, so don't compare yourself to anyone else. People who don't have obvious disabilities still have their own problems. You just can't always see them.

have offered you throughout this book, you'll never go wrong! Here are a few other things for you to remember:

- **Be a friend to the disabled.** They are no different from you—they just have a disability. Remember, that is only one part of who they are. Follow your disabled friends' examples to see how you should act, and don't be afraid to ask questions.
- **Don't feel sorry for them.** Most people with disabilities want to be seen as self-reliant and independent as you. Treating them any differently won't do either of you any good.
- **Don't use offensive or insulting language when you speak of the disabled.** Mean words hurt everybody, not just the disabled.

How to Cope with Being Physically Disabled

If you have a disability, you have probably endured a lot of taunting from unthinking kids. Besides following all of the other suggestions that I've offered in this book, check out the following ideas for how to get the respect you deserve:

- **Get involved in activities you enjoy.** Get a good education that will ensure your future. Choose activities you can excel in. Take risks. You can do whatever you set your mind to.
- **Remember that your disability is only one aspect of who you are.** See the whole you and you will be a lot happier. Do not let your disability define how you see yourself. You are a complex person.
- **Know that while there will be some things you may not be able to do as well as others, you can excel in other areas.** Those who can achieve in spite of their disabilities earn the respect of everyone around them.
- **Accept a good challenge.** Don't be satisfied with doing the bare minimum. Take challenging classes in high school. Reach out for more and you will get it. *Dare to succeed.*
- **Understand that there will always be ignorant people in the world.** You can choose who you want to be with. Don't settle for any friends but the best!

A DISABLED STUDENT SPEAKS OUT

Having a disability in high school can cause problems. People sometimes make fun of you because you're different. Well, they're the different ones. They are the heartless ones who can't see past a disability. Just ignore the fools who crack jokes about you and call you names. Until they experience being "different," they don't know how it is. Don't just sit around feeling sorry for yourself either. Do something! Work out or study or take up art. Remember, not everything is for the "normal." After all, Def Leppard's drummer only has one arm, and Stevie Wonder is blind. Don't let yourself decline just because others don't see you as equal. Remember, you're as good as everyone else.

Ryan

Be bold. Even though you have a disability, challenge yourself to do new things.

TRY THIS! (FOR THE NON-DISABLED)

1. **Think back to how you have treated disabled people in the past.** Have you ever called them names? Have you always treated them as you would want to be treated? If you haven't, try to figure out why you were unkind.

2. **Make a big effort in school to befriend a disabled person.** You'll never know whether Leslie is someone you want to have as a friend until you talk to her. Maybe you will make her day because you are the only person who has talked to her with any kindness. Write down her reaction? Did she react with anger to your overtures? Do you think she just doesn't know how to act when someone is nice to her?

TRY THIS (FOR KIDS WITH PHYSICAL DISABILITIES)

1. **Write about the bad things that have happened to you in your school years.** Have you had lots of bad experiences? Analyze them. What triggered the bad event? How did you handle it? What, if anything, could you have done to change it?

2. **Write about all of the good things that have happened to you.** What was going on when these things happened? Why were you doing so well then, but other times not? Your job here is to analyze what works and what doesn't. Do you smile often and have a courageous attitude toward life, or do you let your disability get you down? Writing all of this down on paper will help you see the patterns in your life.

Losing someone you love is very difficult. Since you may have never suffered the death of someone close to you, knowing what to do is difficult. These tips can help.

GRIEF—A NATURAL PART OF LIFE

Grief is a natural reaction to a loss. Most people think that we grieve only when someone who is close to us dies, but this is not always true. You can experience grief when a close friend moves across the country, when you break up with your boyfriend, when a favorite pet dies, or if you change schools. Grief may occur whenever there's a change in your life. Check out the following tips on how to understand and deal with your grief.

You cannot avoid feeling grief. The sooner you deal with it, the better you will feel. Trying to avoid it will make you feel numb and not live life as joyfully as you could. Dealing with your loss is normal—you must go through it. It will not go away.

You may feel anger when a loved one dies. This could include anger at God for letting it happen, anger at yourself for not being a better person, anger at the doctors for letting the person die, or anger at your friends for not understanding why you feel so badly. This is a normal reaction to someone's death and is especially severe if the death is sudden or violent. Your anger will dissipate little by little as you learn to accept what happened.

You may feel a loss of control over your own life. Someone important to you is gone, so life will never be the same. How will you cope? What will you do to survive? Loss of control is a normal feeling in the grieving process, but it will gradually go away as you learn to cope with and accept your loss.

You might feel disorganized and helpless. So much of your life has changed because you have just had a wrenching experience. You don't know how to get back on track. Be patient and give yourself a break.

Don't blame yourself for someone's death. Many people react like this when someone dies. You must remember that you are not to blame. You didn't cause the accident that killed your father, you didn't cause the cancer that killed your mother, you didn't cause your brother's suicide. It was beyond your control.

Cry when you need to, even if you're usually tough. Crying helps you deal with your grief in a healthy way. It is the human way of dealing with sadness. If you have a hard time crying, listen to some music that reminds you of your loved one or to something sad to help you get in touch with your feelings. Even talking to a stranger can help. After my father died, I was crying in a park. A park custodian, a man I'd never met before, came up to me and asked me what had hapened. When I told him, he said he knew just how I felt because his father had died recently, too. He was feeling the same way. We had a nice conversation that made us both feel better. You never know when a helping hand will reach out to you.

Talk with your family or friends about the death. It is healthy to get together with the people who loved the person. Talk about your memories of her or about her funny way of laughing. Openly grieving with your family and friends helps you deal with your loss and to accept it.

If no one seems to care about how you feel, tell them. They may be trying to shield you from those awful feelings. They *think* they are protecting you, but instead they are making you feel uncared for and possibly very angry. It's always better to be open and honest. Tell them how you feel. They will be grateful they can share their grief with you too.

Funerals are a necessary way of saying goodbye. I used to think they were so ritualistics, but now I realize that rituals provide structure during an uncertain time. They allow you to join others who cared about the person and to share your grief.

Don't get stuck in the grieving process. At some point after you have dealt with your grief, it's time to move on. Realize you have a right and need to enjoy your own life. Good luck!

Things You Can Do to Help Yourself

Join a support group of teenagers who have suffered the same loss. There are survivor groups for the families and friends of people who have died of suicide, accidents, or illness. The members help each other move on, to continue to live, and to accept the death. If you can't find a support group, start one. Ask hospital social workers to help you find others in your same situation. Remember, you still have your own life to live.

Lend a helping hand to someone in need. Remember, there are others in the world who are suffering. Helping others gets your mind off your own problems and makes you feel good and worthwhile. You will have a sense of purpose that you did not feel before.

Write a letter. Even though she is dead, tell her what you wished you had told her before she died. Tell her how much you miss her. Tell her what you are angry about. Write down anything you can think of to get it all down on paper. This will be your way of saying goodbye, keeping her in your heart, and being able to accept her death.

If you can't let go of your grief, find a support group of other teens that will help you get through it.

Get together with family and friends to talk about your loved one and what he meant to you. Share with others what you are thinking. If you're angry about something, talk about it.

Get professional help if you experience any of the following:

- Your grief lasts for an extended period
- You have thoughts of suicide
- You turn to drugs or alcohol to deal with your pain
- Your anger is affecting everyone around you—friends, family, teachers, and fellow employees
- You have no interest in your school activities, friends, or classwork
- You were very outgoing, but now you want to be alone all of the time

You can help a friend with his or her grief by doing the following things:

Get her to talk. When she talks, really listen to her. Let her do all of the talking. Express how you think she must feel.

Talk about the good memories you have of the person. This especially helps if your friend is reluctant to open up to you. Just don't push it because she may not be ready to talk about it.

Tell your friend you care about her. She will feel very happy to know someone is trying to understand what she feels.

Ask her how you can help. She may say that she would like to take a long walk to talk about her loss or she may just want to go shoot some hoops. Either way, she knows you are there for her.

TEENAGE SUICIDE

Suicide is one of the most terrifying subjects to discuss or think about, especially when the victim is young. It is the third leading cause of death of teenagers after accidents and murders, so you need to learn all you can about suicide so you can help yourself if you feel suicidal or a friend who starts to talk about suicide.

Reasons for Suicide

There are many reasons people commit suicide:

- to escape intolerable pain
- to punish family or friends
- to join a loved one who has died

- to imitate famous suicide victims, like Kurt Cobain of the rock group Nirvana, thus trying to become famous like him
- to get the attention in death that they could not get in life

Suicide victims choose to die because they can see no other way out. They feel hopeless and don't believe things will ever get better. Often, they are so ashamed of their feelings that they can't tell anyone how they really feel.

Warning Signs

- a new lack of interest in school activities
- a need to be alone instead of with family and friends
- a lack of interest in eating or a new interest in overeating
- a drastic change in personality—sad, agitated, always sleeping, withdrawn, negative, angry, crying a lot
- excessive use of drugs or alcohol
- talk of suicide
- recent loss—of a girlfriend, boyfriend, job, flunking classes, getting kicked off the football team, inability to deal with someone's death, parents divorcing— anything that has great impact
- unnecessary risk taking
- statements that indicate the person has no hope things will get better
- neglecting physical appearance

We will not always be successful in preventing suicide because some teenagers are experts at hiding their feelings. But with a greater awareness of what causes suicide and of the key changes in a person's behavior that can lead to it, family and friends can keep an eye out for the signs that a teen might be contemplating suicide. The more education we have on this painful subject, the more effective the prevention.

If You Have Suicidal Thoughts

Engage in healthy behaviors. Avoid the use of drugs and alcohol. Get lots of exercise. Eat healthy foods. Don't risk your life doing crazy, dangerous things.

Write down all of your negative thoughts. Write them *all* down. Wait a few hours. Then go back and look at what you've written. Can you see any faulty logic in what you have written? For example, do you think no one loves you? Then write about the people who care about you. Or do you

Where there's life, there's hope. Sometimes, it is hard to see that. If you are feeling suicidal, reach out to others for help.

consider yourself a failure? Write down all of the things you *have* accomplished. Always counter the negatives with positives!

Realize that suicide is a permanent choice. You cannot take it back. You won't be able to see your friends and family or even the consequences of committing suicide. Whatever your reason for suicide, it won't solve anything because you won't be around to see any changes. There's no turning back.

Share your feelings with an adult. Your parent, doctor, school counselor, or teacher will help you. Don't be embarrassed to feel the way you do. Many people have had the same feelings you are having now and have lived through it. People who are trained in suicide prevention will understand the hopelessness you feel. Many of them have loved ones who went through the same thing. Some of them used to be suicidal and learned how to deal with their feelings of despair. Don't give up. There are people who can help you. Reach out to others. Teenagers who have reached out are happy they are still alive. **There is hope for you.**

You Can Help a Suicidal Friend

Get your friend to talk. If you notice he no longer wants to hang out and seems depressed, ask him what's going on. If he tries to change the subject, tell him you care about him and would like to help him if he needs it.

Listen when your friend talks. Don't tell him you know how he feels; simply listen. Ask him if he has been thinking of committing suicide. Never ignore a suicidal statement. Tell an adult immediately.

If you think he is going to attempt suicide, call a suicide prevention hotline or talk to your school counselor and ask for advice. Do not try to deal with this alone. You are not a suicide prevention expert, but you are a very important part of the prevention process because you are the one he has confided in. Remember, safety comes first. Even if your friend swears you to secrecy, *never* keep a suicide plan a secret. Your friend may be mad at first, but you will have saved his life.

If your friend already has a plan to kill himself, has the means, or has already tried, DO NOT leave him alone. Call 911 while you stay with him. Talk to him until help comes.

And if your friend does commit suicide, realize that you are not responsible. You did all you could. No one can force another person to live. You can only control your own life and yourself.

For more information, read:
> *Teen Suicide, Too Young to Die* by Cynthia Copeland Lewis
> *Straight Talk About Death for Teenagers* by Earl A. Grollman

ANOREXIA, BULIMIA, AND COMPULSIVE OVEREATING

Anorexia, bulimia, and compulsive overeating are often interrelated diseases. A person may suffer from anorexia and then switch over to compulsive overeating, then to bulimia to regain control of the weight. There is no set pattern to these disorders, but they do share two strong bonds: their victims suffer greatly and need help to escape from the disorders. These disorders are one of the most serious problems facing teenagers today. The vast majority of teens who suffer from them are girls, but it is not uncommon for boys to also suffer from them.

Reasons for Eating Disorders

- Society tells us that thin is beautiful and fat is ugly. Look at Barbie®. She is thin as a rail. Little girls grow up playing with Barbies and similar dolls, getting that subtle, subconscious message that they must be just like her to look good. We praise teenagers who are thin and make comments when heavier teens eat an extra piece of pizza. Teens get teased in the locker room before gym class if they aren't as skinny as a Spice Girl. They feel fat, even though they are not.
- To have that "beautiful" model's body, teens may start dieting to lose a few pounds, but they keep going until they lose control of the diet. Even though they've lost weight, they still see themselves as "fat." This leads to excessive weight control that causes them not to eat the proper foods, get the proper nutrients, and maintain a healthy lifestyle.
- Some teens have an extreme need for control. They may have suffered from sexual abuse when they were younger or are still being abused. They may have parents who have an excessive control over them. Whatever the reason, the eating disorder is their way of gaining some kind of control over their own lives—their way of saying, "You can't tell me what to do anymore."
- Low self-esteem gives teens the idea that their bodies are not okay and that they have to be as thin as Barbie or a model in order to be accepted by others. They

America's obsession with thinness has distorted teenagers' opinions of their bodies. Many of you think you're fat—but you really aren't.

look up to that perfectly thin popular girl who has the boys waiting in line for her and wish that they could be just like her. The irony is that these popular girls and the too-thin models are often just as miserable and have just as little self-esteem as the kids who look up to them because of the focus on their weight.

- Some girls fear that if they're too shapely or too attractive, boys may become sexually interested in them before they're ready.
- Some researchers in the medical community are beginning to relate eating disorders to brain chemistry imbalances.

Let's look at each of the eating disorders, one by one.

Anorexia Nervosa

People who suffer from anorexia nervosa are literally starving themselves to death. They eat very little to avoid gaining even an ounce of weight. When they first lose a few pounds and get favorable attention from other people, they feel good about themselves and mistakenly think that losing more weight will get even more positive notice from their family and friends. They become trapped in a dangerous program for self-improvement that never seems to end.

Warning Signs for Anorexia

- losing a lot of weight
- continuing to diet, even when they have lost so much weight
- looking in the mirror constantly, saying they're still so fat
- excessive exercising, even though they are not eating enough to have the energy to exercise so much
- constantly drinking diet sodas
- not having a menstrual period every month
- obsessing about food they eat, food labels, calorie counts, and portion size
- skipping meals
- making excuses for not eating with friends or family: *I just ate. My stomach hurts. I'm not hungry.*

Physical Effects of Anorexia

- hair becomes dull and brittle and sometimes falls out
- sleeping becomes difficult
- blood pressure drops

- skin becomes dull and lifeless; nails get brittle and break off
- skin always feels cold
- eventual death due to starvation if help is not received

It has been estimated that 5 percent of people who suffer from anorexia nervosa die from it. If you are one who suffers from this disorder, get help so that you can stop what you're doing. Don't wait, because if you don't stop the disorder early enough, too much damage might occur. Choose to live. Wake up to a better life.

Friends of Anorexia Sufferers

If you know your friend suffers from anorexia, talk to her about it. Tell her you know what she's doing. Ask her to go get the help she needs to escape from this insidious addiction. If she refuses, you must talk to someone she trusts—to a parent, a school counselor, or a kind teacher. Don't assume her parents know what is happening—she is probably hiding it well from them. In addition, they might not know much about anorexia and be unaware of the warning signs. You, as a friend and teenager, have probably heard of other cases of girls or boys who suffer from this and know more about it. Don't sit back and watch her destroy herself. Speak out. You may save your friend's life.

Bulimia

People who suffer from bulimia eat huge quantities of food (bingeing) and then get rid of the food by vomiting or using laxatives (purging) before it has a chance to be digested. Just as with those suffering from anorexia, they are terrified of becoming fat. They have a distorted view of their bodies for the same reasons anorexia victims do. As with anorexia, most of the victims are young girls, teenagers, and young adults.

Some guys on wrestling teams have been known to either starve themselves or purge what they have eaten so that they won't exceed the maximum weight for their weight class. One of my students was as thin as a rail and looked exhausted all of the time. When he was finally able to eat at the end of the wrestling season, he gorged on food and was sick the next day. We had planned a party for him in our class with lots of food, but he didn't show up! Needless to say, he was very embarrassed. I was glad when the wrestling season was over so that he could eat normally again.

Warning Signs of Bulimia

- eating huge amounts of food in an uncontrolled, obsessive manner

It isn't just girls who suffer from bulimia. Boys are just as vulnerable. They might have been teased about their weight when they were younger. Now, they'll show the rest of the world that they can be thin too.

- going to the bathroom after every meal and running the water to hide the vomiting sound
- obsessing about body weight, looking in the mirror constantly
- feeling fat, even when looking like a concentration camp survivor
- looking bloated in the face
- having heartburn
- stopping of or irregular menstrual periods
- dieting when with friends, bingeing when home alone
- evidence of empty chip bags, many candy wrappers, food disappearing from refrigerator
- abuse of drugs or alcohol to forget problems
- irritability, anxiousness, depression, anger
- low self-esteem
- impulsive personality

Physical Effects of Bulimia

- dehydration
- damage to mouth and esophagus tissues because of stomach acids, which results in infection
- electrolyte balance disrupted, resulting in eventual kidney problems
- loss of tooth enamel, resulting in tooth decay
- bad breath
- swollen throat glands
- gum disease
- stomach ulcers
- eventual death if help is not received

Friends of Bulimia Sufferers

If you know a friend who suffers from bulimia, get help. Talk to him first before you go to others for help. It would be ideal to have him agree with you that he needs help. Read the above advice for friends of anorexia survivors for more information about what to do to help. Don't ignore this deadly compulsion. Safety comes first.

Compulsive Overeating

Compulsive overeaters have an addiction to food. Overeating causes obesity, a medical problem that puts people at risk for heart disease, diabetes, and high blood pressure.

Reasons for Overeating

- food is a comfort for the overeater when sad, depressed, mad, frustrated, bored
- food temporarily helps the overeater's self-esteem problems
- the food looks good, and the overeater likes to eat
- to be sociable while out with friends
- because the overeater might feel lonely

The Right Way to Diet

Proper weight-loss diets observe good nutritional practices and balanced food intake, including the recommended daily regimens of vitamins and minerals. With proper dieting and exercise, the fat stores in the body continue to supply some of the dieter's energy needs while maintaining good health. For most people, the recommended rate of weight loss is about 1½ to 2 pounds per week. This can be achieved on diets limited to 1,200 to 1,500 calories a day for women and 1,500 to 2,000 calories a day for men. Calorie needs of children vary greatly, and their rates of weight loss should be prescribed by a physician.

Although some diets may place more emphasis on calorie reduction and others on increased exercise, all of them should emphasize the importance of good nutrition and should maintain a balance of proteins, carbohydrates, and fats.

Overeaters Anonymous is a successful weight-loss program based on the same twelve-step principles as Alcoholics Anonymous. It is a group-support approach to cutting back on eating that emphasizes the whole person, not just the calories and fat content of foods. There are many weight-loss programs, but none will be effective unless the overeater gets in touch with his feelings and the things deep down that are troubling him. Overeaters Anonymous helps the overeater work on his life issues, not just his food issues.

A good weight-loss program must provide foods that give the overeater a balanced intake of necessary food. Diets that cut out protein or carbohydrates are unsafe for more than a week or two. A dieter should try to lose no more than two pounds per week to be entirely safe. By not starving herself, the overeater can gradually cut back how much she eats to a more healthy lifestyle of eating. Sudden weight-loss programs of more than two pounds per week are very dangerous. Most people go off the diets within a short period of time and revert to their old eating habits, putting on even more pounds

Before starting any weight-loss program, talk to your doctor. She can make sure you stay healthy while you diet and might even have a few good tips for you to follow.

We are not born with prejudice. It is taught to us as children.

than before they started the diet. Be careful. Consult your doctor for good medical advice.

Exercise is also an important part of every weight-loss diet. Without it, you will not burn as many calories. In addition, exercise makes you feel better, burns calories, and gives you an overall sense of well-being. A good starting point to losing weight and exercising is to go for a short walk. Gradually build up the amount of time you walk and the distance you go every day. Try to walk with a classmate. It's always more fun to walk with someone, and you can encourage each other in your project. Good luck and have some fun!

PREJUDICE AND DISCRIMINATION

Prejudiced people irrationally judge all members of another race, religion, or group to be inferior to themselves. They make stereotypes about an entire group of people, but they don't even know the vast majority of people who actually belong to those groups! Typical groups who are discriminated against because of prejudice are African Americans, Native Americans, gays, Hispanics, women, and Jews, but this is by no means an exhaustive list.

Prejudice of any kind damages all of us. People who make blanket statements about any group of people are hurting all of us because they keep the human race from reaching its full potential. Think about how much better our world would be if we could all accept each other. Look at small children playing together. Do they reject another child because he's a different color? No, they play together as equals unless they're taught otherwise.

Prejudice is learned first in families. It occurs as a result of a limited world view. Children see how adults, especially parents, treat and speak about people of different groups; kids imitate their behavior because they think it is the right way to behave. I don't think a lot of adults realize the negative effect they are having on their children. Learning about other cultures and the communication styles inherent in those cultures helps people understand each other and get along. When these types of lessons are passed on to children, we all benefit.

Examples of Prejudice

1. A well-educated African-American friend of mine was recently stopped by the police for speeding. He was

driving a BMW. When the policeman came up to his car to talk to him, his first question was, "Is this your car?" as if it were stolen. As a white person, I thought about this and knew that no policeman would ever ask me the same question. The policeman was stereotyping black people as not having nice cars, as being poor, and as being criminally inclined. Is it any wonder that African Americans feel as though they are the victims of so much prejudice?

2. Gays are one of the groups who are most discriminated against in our society. News of gay bashings is not unusual. A young gay man who came out in high school was harassed so much that he finally committed suicide because he couldn't take it any more. He was just trying to be himself. Is this fair? It's a sickening commentary on how narrow-minded so many people are.

3. More than six million Jews were murdered in the Holocaust during World War II. Is there anything more horrifying than branding an entire group of people as unfit and subject to extermination? We must never forget this wholesale slaughter of a people. We know from the Holocaust that mankind is capable of great evil. We must always fight any kind of discrimination when it first begins in order to keep it from getting any worse. Prejudice and discrimination hurt all of us. These injustices make us less human.

4. Teenagers are stereotyped by many adults as loud and obnoxious and are treated like children. In my own experience, though, most teens are not loud and obnoxious. You have a lot of wonderful characteristics—your openness to new things, your enthusiasm, your honesty. I believe that teenagers are capable of so much. We could use your help in so many ways to make this world a better place.

Prove the people who stereotype you wrong—excel at all you do!

Advice for Students Who are Members of Minority Groups

If you are a minority student, you will be swept along by the majority culture's value system and rules. Learn how to get along with other cultures, but keep your own cultural identity. It's important not to lose your sense of who you are. Read the following tips for how to survive as a minority student of any group, whether you are Hispanic, Black, Native American, or Vietnamese.

No two people are exactly alike. We should embrace our differences, not condemn one another for them.

Play the game of the school you are attending. If they want you to follow certain rules, go along with them. You will have a much easier time if you don't fight the system. If the system is really unfair, work to change it in a peaceful, rational way. It's always a good idea to speak up and give your opinion. Your opinion counts!

Excelling academically will put you at the top of the game. In order to excel, you will need to study hard, do all of your homework, and participate in class. Prove those people wrong who say your race or nationality can't cut it. Show them you can.

Be a gentle person. If it makes you angry to be attending a school as a minority student, it is best to let your anger go. You will only be hurting yourself if you turn people off with a defensive attitude. Your goal should be to get the best education possible, to prepare for getting the best job possible.

Get involved in your school's activities. If you sit back and don't participate, how can you expect anyone to care? They need to get to know you, to see the good qualities you can bring to the school. Toot your own horn. I believe most teenagers, teachers, and administrators will give you a chance. If there are a small percentage who don't, it's really their loss, not yours. They are not taking the time to get to know you.

Whatever culture you come from, be able to learn from your teachers who belong to other cultures. Remember, you are in school to learn. Get the best education possible to prepare for your future.

Get to know your teachers. You're probably terrified of all of those different faces. It's hard to walk into a school when you're a minority student. Be courageous, pick your head up, and do your school work. People will start to notice you in a favorable way. You can do it.

Religious Tolerance

If you were taught that your religion is the one true religion, look with tolerance upon other religions and even study about other religions. You will find that while another religion might worship a different god than you or you might read from different books, there is a single unifying force among all religions—a belief in something greater than us all.

BEING GAY

Some teenagers have to deal with sexual orientation issues while in high school. Talk about trauma! Students who know they are different often try to deny it. Many turn to drugs and alcohol or other destructive behaviors to deal with their conflicting emotions.

Read what a high school student, Brian, has to say about coming to terms with the fact that he is gay. His story will show you that you are not alone. He, too, had difficulties with coming to accept that he was gay.

Imagining yourself in another person's place lets you see that we all struggle against stereotypes.

BRIAN WANTS YOU TO KNOW

There wasn't enough room for the two of me in my body—so I came out of the closet. The journey to that point, though, wasn't exactly easy. Like many gay teens, I realized that I was gay around the age of 12. Not only was I scared, but I felt extremely alone. I had no gay role models, I had never met anyone who was openly gay before, and I thought that I was doomed to a life similar to how the media portrays homosexuals. I hated myself. After numerous futile attempts of trying to change my sexuality (of course, I now realize that you are who you are), I entered high school deeply depressed. Desiring only to be "normal," I found it difficult to connect with other kids because I was afraid that they'd reject me if they found out who I really was. At times, I even believed that taking my own life would be the easiest way to solve my problems. Fortunately, after years of self-hate and denial, I found the strength and courage to attend a gay youth support group meeting and eventually to tell my parents. Although we've had our rough times, they love and accept me just the same. They realize that I'm still the same Brian I've always been and that being gay doesn't change anything—only that my partner won't wear a skirt. My school friends have told me that they admire my coming out. I hope that I've made it easier for others at my school to face their sexual identity and accept themselves for who they are. I now strive to raise awareness, be a role model, and advocate equal rights for all human beings, regardless of their sexual orientation. I finally can love myself and others; coming out was the best decision I've ever made.

For more information, read:
The Journey Out by Rachel Pollack and Cheryl Schwartz

TRY THIS!

1. **Imagine yourself in the following scenarios:**

   - You are a black man crossing the street. You hear a white person in a car locking his car doors as you pass by. As a black person, how does it make you feel to be stereotyped as a criminal and a bad person? Can you see how much that hurts the black man and how angry he must be?
   - You are a white student trying to be friendly to a group of black students. They give you the cold

shoulder. How do you feel about this? Do you think it's because you're the "wrong" color?

- You are of Arabic descent and of the Muslim faith. You hear students using a racial slur about Arabs. How do you feel as an Arab? Does it make you angry that these kids are stereotyping all Arabs? Is that fair? What would you say to them? Or would you say anything to them at all?

- You are a Hispanic teenager. You overhear white kids using racial slurs against Hispanics. What is your reaction to that? Will you say something to them?

- You are a gay teenager. You constantly hear other teens calling you names. Can you speak out against this type of discrimination? Would you be able to tell your fellow students that they are being ignorant? Can you tell them that all people are individuals and cannot be put into categories? Can you tell them that life and people are much more complex than that?

   NOTE: I put all of these examples in this section for you to think about how you would react if you were the student being discriminated against. Would you have the guts to speak up and tell them they are wrong to stereotype a whole group? I have seen many teenagers of minority groups of all kinds keep quiet when students are bashing their group. Teenagers will respect you for calmly telling them how faulty their logic is. You owe it to yourself, to your self-respect, and to your whole race, nationality, or group. Don't be afraid to say what you think. You'll be glad you did. Notice, however, that I said to do it *calmly*. If you reply to others in anger, your whole message will get lost in the emotion. After all, you are proof that what they are saying is baloney. Show them they are wrong.

2. **Brainstorm with a friend different ways that you can create more racial harmony in your school.** Get friends from different nationalities and races involved. You could make this a fun experience for everyone. It feels good to make things better in your school. Believe in your power. You have great potential for doing good things. Use it!

3. **Start noticing prejudice of all kinds in our society.** You will see it everywhere. Men discriminating against women, blacks against whites, whites against blacks,

heterosexuals against gays, and so on. When you notice these situations, ask yourself why this discrimination is happening and why we can't all get along as equals.

SEX

Sex is full of emotionally contradictory feelings for teenagers. Maybe you know some of your friends are "doing it," but you aren't sure if you want to or if you're ready to yet. Let's face it, engaging in sexual activity is appealing, but the issue is a complicated one that can have dangerous and serious consequences.

I met with a group of students, some high school age and some college age, to get their views on sex. The viewpoints varied from person to person, but they all agreed that each person has to know what his or her own values and beliefs are about sex before engaging in any sexual activity.

It is sad that teenagers often become sexually active before they are ready to deal with the emotional and physical consequences. Check out the questions the students said you should ask yourself and your partner before becoming sexually active. I feel they did a great job covering the issues. See if you agree. Can you think of any other questions?

So many teenagers are having sex before they're ready and know what they're doing. Abstinence is the only safe way to avoid pregnancy and sexually transmitted diseases.

Questions Teenagers Say You Should Ask Yourself Before You Engage in Sex

1. Can you talk openly to your partner about sex? Are you or your partner afraid to talk about it?
2. Who will take the responsibility to prevent pregnancy and sexually transmitted diseases (STDs)? What precautions will one or both of you take?
3. What will the two of you do if a pregnancy results from sexual intercourse? Will you have an abortion? Will you have the baby and raise it together? Will you get married?
4. Do you feel your partner will dump you if you don't have sex? Do you feel that your partner is pressuring you to do "what everyone else is doing?"
5. Do you know your partner well? Is your partner a person with integrity who really cares about you? Do you love each other? What is love?
6. Do teenagers who love each other necessarily have to have sexual intercourse? Is there another way to

If you have already had sex, you can still choose to be abstinent in the future. If you have not had sex, do not get talked into doing it by peer pressure. Being a virgin is not a crime—stay true to your beliefs and be strong.

express your feelings of love toward each other without "going all the way?"

7. How will you feel about yourself the morning after? Will you feel good? Will you be ashamed? Will you feel better or worse about yourself?
8. What would it be like to have sex and then later break up?

After answering all of these questions, the students I spoke with feel that you will definitely know whether or not you should engage in sexual activity with your partner. Having sex is a serious commitment that requires much thought before getting involved in it.

Reasons Teenagers Say to Wait Before Having Sex

The students saw the following advantages to waiting:

1. You decrease the chances of getting sexually transmitted diseases.
2. You can wait for the special person to make a lifetime commitment.
3. You feel the stakes are too high at this time and are too involved in other activities to give a sexual relationship the time and energy it needs.
4. You do not feel physically or emotionally ready for such a commitment.
5. You won't get pregnant.
6. You prefer to wait, for moral or religious reasons.

If You Are Pregnant

There are risks involved when a teenager gets pregnant. Here are some things you should do or avoid if you are pregnant and decide that you want to have the baby.

Tell your parents and see a doctor as soon as you find out you are pregnant to start your medical care. Your parents can help you make important decisions, and the doctor will advise you on what you need to do to ensure that you and your baby will be healthy.

Do not drink alcohol, smoke, or take drugs. Doing so increases the chances of premature birth, birth defects, and low birth weight.

Eat a balanced diet. Remember that you are feeding not just yourself, but also your baby. Lay off the junk food!

Take a community college class on parenting with your partner. That way, you will both be better able to cope with the stress of raising a child.

A Sex Wrap-up

Some of the students I talked to admitted that sex for them while in high school was not enjoyable. They felt pressured to do it before they were ready. One girl said she felt used by her boyfriend. Do not let yourself be exploited by anyone. Do not let someone require you to have sex as "proof" of your love for him or her. Remember the story I told you a couple of chapters ago about the girl who had sex with all of those guys on Spring Break and then didn't get invited to the Senior Prom? People who truly love each other don't put this kind of pressure on each other.

And remember, you can always postpone sexual intercourse. It's your decision. An increasing number of teenagers are committing themselves to wait until marriage. Don't be fooled by feeling that you're the only virgin in your school. According to statistics, that's not true. Many teens are not doing it. Take charge of your own sexuality.

Many teens are choosing abstinence for several reasons: they are not ready to have sex, they do not want to have sex just because "everyone else is doing it," or they want to wait until marriage to have sex.

SEXUALLY TRANSMITTED DISEASES

Engaging in sexual activity risks exposure to sexually transmitted diseases (STDs) such as gonorrhea, chlamydia, genital warts, genital herpes, hepatitis A and B, and AIDS. The occurrence of these STDs is growing, especially among teenagers. No one is immune to their attack. One of the problems today are new strains of these STDs that are harder to cure.

Here are some of the facts you need to know about STDs:

- You can get an STD even if you don't have sexual intercourse.
- You can get several STDs with one sexual act.
- You *can* get STDs or get pregnant the first time you have sexual intercourse.
- You can't always tell who has STDs. The finest dressed person can be infected. The only way to know for sure is to have a medical exam and in some cases, a blood test.
- Condoms cannot be used for more than one sexual act.
- AIDS attacks both heterosexuals and homosexuals. No one is safe from it.
- Even if the person's medical exam shows no STDs, this is still no guarantee that he or she doesn't have one. Sometimes the infection doesn't show up until six months after exposure, especially in the case of AIDS.

STDs are an unfortunate by-product of the casual sexual activity engaged in by many people. You must always be aware of the dangers of sex. The worst STD—AIDS—can kill you. It has happened to other teens, and it can happen to you.

New STDs have appeared on the world scene in the last 25 years. Chlamydia and AIDS were unheard of before then. More than 5 million people in the United States are HIV positive. If you are going to be sexually active, you must talk to your partner about past partners and about methods of prevention of pregnancy and STDs, such as the use of a condom. Teenage girls should know that many STDs can cause sterility so that they will never be able to have children. But if you take proper precautions *before* you engage in any sexual activity, you will protect yourself and future partners.

IMPORTANT: The more partners you have sexual relations with, the greater your chance of getting an STD. Remember that every time you have sex, you are having sex with all of the people your partner had sex with. Why is that, you ask? Because your partner can be a transmitter of an STD that he or she received from one of his or her other partners. Many teenagers think that getting infected can't happen to them, but the truth is, teenagers are getting STDs at an alarming rate. Some people have said that teens don't want to talk about taking precautions, such as using a condom, because then they will be saying that they're intending to have sex. Does that seem crazy to you? If you're doing it, you're doing it. Take the necessary precautions. Talk to your partner about his or her past sexual experiences. It's your life. Don't just hope nothing will happen. That kind of attitude is almost a guarantee that something bad will happen to you. Love yourself and love life enough to take good care of yourself.

In addition, if you have an STD, you will need to be totally honest with your partner. It is reckless and unfair to transmit disease to others just because you are too embarrassed to admit you are infected. Sexual activity is a grownup thing to do, so you must be grownup about this. You can hurt other people. Wake up to the dangers out there. You ought to be more than a little scared about what's out there. It's no joke.

Educating yourself is the key to avoiding the dangers of having sex. Talking to your partner is another way to avoid them. If you can't talk to your partner about these things, ask yourself if you should be engaging in sexual activity.

It is beyond the scope of this book to go into detail about the nature of all of these sexually transmitted diseases. It is a good idea to do research on them *before* you become sexually active.

For more information, read:
   Straight Talk About Sexually Transmitted Diseases by Michael Brodman, M.D., John Thacker, and Rachel Kranz.
   Teens with AIDS Speak Out by Mary Kittredge
   What You Can Do to Avoid AIDS by Earvin "Magic" Johnson

TEENAGE PREGNANCY

Most kids don't believe they could ever become pregnant while still teenagers or that they could get their partners pregnant. Most say, "That'll never happen to me." The fact is, though, that many teenage girls do get pregnant because they and their partners did not take the proper precautions or their birth control method failed. Read the following section on teenage pregnancy to get the facts. Much of the information in this section comes from the March of Dimes' Web site (http://www.modimes.org).

You only have to forget to use birth control once to get pregnant. Use it AT ALL TIMES! And guys, you are just as responsible for using birth control as your girlfriend. Don't make her do all of the work to ensure safe sex.

Statistics

- 560,000 babies are born to teenage girls every year.
- Almost one-sixth of all U.S. births are to teenage girls.
- Babies born to teenage mothers have a higher risk of birth defects and serious health problems.
- Teenage girls under age 15 who give birth have more pregnancy complications than older mothers.
- During the first three months of pregnancy, seven out of ten teenagers do not see a doctor or go to a clinic. Many times this is because they don't know they're pregnant or are afraid to find out.
- Poor nutrition, alcohol, drugs, and smoking increase the risk of having a baby with health problems.

Risks to the Baby

Low birthweight is the main health problem because often babies born to teenage girls are born too soon (premature). This low birthweight can cause the following health problems such as mental retardation, a risk of dying in early infancy, or immature organ systems (heart, brain, lungs).

If you are pregnant, be sure to see a doctor as soon as possible. Good pre-natal care is essential for having a healthy baby. Do everything the doc-tor tells you to do.

Effects of Having a Baby When You Are a Teenager

- You will miss excessive days of school. Many teenage mothers do not graduate from high school.
- Your earning power will be drastically reduced if you do not graduate from high school. It will be roughly half that of women who gave birth in their 20s. Note: In order to help pregnant girls, many high schools have day-care centers, and girls get money to help pay for childcare. Your school might have one of these services.
- Usually the teenage mother becomes dependent on her family for financial support and help to raise the baby. You won't become independent from your parents until you're a lot older.
- Your friends will be going out and having fun while you'll have to stay home and take care of the baby.
- You may have to go on welfare to take care of your baby, especially if your family won't help support you.

To Have a Healthy Baby

All of the above sounds terribly negative, but these often are the kinds of things that happen to teenage mothers. It's important to give you the facts so that you stand a better chance of having a healthy, normal baby. Be sure and do the following:

- If you are not using any kind of birth control or skip a period, go to the drugstore and get a pregnancy test kit. You need to know as soon as possible if you are pregnant. Your baby's welfare is at stake.
- Get prenatal care from your doctor or a clinic as soon as you find out you're pregnant.
- Don't drink, do drugs, or smoke cigarettes. This is a must. If you continue to do any of these things, your baby may be born with a birth defect. Some babies with fetal alcohol syndrome have abnormally small heads, heart defects, mental retardation, hyperactivity, and other problems.
- If you are taking any kind of prescription drugs or over-the- counter medicines or herbs, ask your doctor if you should continue to take them. They may have a bad effect on your baby.
- Follow your doctor's instructions carefully. Go regularly for checkups to see how your pregnancy is progressing.

If You're Pregnant and Are Unsure What to Do

When you discover you're pregnant, your initial reaction might be joy at having a baby, but in most cases your first reaction will probably be, "Why me?" Once you get over the initial shock, you will have to make some decisions. You have three choices:

- You can continue the pregnancy and keep the baby.
- You can continue the pregnancy and give the baby up for adoption.
- You can opt to have an abortion.

Looking at the three choices, none of them probably seems good to you. You are young, just starting to become an adult, and now you are faced with having a child who will depend on you totally for its care. This is a real dilemma for teenage girls who get pregnant because each of the options will be difficult for you to face. If you decide to keep the baby, your youth will be over. You will have the responsibility of being a mother. You may decide to quit school because the stress is too much for you. If you decide to give the baby up for adoption, you will always wonder where the baby is and whether he has good parents. You may feel an aching in your heart, an empty place that you cannot fill. If you choose to have an abortion, there's a chance that you will always feel as though you never got to know your baby, and you might even feel conflicted about having had an abortion.

When you find yourself faced with this situation, get help from your parents, your school counselor, or a pregnancy counselor who can help you sort through your feelings. You might have different family members telling you what to do. Your mother may want you to keep the baby, but your father might be telling you to have an abortion, and your boyfriend might take off because he doesn't want the responsibility of being a father. You will be confused, and it's important that you get your head clear before you decide anything. That's why it's always a good idea to get impartial, outside help to give you the opportunity to weigh your options.

The following story was written by a 26-year-old woman who has had to make some difficult decisions in her young life. To protect her identity, we'll call her Kelly.

Teenage mothers are at a big disadvantage in the job market because most of them cannot continue their education and raise a child at the same time.

KELLY WANTS YOU TO KNOW

I want to share with you not only the details of my battles with drug addiction, mental illness, and teenage parenthood, but also how you can find joy, hope, peace, beauty, and, most important of all, balance in your life.

First, a brief history. A friend of my family molested me between the ages of 7 and 9. My problems started there. Since I was lured into my role as a victim, drugs and alcohol became very comfortable ways to avoid the pain I felt daily. By the age of 11 or 12, I was already quite ill emotionally. I thought about death daily; my behavior was erratic and unpredictable. I would sneak out of the house to use drugs and find the only thing that felt like love to me—sex. It may be difficult for some of you reading to understand, but when as a young child you are told repeatedly that this is okay, you accept this as the truth—especially when you are overweight, have zero self-esteem, and have no healthy people around you willing to share the real truth with you. Sex is a biological function of the human body; it can be a wonderful expression of trust and commitment if you are saying to a person, "This is my body and these are my most private thoughts; here take them, hold on to them for a moment, and cherish their uniqueness." My problem was that I kept saying, "Here take these; they are fairly useless anyway, but you can keep them." Every time I did that, I felt less and less worthy of myself.

But deep down inside, something kept saying to me, "Um, excuse me, this isn't the way childhood is suppose to be." That voice eventually helped me to overcome many obstacles, reflect on them, and then eventually accept what had happened to me.

I raged on in my youth until I found out I was pregnant at fourteen. I was apathetic about it at first. Many people wanted me to terminate the pregnancy. My gym teacher even looked up the number to an abortion clinic and dialed the phone. I made the appointment but on the way to hock some stolen jewelry to raise the $350 for the procedure, I changed my mind.

My boyfriend, who later became my first husband, and I broke the news to our parents. They were devastated. My mother left town for several weeks, leaving my father to cope with the mess. My father and I did a lot of arguing, yelling, and screaming at each other the first four or five months. I spent nearly every night in tears.

He and I spent the last four months taking long walks together, sometimes in deep conversation, other times in silence. I knew he wanted me to consider adoption, but I was too immature to think about the ramifications my lifestyle would have on a child. Now, as I see my beautiful daughter's face crumble when she realizes her biological father has yet another excuse why he cannot come see her, or write once a month, or call, or I see her antagonize her stepfather because somewhere in her mind she thinks if he were not around, her dad would be, I realize what my dad was thinking.

I hope my daughter will be wise enough to choose abstinence. I want you to know that I love my daughter and it is because of that love that I wonder now how her life might have been if she had been reared in a home filled with love from the beginning. What I don't wonder about is the abortion issue. I know where I stand on that.

January 4, 1991, will live in my mind forever. After my daughter was born and I had married my boyfriend, I began drinking again, had an affair, and ended up in a psychiatric hospital, where I spent the better part of a year. I became pregnant again.

I had only been out of the hospital about a week when I had the abortion. I was still mentally sick, and if anyone had been interested, I am sure they could have seen that during the pre-abortion counseling. All I can think is that they must have thought, "This kid doesn't have a chance anyway." I remember only bits and pieces of the day because you are given a type of sedation that inhibits memory, but I do remember the nurse saying, "It looks about eleven weeks." I asked whether they could tell from the remains whether it was a boy, while sitting in a row of recliners surrounded by other girls who had made the same choice.

Abortion is by no means an easy way out. Think, think, and think before you choose. I wonder what that baby would have looked like, and when I look at my family now, it seems so unfair that he missed the opportunity to share his courage and love with the rest of our family. I am only comforted knowing I did the best I could and I believe that he is okay now—wherever he is. I hope someday, when I leave this earth, I will be able to say I am sorry.

How do you get over living on the streets, a slutty reputation, drugs, insanity, and everything else? The event I just mentioned was a real turning point. I decided I needed to get it together and take care of the child I had. It took a long time. I saw a therapist, and took some medicine, went to college, met my husband, got married, regained custody of my daughter, had a son, and found God. That is key. I never was a big believer in prayer until I looked back on my life and reflected on just how dead I should be.

Helping other people in your community is another excellent way to refocus your anger and pain. You can use all that experience and energy to lift someone up who is in trouble. Start today by looking in the mirror and saying, "I am a beautiful child and I deserve good things to happen to me." Reflect at the end of the day. Keep a journal and set two goals for the next day that are simple and attainable. For me, getting to school was one. Saying hello to my parents was one. Not yelling at my children later became one. You can read your progress and in several years, you will truly be amazed by the places you have been and where you are going.

Today, I am a nurse—a psychiatric nurse. I have a beautiful family that at times bears the scars of my past but overall is pretty safe. I can accept that no matter how much I want to control things, life doesn't work that way. I love my life and all of the people in it. Most importantly, I know that I am using my life in the way in which it was intended to be used. You can too. Never give up! You can make it one more day. I'm 26 now, but I wasn't expected to live past 18.

Take your time when you have to decide if you are ready yet to be sexually active. It is a huge responsibility to deal with.

Tough Choices for Girls

Many students have asked me to write the following information for you. Because the decision to have sex is so difficult for most girls, it's a good idea to ask yourself if you're truly ready for it and the consequences it brings, such as pregnancy and STDs. Many girls have chosen to abstain from sexual intercourse until they are a lot older and are emotionally ready for it. When you are 14 or 15 years old, you are still figuring out who you are and what you want to do with your life. You've got lots of time to be sexually active.

SOME TEENAGERS WANT YOU TO KNOW

True love waits! As best friends, we keep each other accountable to this motto. Life is full of choices, and we have made the choice to wait to have sex until marriage. We highly recommend this to all teenagers. Imagine being able to say to your husband/wife that you saved yourself for them and only for them. What a wonderful gift! This is what keeps us going. It gets hard at times knowing where to set the boundaries, but with God's help and the help we give each other, it makes it a lot easier. This also gives us something to look forward to. *Save sex, not just safe sex.*
    —Lindsey and Becca

I was fifteen years old and a freshman. It was one of those times when it just hadn't been my day, week, or month. Nothing had been going right. So, when a tall, cute, popular senior asked me to do something with him after school, I thought this would be the solution to all my problems. He told me that he liked me, and that felt so good. He only wanted to have sex with me. It seems so obvious and simple, but it wasn't. I didn't want another problem or another lost friend. So, I had sex with him because maybe it would bring us closer together. Wrong. He was the first person I had sex with, and I wasn't at all ready for the feelings that came along with intercourse. I thought it would be no big deal, but it was. He never really talked to me again or even looked at me the same. That was a year ago and it still hurts. Now I realize what sex is supposed to be about and what caring about someone is supposed to feel like. But I learned it the hard way.
—*Cassandra*

SEXUAL HARASSMENT

Many teenagers are sexually harassed in high school. I have heard many negative and sexual things said to students while walking down the hall. It's usually girls who have to put up with sexually motivated comments made about their breasts, legs, and hips and their weight. Less frequently, boys also pinch girls, back them up against lockers in a threatening manner while making sexual comments, or grab at their breasts. I have asked many girls why they put up with such treatment, and they can't give a good answer. They seem to be allowing these things to happen so as not to rock the boat and create more problems for themselves. Sometimes, they don't realize that what the boys are doing is wrong.

Girls, you do *not* have to put up with these comments or actions. If they persist or if a group of boys gangs up on you every day while on your way to class, report them to the principal. If the principal does nothing, go to your counselor or parents for help.

Some guys also get sexually harassed. Girls make comments about their "cute buns" or their muscles, thinking nothing of it. Some guys like it, but others don't. If you don't like it and it makes you uncomfortable, you have a right to say so. You don't want to be treated like an object, either.

If you are a boy who is sexually harassing a girl or who makes sexual comments to and about girls walking down the hall, stop it. You are objectifying the girls and bringing yourself down to the lowest level possible. You don't need to go along with other guys to be "cool." If you are a girl who is sexually harassing boys, stop it. You don't want to be treated that way, so what makes you think guys like it any better than you do?

Listen to one student's very painful story about the sexual harassment she endured for an entire school year from male students and her male teacher because she didn't know how to stop it. Put yourself in her place, whether you are a boy or a girl, and think about what you would do if you were in her situation.

If you are sexually harassed, go to your school principal for help. She is bound by the law to help you. Harassment is illegal.

MEGAN WANTS YOU TO KNOW

I will never forget the year I spent in Mr. H's chemistry classes. Chemistry class sophomore year was interesting and fun. Mr. H was always good at explaining chemical bonds and other related material in terms that any high school student would understand. He utilized humor and made chemistry interesting. I enjoyed chemistry, so I enrolled in advanced chemistry for my junior year.

My advanced chemistry class was composed of three girls, including myself, and about fifteen boys. Mr. H began joking about the girls. In the beginning, the jokes were funny. As the weeks went by, I began to notice that Mr. H's jokes were implying that the girls were not as smart as the boys. Class became a competition every day between the girls and the boys, and as the competition grew so did the "jokes."

I remember one particular instance that made me the center of attention for several jokes. We were going over homework problems. Mr. H always called on the boys to demonstrate how to correctly solve a problem, but on this day, there was a bonus problem that none of the boys could solve. I stated that I could solve it, and Mr. H laughing said, "Go ahead and try." I went to the board and correctly solved the problem. Mr. H and the boys were amazed. Mr. H said that I would receive an *A* for the day and then stated that everyone could "party in place." "Party in place" meant that homework could be worked on or talking quietly was permitted.

As the weeks continued, "party in place" turned into "party in Megan's place," followed by a laugh. Immediately following the announcement of "party in Megan's place," the boys in the class began chiming in with crude statements of how to "party in Megan's place." Their comments were full of sexual innuendoes, referring to parts of my body. The comments got worse and more sexually explicit as time went on. I was so embarrassed that I would laugh, but on the inside I was crying.

"Party in Megan's place" became a regular phrase in class, especially if I answered a question correctly or did well on a test. The other girls in the class never said much or laughed, but the boys began to take the phrase outside the classroom. I became a big joke. Mr. H would just laugh and laugh. He allowed the boys to continue their sexually explicit talk. I never spoke up; I just smiled and told the boys to shut up. Not only did I have to deal with the horrible comments, I had to prove myself every day in class that I was just as intelligent, maybe more, than all of the boys.

I realize now that I should have defended myself and that I should have gone to someone in administration and put a stop to "party in Megan's place." I did tell my parents, but at the time I do not believe they knew how to handle the situation either. My parents told me to ignore the behavior and not to acknowledge that it bothered me. I tried to do that, but sometimes I could not. At the time, I did not think that I was being sexually harassed, but now I realize how wrong it was.

If someone in your family is sexually or physically abusing you, you have the right to say, "NO!" If you do not feel strong enough to stop it, there are many people who will help you get the strength you need to put a stop to it.

DOMESTIC ABUSE

Domestic abuse happens in homes more frequently than anyone imagines. Experts estimate that between 10 and 25 percent of children are abused by a family member or close friend of the family. The abuse can be physical, emotional, or sexual. If you have been victimized by someone's abuse, report it to an adult who will listen to you. Nobody deserves to be abused. You have a right to grow up without anyone hurting you physically, sexually, or emotionally.

Many kids who are abused do not report the crime because they are afraid a parent will be sent to jail, breaking up the family and creating a serious financial loss. While it is true that this sometimes happens, social agencies can intervene for you and get help for both you *and* the abuser. You do not have to suffer in fear and silence. There are many agencies that are devoted to helping victims like you.

Sexual abuse in families is a well-kept secret that happens more often than we would like to think. If you have been sexually abused or are currently being sexually abused, you must get help. The problem will not go away until you get someone to help you work through all of your feelings. Even if the abuse happened when you were only six or seven years old, you need to talk to someone because this abuse will affect your adult life. It won't go away. You may hide your feelings and be numb to them, but it will affect your ability to trust others, especially in sexual situations. Talk to your school counselor for information on counselors who specialize in dealing with sexual abuse issues.

Teenagers Who Suffer Abuse From Other Teens

Physical abuse. Physical injuries resulting from abuse are the easiest to detect. Some examples of physical violence are slapping, kicking, biting, pinching, hair pulling, throwing things at the person, punching, or brandishing weapons as a threat. Often, marks are left on the victim's body. The physical abuser is even more dangerous if he or she is drinking alcohol. More than half of the murders committed in the United States are alcohol-related.

Verbal and emotional abuse. These include calling the victim names, swearing at her, accusing her of dating other boys, and insulting her. More teens verbally abuse their boyfriend or girlfriend instead of resorting to physical abuse. However, if the teens stay together long enough, the verbal abuse can turn to physical abuse. A victim might have to account to her boyfriend for every moment they're not together. If she isn't home when he calls, he might accuse her of seeing other boys, even when he has no proof of this. In short, this verbal abuser will make the girlfriend feel trapped and hopeless.

The abuser might ask her boyfriend to stop seeing his guy friends, trying to control his every free minute. She might get angry with him because he's five minutes late to pick her up. She might verbally assail his past girlfriends or demand he stop talking to any girls. She might drive by his house, checking to see if his car is there. If it isn't, she might accuse him of seeing other girls. In short, she will make his life a living hell. He will not be able to have his own life, have his own opinions, or have his own plans for the future. She owns him, emotionally and physically.

Sexual abuse. A teenager who forces his date to have sex is guilty of rape. In addition, some teens believe that their boyfriend or girlfriend won't love them if they don't have sex. They often get talked into doing something they don't want to do. Don't let anyone force you or talk you into having sex before you're ready. You always have control of the situation, except in the following extreme situations:

- Your date slips a drug called rohypnol in your drink. Rohypnol is called the "date rape drug." Anytime you are with someone you don't know well, do not accept a drink from him. Be sure you don't leave your drink sitting on the table while you go to the bathroom. Take it along with you. Sounds super-paranoid, doesn't it? Just the other day, I was reading in the newspaper that some teens from Michigan put rohypnol in their girlfriends' drinks, disabling them, which enabled them to subsequently rape the girls. Granted, most boys are *not* going to use this drug to rape you, but you can never be too cautious, especially with guys you just met.
- You are drinking alcohol. Alcohol lowers your resistance. You are much more vulnerable when you are drinking. Your judgment is clouded and your intuition (that voice that warns you of danger) shuts down. Be careful of alcohol. It causes many problems. Besides, it's illegal to drink it until you're 21.

As you can see, you must always keep yourself safe. You can do that by not getting drunk on dates and by going out in groups of friends whom you know well. Be careful of that guy or girl you just met.

It seems crazy that there are people who abuse others, but there are. Abuse is no joke. If you are a victim of physical abuse, you must report it. Don't let yourself be victimized. Fight back.

Advice to Teenagers Who Date Abusers

Talk to someone about the abuse. You will be able to be more objective about the abuse when you talk to your school counselor or to your parents. You are not being treated normally. You deserve better.

Ask yourself if you really love the person or if you believe that you don't deserve someone better. Often, teenagers who put up with abusers feel that they don't deserve anyone any better and that they have to settle for less. Not so! You have every right to demand that your boyfriend or girlfriend respects you and does not treat you abusively.

If you do feel you are in love with the person, take a timeout to reassess your feelings. Perhaps your parents could send you out of town to an aunt's for several weeks. Or maybe they could send you to a different school.

Do not drink alcohol with your boyfriend or girlfriend. He or she might turn into an angry beast at the slightest provocation.

If your boyfriend or girlfriend shows no signs of changing, leave while you're still in one piece. When someone strikes you but then apologizes profusely afterwards, don't forgive the person and keep dating. The abuse will only get worse. The third or fourth time could find you with serious physical and emotional injuries that will haunt you for the rest of your life.

One of my students was dating an abusive boy. She told me that he would shove her up against the lockers if he saw her talking to another guy. He started hitting her. When he called her and the line was busy, he accused her of talking to other guys. She was really scared and couldn't concentrate in classes, so her grades went downhill. I got her the help she needed. She was able to see that she didn't have to settle for someone like him. Yes, he was cute and had a winning personality. But when his dark side came out, she wasn't safe. Luckily, she was able to get him out of her life.

Self-Abuse

Some teenagers injure themselves—cutting their wrists or legs—to cope with stress and express their fear, frustration, and anger. For more information on self-mutilation, read the book *Bodily Harm* by Karen Conterio and Wendy Lader. It will give you hope that there is a way for you to stop hurting yourself. If you are a friend of someone who does this, you can read the book to get an idea how you can help him or her.

It is always a good idea to report this self-abuse to someone you trust. People who abuse themselves are crying out for help but don't know how to get the help they need. They don't understand why they're doing it to themselves any more than you do.

EMBARRASING BODIES

Gynecomastia

Never heard of it? If you're a guy who has this problem, you know what it is even though you may not have ever heard its name. Gynecomastia is a medical term that comes from the Greek words for "women-like breasts." No one ever talks about it, but for many boys who have them, it is a humiliating experience, especially if you have to dress for gym class or when your friends want you to go swimming. One year, a student of mine told me that he didn't ever get changed for gym and was going to take an *F* for the semester. I knew why he didn't dress out—he had enlarged breasts. I'm sure he was taunted by the other guys in the locker room.

Heavy-weight guys often look like they have gynecomastia, but they simply have an excess of fat. When they lose weight and exercise, the "women-like breasts" disappear. The real gynecomastia, however, is caused by changes in hormones in young men at puberty or by steroid use, marijuana use, or as a side effect of taking certain medications. More than half of 13 to 15 year old boys have enlarged breasts. They usually disappear after a couple of years when the hormones in their bodies stabilize.

Treatment for Gynecomastia

In most cases, no treatment is needed because it usually goes away in two or three years. For the guys who still have the enlarged breasts after a few years and who are not overweight, surgery is a possibility. Liposuction is used to remove the fatty tissue. The fat is removed by suction, returning them to a more acceptable shape.

Traumatizing Effects of Gynecomastia

Many of you guys can relate to this if you have suffered a lot of humiliation at the hands of friends and classmates in gym class. You feel a sense of shame because you think you look like you have a girl's body. Guys aren't supposed to have "women-like breasts." Basically, you are powerless over this and will just have to wait it out, or, if possible, lose weight to

Boys taunt other boys in the locker room if they have "women's breasts." If you're a guy who doesn't have these, don't tease the boys who do. They are often traumatized by it. What if it was you who had the breasts?

If you deal with your body image as a kid, you won't have major hangups when you're an adult.

get rid of them. Even then, some of you will still have the enlarged breasts and will never want to take your shirt off in front of *anyone*.

If you are suffering severe embarrassment and low self-esteem because of gynecomastia, you can look into surgery as an option to get rid of them. Everyone is different. Some guys adjust to them and learn to accept their appearance, but others feel extreme humiliation. I had another student (also failing gym class) who seemed very depressed because he had the enlarged breasts. After watching him for a couple of months—he never smiled, never laughed, and sat in the back of the room—I called up his mother and told her I thought he was depressed. She was angry with me and said that, no, he was *not* depressed. Six months later, she called me to tell me that he had tried to commit suicide. Luckily, he was unsuccessful. If you are feeling like this, please get some help. Talk to your doctor. He can tell you what options are available to you. Feeling self-conscious is a common problem, so don't be embarrassed to level with him. Tell him how this is affecting your life. There is help out there.

Deal with the traumatic effects of gynecomastia when you're young. Otherwise, you'll take your poor body image and low self-esteem with you into adulthood. It will affect every aspect of your life. Confront it now. Enlarged breasts do not make you any less worthy than the next guy. Reach out to others. Tell your parents, counselor, or doctor how miserable you are. They will understand. We cannot heal what we do not acknowledge.

ANDREW WANTS YOU TO KNOW

I'm a successful male executive in my mid-thirties. When I was in second grade, I suddenly started developing breasts for no apparent reason. The first problem I remember was kids making fun of me. They said I was a girl because I had enlarged breasts. Kids are brutal. I played basketball on a team in grade school and high school. Waves of fear would envelope me when we had to divide into "shirts" and "skins." I always hoped I was a "shirt," but sometimes I had to take my shirt off and tough it out. I was miserable, so I quit the team. Back then, I had never heard of any treatments available, so I just adjusted my life around the problem. To this day, I still buy oversized, very thick shirts to cover up my problem.

It wasn't until a few years ago that I realized I significantly control how my breasts look. I should note that I have always enjoyed eating much larger than normal amounts of sweets and junk food. I was doing some aerobic exercises, combined with light strength training and a lower fat diet. The results after a few months were dramatic. I actually didn't mind going to the swimming pool! Like a lot of people, though, I slacked off and my problem eventually came back. I think strength training is crucial to look better.

For young boys who have the condition now, I would advise them to analyze their situations. If they don't think it will bother them, fine. If they are like me, though, they should seek help. They should run, not walk, to their doctor and get an examination and treatment, if the doctor recommends it. I wouldn't want to see a boy go through what I have, since there are treatments available to remedy the problem. I could still go through treatment myself, but at my age it is rare that I have to worry about it any longer. I still can't take my kids to the swimming pool, but I do lots of other things with them to compensate for that. Besides, I reason, if I started taking my shirt off while cutting the grass, I would just expose my upper body to increased risk of skin cancer!

Don't be afraid to talk to your doctor about embarrassing problems. He's there to help you, not to make fun of you.

Acne

Many teenagers live in dread of acne. All you need are one or two zits to feel miserable. No one wants these gross-looking things on their face. Read the following information on acne to find out what you can do to avoid it or to get rid of it.

How Do You Get Acne?

Acne can develop under the following conditions:

- The glands in the skin produce too much sebum—an oily substance.
- Bacteria in the skin's pores get trapped along with the sebum, plugging up the pores. This causes the skin to break out
- Acne is often made worse by the person's scratching, pinching, or squeezing the pimples.
- Scientists feel that heredity plays an important part in developing acne.
- Scientists also believe that the hormone androgen stimulates the sebum-producing glands. Because boys produce ten times more androgen than girls, they get more severe cases of acne.
- Chemicals can cause acne—one of my nieces got outbreaks of acne when she used perfumed shampoos. In addition, oily cosmetics, in combination with the over-production of the oily sebum, can cause acne.
- Stress has also been given as a cause for acne outbreaks.

The face, back, chest, and shoulders can break out. Acne usually starts in the teenage years and sometimes continues into the twenties. Most teens get what is called noninflammatory acne, which can be controlled more easily. Teens who have the inflammatory acne have a harder time getting rid of the zits. For them, the acne covers the face and often the back and neck.

Take good care of your skin. Read the tips on this page to find out how to get rid of acne or avoid it.

Taking Good Care of Your Skin

If you have started to get zits on your face, do all of the following things. You may be able to get rid of them and avoid getting them again.

Use a mild soap to wash your face. Keep your face clean to remove dead skin, dirt, and accumulated oils. Be gentle when you wash your face because rigorous scrubbing can irritate your skin. If you already have the zits, you will make them worse by trying to scrub them away. That won't work.

Eat the right foods. Although it has not been proven that fatty foods, fast foods, and sweets cause acne, many teens report that when they eat good meals, they don't have so many outbreaks of acne, but when they hit the burger and taco places, they have more problems.

Don't use oil-based makeup. Ask the cosmetics clerk to steer you to the water-based cosmetics.

Get products that contains benzoyl peroxide from your drugstore. Use these products with caution at first, because some people are allergic to benzoyl peroxide. Follow the directions on the package. Be vigilant or the acne will return.

What to Do If None of This Works

Make an appointment with a dermatologist. He may recommend you take a drug like Accutane if you have a severe case of acne. If you do have to take Accutane, be very careful. If you are a girl who takes the drug and becomes pregnant, there is a good chance you will give birth to a baby with birth defects. Your doctor will give you a brochure that tells of all of the possible side-effects of the drug.

SHORTCUT TO ACTION

1. If you're shy, talk to other kids. You can help each other break out of your shyness.
2. Treat disabled students just as you would other students. Their disability is only one part of who they are.
3. If disabled, find things to do that you enjoy. Just because you're disabled doesn't mean you can't do cool things.
4. When a family member or good friend dies, deal with your grief. It's okay to cry and talk about it—even if you're a guy.
5. Suicide is permanent. If you are suicidal, talk to someone about your feelings. Ask for help. There *is* hope.
6. If you know your friend is anorexic or bulimic, tell her you know. Explore with her ways to find the help she needs.
7. Do not judge others. When you start to have prejudicial thoughts against a group of people, ask yourself how *you* would feel if you were a member of that group.
8. It's okay to abstain from sexual activity. You'll avoid sexually transmitted diseases and pregnancy.
9. Do not allow others to sexually harass you or grab you in inappropriate places. Stand up for yourself and say, "No."
10. If you have acne and have already tried over-the-counter products that don't work, see a dermatologist for help.

CHAPTER 10

Bold Is Beautiful—
Take a Risk and Create

Have you ever felt like you are on a merry-go-round and can't get off? That life just seems to be moving so fast and you can't stop it? That changes sometimes overwhelm you? Face it, this is our modern way of doing things. Change happens. Working on how you react to stress will help you face every new challenging change that comes along. Without challenges, your life would be terribly boring. If you're bored often, ask yourself if you have enough challenges in your life. Many students go home, turn on the TV, and zone out until dinnertime. Maybe doing something vigorous after school and having goals would help you not to feel bored so much of the time. Find new challenges and new things to do that max you out in a good, fun way.

Risk taking is important if you want to be successful in life. Risks are what enable people to do great things. You don't have to be an Einstein or an Edison to be successful. You can make your own mark in your own way.

We have many ways to eliminate risk taking in our lives. Look at some things people say to avoid having to take risks and be challenged and ask yourself if you ever say the same things. What else do you say that eliminates risk from your life?

- *I can't.*
- *Ooh, that sounds hard.*
- *No one I know has ever done that.*
- *No one I know has ever tried that.*
- *It's impossible.*
- *I couldn't begin to think of doing that.*
- *You think I could do that? You must be crazy.*
- *It's just too much trouble.*
- *My friends wouldn't like me anymore if I did that.*
- *What would my parents say?*
- *Are you out of your mind?*
- *It's a good idea but . . .*
- *I'm afraid.*

Do any of those resistances to change and risk sound familiar to you? The next time you want to do something good and sensible that seems too risky, tell yourself you can do it if you work at it. You say you'd like to try your hand at a book written *by a student* to help kids in school? Go for it. You'll learn a lot while doing it and may even write a bestseller.

HOW TO LIVE WITH CHANGE WITHOUT FREAKING OUT

Accept that change is inevitable. It will happen whether you like it or not. That's a given in anyone's life. It's hard to accept sometimes, but you will adjust to it. You have to or else you will drive yourself crazy.

Make gradual changes. If you want to improve the way you operate in school in order to do better, change things gradually, step by step. Too radical a change will get you discouraged easily. Start by doing the *Try This!* activities in the book. Remember, a couple of small changes add up to a big change. Look upon it as exciting to do things differently.

Enlist your friends and parents to be your cheerleaders. They can help get you pumped up.

Reach out to others. Ask a trusted friend, teacher, or parent to help you deal with a change you have to face. Sometimes just talking to someone about it helps you let go of your fears and anxieties. Often, the person you ask will help you see a new perspective on a problem and enable you to make a change.

RISK TAKING

Taking risks in life is necessary to ensure your growth as a human being. When we risk doing something, we cannot be certain of the outcome. That is why many people are afraid to take risks. Every once in a while as I was writing this book, I had the fear that it would be a failure. Luckily, each time I experienced that fear, it only lasted for a day, and I continued writing the following day. For me, it was a positive experience to write the book because I could have become complacent as a teacher. Writing it forced me to reassess what I was doing in the classroom and also enabled me to see some good things I could do to make students' lives in school better and more efficient.

It's important to take risks—that's what keeps you alive and interested in life. You never know what you can do until you try. Have some fun.

Fight fear's influence in your life. Fear can paralyze you, keeping you from making good changes.

The positive benefits of risk-taking:

1. You learn more about yourself.
2. You find out what does and doesn't work.
3. You become more confident and will try to do more new things.
4. You learn a lot in the process.
5. You learn how to deal with the fear of failure.
6. You learn how to think smarter.
7. When you fail and keep trying, you become a more courageous, gutsy person.

Check out this poem on risk-taking. Do you think that what the author is saying true?

Risk-taking is free

To laugh is to risk appearing the fool.
To weep is to risk appearing sentimental.
To reach out for another is to risk involvement.
To expose feelings is to risk exposing your true self.
To place your ideas, your dreams, before the crowd is to risk their loss.
To love is to risk not being loved in return.
To live is to risk dying.
To hope is to risk despair.
To try is to risk failure.
But risks must be taken, because the greatest hazard in life is to risk nothing.
The person who risks nothing and does nothing . . . has nothing and is nothing.
We may avoid suffering and sorrow, but we simply cannot learn, feel, grow, love or live without taking risks.
Chained by our attitudes, we become a slave and forfeit our freedom.
Only a person who risks is free.
—Anonymous

When we try new things, whether in school or in the business world, we are taking a risk. When we exercise our creativity we are taking a risk. I took a risk when I started writing this book because I did not yet have a publisher—I was too busy writing to find one! My reason for writing is to help kids. If this book helps even ten people, I will at least have bettered those ten kids' education. The bottom line is that I believe in what I'm doing, and that made the risk worthwhile.

TRY THIS!

1. Think about some changes you need to make in your life. Write them down and write down what fears you have about making the changes. What bad things could happen if you make the changes? What good things could happen? Does the good outweigh the bad, and are the changes sensible and safe or will they hurt you or others? If you decide the changes are good for you and won't hurt others, decide how you are going to start to make them happen.

2. Write down in your journal some changes you need to make in school. Do you need to pay attention in class and do your homework? What will your friends think of you if you start doing your schoolwork? Will that cause problems in your friendships? How can you make the changes and still keep your friends? Or do you need different friends? Analyze the situation and ask what's good for you. What do you need to do to make your life better? Make up an action plan for making the changes happen.

3. Analyze the changes friends and family members have made that upset you. Why did they upset you? Were they good changes or bad changes? Did you feel you had to go along with them and make the same changes even if you felt they were not good for you?

CREATIVITY

When a person is being creative, she gets an idea to create something and then sets about doing it. The inspiration that comes to her is the act of creating but then she also must apply her idea. If she does not, she has not completed the creative act. The actual application of the idea can take her weeks, months, or years to finish. Many factors enter into the equation: How much free time she has, whether her life is stress-free, how persistent she is in carrying out her idea, and how confident she is about herself.

I'd like to give you an example of a man I'm sure did not think of himself as creative—my father. I'm mentioning this because what he did creatively does not fit our stereotype of what it means to be creative. He could fix anything that was broken, even if he did not have the proper part to fix it. He could create his own solution, and many times invented his own piece to fix a machine. He came up with some hilarious

You can do creative things if you have a positive focus on life. Nurture the part of you that can look at life creatively. It's fun!

Creative thoughts can strike you at any time. Write down your ideas so that you won't forget them. Start to notice your environs, writing down what you see.

solutions to problems, but the bottom line is they *worked!* He got tremendous satisfaction out of his ability to create workable solutions.

Don't be limited by what you previously thought it meant to be creative. You have the potential within you to create something that will give you a good feeling of accomplishment and will make your life full of fun. Try it.

How To Be Creative

Allow yourself enough time to relax. A person's most creative thoughts come when he is not thinking—he is simply being. Don't rush around during every waking moment. Take time to just be.

Do not constantly obsess about grades. Allow yourself time to enjoy learning. You will come up with a lot more creative ideas that way.

Brush off criticism. Don't let other people's criticism keep you from creating—believe in yourself.

Tell yourself you are creative. We are all capable of being creative. We just have to know how to access it—how to nurture it.

Get out into nature. Sit under a tree, feeling the breeze caressing your cheek. Hear the rippling sound of the water and the leaves blowing in the trees. Go into a relaxed state. **IMPORTANT:** Do not use drugs and alcohol to get into a relaxed state because they will numb you instead.

Just enjoy what comes up for you at any moment. If nothing does, don't try to force it. It will happen if you're patient.

Stay away from mind-numbing things like game shows, soap operas, and talk shows on television. You cannot create when you are looking at someone else's creation. Besides, you can create something better than that!

Keep all of your relationships as peaceful as possible. When your family and friends are having personal problems, this can drain your energy, depleting all of your creative impulses.

Be open to new things, new people, and new ideas. If you are very rigid in your viewpoints, you will tend to eliminate many possible creative ideas.

Be kind to yourself. Creativity is like anything else—you have to work at it. Your creative mind will naturally improve with practice. You simply need to start doing it. Don't think that great writers, painters, and musicians immediately started turning out masterpieces. They started from point zero just as you will have to. Their initial output was not brilliant.

Practice creating new ways of looking at things in your life. Look at problems as opportunities to create solutions. Brainstorm ways to change your perspective on a preconceived notion. Let your imagination run wild. Then start making the changes you need to make. Have fun. Make this an adventure.

Creativity is everywhere. Recognize that your creativity may come in any field in which you specialize. An engineer needs to come up with a creative solution for designing a superhighway that crosses over a steep gorge and waterfall. How is he going to do it? He uses the knowledge he has learned in classes and then lets his creative thinking help him come up with a workable idea to solve the problem. He will not always be able to find answers in books. He will have to look within and access his creative mind. This example comes to mind because when I was at Malad Gorge State Park near Twin Falls, Idaho, I saw that Interstate 84 was literally built over a steep gorge and waterfall. I stood there transfixed in amazement, asking myself how they did that. That is not something I could do, but I am grateful there are others that have creative talents in those areas. Truly amazing!

Have lots of interests. Be curious. Ask questions. Research new things. Explore a new section of town where you have never been. Learn all you can about it. Walk down the streets soaking up everything you can.

Do boring tasks in a new, unusual way. If you have to clean the house, why not dance and sing as you run the vacuum cleaner? Who knows, you might get some great creative ideas when you are doing something in a new, different way. If people think you're crazy, that's *their* problem, not yours. You're just "doing your own thing" in order to get a different perspective of those everyday tasks we all have to do.

Read The Artist's Way *by Julia Cameron. It's a great book to get your creativity jump-started. Do all of her exercises. It really helps.*

TRY THIS!

1. **Exercise your creative brain to come up with at least five ways a person can be creative in a non-traditional way.** Most of us feel that if we want to be creative, we have to be a painter, a poet, or a composer. Because of this notion, many of us do not

Creativity is like your muscles; you have to exercise it. Opportunities to create are all around you. Find ways that enable you to feel the joy that comes from exercising your creativity.

---

even think we have the capability to be creative *because* we can't paint, write poetry, or write music. Prove that notion wrong!

2. **After you have done the first Try This!, name some ways you can be creative.** Let your imagination run free here in order to give yourself permission to believe in yourself.

3. **Look around you at your fellow students.** Which students do you think are creative and why? Do you think your previous definition of creativity was too limiting? Can you see yourself and your friends as creative when you see creativity in a different light?

4. **Know what you're interested in.** Go to a place where you can relax and get all stressful thoughts out of your mind. No exam or homework thoughts allowed here! Think of something you can create. Take your time doing this and come back to it again if nothing comes to you this time. It will eventually.

5. **Be ready with your creative ideas at any time.** Have paper and pen next to your bed. Some of my best ideas come in the middle of the night or early in the morning. Pay attention when your creative thoughts start coming and focus entirely on them. Make this lots of fun.

6. **Think of ways you can make your participation in your classes more creative.** You get bored a lot in school, so what can you do creatively to make things better for you? Write these ideas down and start using them in your classes.

7. **Now that you've read about creativity and done some Try This! activities, give some reasons why being creative would enhance your personal life.** How would it make you more excited about your life? Give some ideas about where you could possibly take this in your coming years. Start being creative now and enjoy life more.

8. **Write down any possible reasons why you can't create something.** Then after you have finished finding all of the reasons why you can't create, use your creativity to figure out how to get rid of all of those negative reasons.

SHORTCUT TO ACTION

1. Are you bored with your life? Make some changes. Maybe you just need to do something different.
2. Instead of saying, "I can't," say, "I can." You'll never change your life unless you have a can-do attitude. Take a risk.
3. Don't try to change your entire life overnight. Go step-by-step. You won't get discouraged that way.
4. Fight fear's influence in your life. Fear can paralyze you, keeping you from making good changes.
5. When you take risks, you learn more about yourself and gain new confidence in yourself.
6. When you take risks and succeed, you can conquer your fears.
7. Everyone has the power to create. *You* can do creative things if you have a positive focus on life.
8. What is your definition of creativity? Think about ways you can use your creativity.
9. Look at the mundane things you have to do every day. Can you do them more creatively?
10. Be ready with your creative ideas at any time. Have paper and pen next to your bed.

CHAPTER 11

BE A CLASSY COMMUNICATOR

Communication is one of the most important skills you can work on and improve. The way you communicate with others will determine whether or not you get the job you want or that boyfriend or girlfriend you want.

The following sections include such things as listening skills, speaking skills, body language, facial expressions, tone of voice, eye contact, posture, vocabulary you use, and the ways you might communicate that turn people off.

Read and study this chapter to learn how to be a more effective communicator. I promise you, you won't be wasting your time. This chapter will help you in future job situations and in your dealings with all different kinds of people.

Enjoy!

LISTENING SKILLS

I'm starting with this part of communication because it is usually the most neglected skill of all and often is the one that will give you the worst problems with your parents, teachers, friends, and classmates.

When you get a certain grade, a teacher will either praise you or give you hell, ostensibly based on your test scores, homework, and quizzes. But the bottom line is this: You need to *listen in class* in order to do well in your schoolwork. The student who listens hears what a teacher feels is important, knows when a homework assignment is due, knows how the homework is supposed to be done, and knows what to study for quizzes and exams. Please don't tune out in class. You will be well rewarded if you tune *in*. Tuning in separates a good student from a mediocre student.

What Kind Of Listener Are You?

To find out what kind of listener you are, take the following survey, answering *yes* or *no*.

	yes	no
1. Do I interrupt when others are talking?	❏	❏
2. Do I constantly use *I* and talk only about myself?	❏	❏

In your next conversation, be quiet and listen.

3. Do I change the subject all of a sudden when others are talking? ❏ ❏

4. Do I constantly think ahead to what *I* want to say next instead of listening totally to the other person? ❏ ❏

5. Do I get distracted by the pimple on the person's face instead of hearing what he says? ❏ ❏

6. Do I daydream when he is talking about something that bores me? ❏ ❏

7. Do I look at what she is saying from *my* viewpoint instead of hers? ❏ ❏

8. Do I sound bored and look around the room for someone better to talk to? ❏ ❏

If you answered yes to any of these questions, you may need to improve your listening skills. Let's look at each individual question.

1. **Do I interrupt when others are talking?** If you answered *yes* to this question, people probably feel frustrated when talking to you. I used to interrupt a lot until a friend brought it to my attention. I would even sometimes finish her sentences. I stepped back and put myself in her place to see how it made her feel. I understood how angry she was when she did not feel heard.

2. **Do I constantly use "I" and talk only about myself?** In your next conversation with friends, examine how you talk to them. If you find that you are always talking about yourself, you need to be less "I"-centered and become more "Other"-centered. Ask yourself how you feel when others are always talking about themselves? Do you feel shut out? Well, you may be doing that to others, too. Check it out.

3. **Do I change the subject all of a sudden?** When a friend is talking about something important to him, do you abruptly start talking about something else? Changing the subject is a big turn-off to the speaker because what you are really saying is that you don't care about what he has to say and that you want to talk about something else.

4. **Do I constantly think ahead to what I want to say next instead of listening totally to the other person?** Focusing on your next thoughts instead of the speaker's words is a common mistake people make when talking to others. It's as if each speaker were a

Try to hear the other person's point of view. Sometimes it's just easier to accept it rather than try to change it. Remember, the only person you can change is yourself.

television set talking to the other and no one is really listening. This a bad game to play because you will never get close to the other person if you cannot totally focus on what she is saying.

5. **Do I get distracted by the pimple on the person's face instead of hearing what he says?** How many teachers do you know who have weird facial gestures, wear awful clothes, don't smell nice, or say bizarre things? Do you get distracted by these bizarre things so that you can't hear their message to you—what you are supposed to be learning? If so, accept them totally for who they are, what they look like, and how they act. When you accept them, you can then concentrate on *your* bottom line—learning their subject so you can get one step closer to your goal of doing better in school. If you don't judge others harshly, they will be much more accepting of you, too. Acceptance is a very important lesson in life—"Judge not, lest ye be judged."

6. **Do I daydream when he is talking about something that bores me?** This can be a big problem. Sometimes people talk about the most boring things imaginable. But it helps to remember that while the conversation is boring to you, it is not boring to the speaker. Once I was dating an engineer who would call me up every night and tell me *every* detail about his life, including things like what rental car he got on his business trip and the mileage he got from it. I used to lie on the couch while I listened to him, with the phone cradled on my shoulder. Once I almost fell asleep. Because he droned on and on, I decided not to date him any more. Ask yourself, "How important is this person to me?" If you decide that he is important, it would be a good idea to start getting interested in some of the things he likes. If he likes sports, you can at least become knowledgeable about the subject so that you can talk about it once in a while. That doesn't mean you have to eat, drink, and sleep sports—just take an interest in what the other person likes. Who knows, you might become a real sports fan.

7. **Do I look at what she is saying from my viewpoint instead of hers?** It is always helpful to try to understand the other person's point of view. She has her unique perspective on life and simply wants you to hear her out. Beware of jumping in with your own experiences or giving advice. Most people don't want to hear it. They just want to be heard. Also try to avoid

saying things such as, "I know how you feel." That can make your friend feel that her own feelings are not important. Instead you can mirror back to her the things you just heard her say with comments like, "So, you feel mad that Jeff stopped dating you," or "You are angry that your parents won't let you stay out all night for the prom."

8. **Do I act bored and look around the room for someone better to talk to?** Acting bored can be very hurtful to the speaker. As a teenager, I was at a party with a date but was looking around for a guy I had a crush on. I was transmitting to him that I was not interested in him and was looking for someone better. I didn't realize he knew what I was doing until later on when he said to me, "Come on, Searchlight, let's go." I knew then that he was aware of my lack of interest and I was embarrassed by the crass way I had treated him. Needless to say, it was our last night together.

A Listening Wrap-up

Check out these additional helpful hints for how to listen, learn, and land yourself some good friends.

Look the person in the eye when he talks. Show him with your eyes that you are really interested in what he has to say. By your attentiveness and interest, he will feel that you really care if he is happy, sad, angry, or hurt. Active listening shows acceptance. It is in accepting others that you can also truly accept yourself. You can then become aware of what you need from others.

Concentrate on what the other person is saying. If your mind drifts off, you might miss something really important. Your friend will know you are not paying attention. Concentrate on words that show you are listening, such as, "Really?", "Oh, no!", "uh-huh." These phrases will keep the person on track to tell his story without interruption from you. It will also help you pay attention.

Refrain from asking a lot of questions. Your friend does not want to be pestered. He wants to do the talking—you will be distracting him when you keep interrupting him with questions, unless you are asking for additional information. He'll tell you what he wants you to know. Remember, you are not a policeman interrogating a witness.

Avoid pat phrases that you think will make him feel better. Avoid these at all costs. Saying things like, "Things will get better" or "You shouldn't get so upset. It's not that big a deal" will only make him mad and feel worse.

Don't tell your friend he shouldn't be so upset about something. Let him vent how he feels. He needs to get it off his chest.

Be sure your facial reaction to what your friend is saying is appropriate. For example, if he is talking about something that makes him sad, a smile on your face would make him feel made fun of and angry.

TRY THIS!

1. **Think about what your listening style is.** After your next conversations with friends, parents, and teachers, write down what you did when listening and then what you can do to become a better listener. Start "hearing" how you listen. By analyzing this, you will catch yourself in any negative behaviors you might be displaying.

2. **Think about how the people in your life listen.** Are your parents good listeners? If they are good listeners, do you feel like an okay person because of it? If they are not, do you feel angry because you don't ever feel heard? Brainstorm ways you can change your relationship with them. Would it help to change your own listening style with them?

3. **Do roleplays with a special friend** in which each of you do several of the eight negative listening behaviors just mentioned. Trade roles so that you can see what it feels like to be on the receiving end of these bad listening styles. These experiences will help you be able to change.

4. **After you have made an effort to change the way you listen to others for several weeks, write down how your friendships with others have improved.** Have you told your friends what you are trying to do? Maybe you can get them interested in working on listening skills with you. You will become closer to them just by showing them you care so much about being a better listener. They will be flattered that you are really there with them 100 percent.

5. **Examine how you listen to teachers and fellow students.** Do you criticize them or make fun of them when they talk? If you do, write down how they react to you when you do it. Are they hostile and fight back? Do they act hurt and try to ignore you? Do you feel like a good person when you do these things or do you feel bad about yourself? Remember what I said about catching more flies with honey than with vinegar in all

of your relationships. You'll have better communication with people and as a result be a happier person.

Listening to Yourself

In this section you will be able to see that how you talk to yourself will determine how you are treated by others. You have already seen a section on positive self-talk earlier in the book, but I am including it here as well because self-talk is the foundation for all of your interpersonal relationships. Improving your self-talk will enable you to become a happier person and a better listener. Good listeners feel good about themselves—that's the bottom line.

When talking to yourself (either verbally or in your mind), see if you do the following:

Don't use extreme language such as "I always..." or "I never..." These phrases are guaranteed to lead you to negative feelings. Let's examine extreme language using an example of a high school girl named Jennifer. She often says to herself, "I always say the wrong thing when I'm with Steve. Nothing I say comes out right." First of all, Jennifer is very nervous any time she talks to Steve. Because of her nervousness, she is not thinking clearly. She actually will say the wrong thing *because* she is nervous. Learn to relax. Believing in yourself will help you a lot. Jennifer's acceptance of herself as nervous will allow her to see that sometimes she has difficulty, but not always.

Never say, "I can't." Saying you can't do something will actually come true. Eliminate this defeatist talk from your vocabulary. Practice telling yourself, "I can." By taking risks, you will eventually see that you *can* do many things you did not think you could do before.

Consider each person as a possible friend. Do you automatically eliminate certain kids in your school as possible friends because you feel that you do not measure up to them? Analyze what they have that you want. Are they considered the cool people—the ones everyone wants as friends? What makes them so special? Before you invest a lot of time, effort, and nervous feelings, ask yourself if they are really nice people. In some cases they will be, in some cases they won't be. Do you really want to be associated with them? If so, start to see what *you* have to offer them. It helps to remember that you also have special qualities that are of value to them. If they cannot see your specialness, it's time to make friends with those who do. Maybe Joe Cool or Susie Somebody are just too wrapped up in themselves to see anyone else's importance.

Always talk to yourself in a positive way. Pat yourself on the back when you do something good and remember that when you mess something up, nobody's perfect. You'll get it right next time.

Don't be a phony.

Say what you mean

and mean what you

say.

Listen to your self-talk. Do you insult yourself a lot when you make a mistake? Write down the things you say to yourself. Are you really that bad a person? I truly doubt it. Sometimes we are our own worst enemies. If you don't feel good about yourself, it is likely others won't either.

SPEAKING SKILLS

How you speak to others can make or break your relationships with them. Check out the following tips to help you speak more effectively.

Say what you mean. Say what you mean and mean what you say. Many of us are afraid to be honest, but when we don't tell the truth, we feel miserable. We walk away feeling misunderstood, but it really isn't the listener's fault—it's ours—because we have not said how we really feel. Little by little, you can start being more honest with your family and friends. How they react to what you say isn't as important as it is for you to take your own power and run with it.

The Manipulation Mess. Have you ever felt manipulated by others? Have you ever felt they are trying to get you to do something because it's what *they* want and need? Let's give an example. One teenager, Beth, told me about a friend who often asked her to go to Big Bob's Burgers. When they got there, she always said she didn't have any money. Beth paid for her food several times, but finally got angry because she felt used. The friendship almost ended, but her friend finally got the message and started to take money with her to pay for her own food.

Don't do triangles. When you have a problem with a friend, do you talk to another friend about it? Ask yourself what good that ever does you. How can your other friend possibly help you out of your bad situation? He can't. The only people who can resolve an issue are the two people actually involved—you and your friend. Have the guts to confront him and talk *to* him instead of *about* him. He deserves that.

Speaking Do's and Don'ts

Enunciate. When you speak, make the extra effort and speak clearly. Because I had seven brothers and sisters, a grandmother, and two parents who could potentially hear my phone conversations, as a survival tactic I got into a bad habit of speaking indistinctly. I did not want to enunciate well because I didn't want anyone to eavesdrop on me. Later, I had to break myself of the bad habit. Now as a teacher, I have to speak distinctly. Impress others and speak clearly. Then you won't have to waste time getting rid of your old way of speaking.

Speak up. Practice this one first with your dog, your cat, or your pet fish—a captive audience that won't break out into laughter when you speak. Tape record how you sound talking. You might be surprised. Keep recording your voice until it gets louder. Improvement is simply a matter of practice and believing in yourself. Speaking in a louder voice was hard for me at first. I was given a job teaching Spanish as a graduate student. I had never spoken before a group and was scared to death. The first several days my students said, "We can't hear you." I knew it was do or die. I found my answer to getting louder when I tripped over the wastebasket and the students laughed. I decided to have some fun teaching. My voice automatically got louder. I also learned how to laugh at myself. I sure felt better about myself by learning how to loosen up.

Not so loud! Are you a person who is so loud that your voice enters the room before you do? We all know some of these people. They often are the people who will do most of the talking, too. Tape record your voice to hear how you sound. Would *you* want to listen to yourself if you were another person? If the answer is no, then do something about it. Just be glad you found out about this irritating speaking trait before you get out of school and into the job market. By the way, don't ask friends if you talk too loudly. Ask your teachers. They'll be honest.

Don't whine. No one wants to listen to a whiner. Whenever I hear one, I excuse myself as fast as possible. Always ask yourself how you sound to others. Step back from the situation. See yourself objectively.

No swearing, please. If you need to swear, pick a place that is socially acceptable, like the locker room or in the car with your friends. If you swear when you first meet someone, she will form a very bad impression of you.

Don't constantly use filler phrases like "you know," "like," and "um." Once in a while they're okay, but don't overdo it.

Talk fast enough, but not too fast. When you speak too quickly, you are probably just nervous. Breathe deeply, consciously slow down your pace, and wait for the other person to respond to what you said. Trying to fill up silent moments with speech the speed of a flash of lightning will not win you friends. They will get frustrated and feel that it is useless for them to respond. You want to have good

Do you speak as if you had a mouthful of marbles in your mouth? Spit those marbles out. Speak clearly.

relationships, don't you? Remember, *to relate* means to interact and connect with others in a meaningful way.

Drop all exaggerated language; use fewer adjectives. Especially avoid such phrases as *You never, I always, I'll never be able to, terrible, awful,* and *impossible.* You can add to this list because there are many more exaggerated phrases that people often use. In your next conversations, listen to yourself talk. Check out whether you use exaggerated language.

Find better ways of saying yes and no with honesty, instead of making up bizarre excuses. Once a student told me she couldn't take a test because her grandmother died. Her grandmother actually died three weeks later. She was very embarrassed that she had lied to me.

Take a breath when speaking. Don't run your sentences together. Let people absorb what you're saying.

TRY THIS!

1. **During your day, make a mental note of the extreme language you use when talking to yourself or others.** Do you often use such words as *never, always,* and *terrible?* Take notes at the end of the day. Always check your language after you have said something in order to see what you need to change. You will be a happier person.
2. **Check out how fast you talk.** Do you speak at the speed of lightning? Do people have a hard time keeping up with you when you talk? Do friends have trouble getting out a sentence because you fill up all silent moments? Let conversations happen naturally instead of trying to control them.

BODY LANGUAGE

Knowing more about body language will help improve your non-verbal communication. Experts have found that words alone account for only 7 percent of our communication, whereas 38 percent of our communication includes our tone of voice, inflection, and other sounds. But a whopping 55 percent of the way we communicate with others comes from our *body language.*

Body language shows the way we really feel in any given situation. How many times have you seen a teacher say he is not angry but his fists are clenched and his jaw clamped shut? You can almost see the smoke coming out of his ears and nose. And those eyes—oh, good heavens, they are like piercing arrows. And how about your parents, who say they are not angry with you but their body language tells the opposite? People can say one thing but their body language gives them away. We know that what they are saying is not true.

Your body communicates through the eyes, head, arm, lips, shoulders, hands, and gestures. Take the following "quiz" to see how well you understand body language. Mark positive or negative for each type of body language.

	positive	negative
1. fidgeting	❏	❏
2. making eye contact with listener	❏	❏
3. slouching posture	❏	❏
4. smiling sincerely	❏	❏
5. hands clenched	❏	❏
6. nodding in agreement with speaker	❏	❏
7. yawning	❏	❏
8. drumming your fingers	❏	❏
9. relaxed posture	❏	❏
10. arms crossed in front of you	❏	❏
11. eyes show disbelief or anger	❏	❏
12. lips clamped shut	❏	❏

If you answered that 2, 4, 6, and 9 are positive and the rest are all negative body language, you understand how your way of communicating through your body can make or break you. Congratulations. If you missed more than two, you need to check out the following information on these negative, silent but deadly ways of communicating how you *really feel*.

Positive Body Language

Arms relaxed (not crossed in front of you). You give the impression that you are approachable. You want that cute guy or that gorgeous girl to come over and talk to you, don't you? Well, loosen up. Practice feeling full of confidence.

Good eye contact. When you speak or listen to someone, you look him in the eye. Eye contact shows you are interested in what he has to say.

Relaxed posture. Normal posture is not too relaxed but also not too stiff. Posture shows you are open to what the other person is saying. He will feel accepted and not threatened in any way. When you stand up straight but in a

Watch the body language of your friends, parents, and teachers. Can you read how they feel? Can you guess what they would like to say? Just remember, if they are transmitting their feelings, so are you.

Learn positive body language. When you're able to read your own body language, you'll know when you're tense and when you're judging yourself or others.

relaxed manner, you show confidence and zest for life. You immediately draw other people to you because they can see you feel you are a person worth getting to know.

Smiling and laughing. You should smile or laugh whenever it is appropriate while the speaker is talking. Remember that we all like to be with upbeat and positive people, not complainers or whiners. Of course, if the speaker is talking about his grandfather's death, you don't want to be smiling—you should have a serious look on your face.

Nodding agreement. When the other is speaking, nod in agreement to show him you understand what he is saying. Be sure your "nods" are sincere though. Once I had a friend who was talking with another friend who had a habit of droning on and on. She would say "Uh-huh," at well-spaced intervals. The problem was that in the midst of this, he asked her a question and she said, "Uh-huh." She never did hear his question. Listening is an *active* skill, not passive. Be careful.

Negative Body Language

Using some of the following negative body language doesn't mean you don't care about the speaker or yourself or that you are a negative person. Negative body language often means that you are uncomfortable in certain social situations. Your job is to boost your confidence by working on accepting who you are and by being proud of what you do in life—whether it means getting good grades, being a beautiful singer, making the cheerleading squad, being an ace chess player, or being an all-around good person.

Fidgeting. This shows that you are nervous or bored. Do you want to run from the situation you're in? Identify and explore what's causing your feelings. Try to see how you can make it positive. Could this be an opportunity to practice how to feel comfortable in different situations? You'll have to conquer this sooner or later.

Slouching. This is a big one in school. I have seen many students slouching in their seats, which sends me, as a teacher, a negative message. When I see a student leaning back with his head on the wall, he's sending me a very clear message—that he's bored out of his mind. I have also found that this posture often indicates the student has no self-confidence or motivation.

Yawning. Yes, maybe you're tired and didn't get much sleep last night because you were up all night writing a paper. Be sure and tell your teacher why you are so tired *before* class. She will be appreciative to know why you're yawning. It always helps to communicate with the teacher.

Wandering eyes. Looking away can indicate that you are bored with what the speaker is saying and would rather be doing something other than talk to her. Your body language says it all. Look at the person speaking in the eye and concentrate on what she is saying. Both of you will get along better that way.

Sloppy appearance. The way we dress tells others how we feel about ourselves. Do you wear clean, neat clothes that give a good appearance, or do you wear sloppy clothes that are dirty and hang off of you as though they were two sizes too big?

Distracting gestures. At different times, I have had difficulty listening to speakers who have distracting gestures. One time, a woman constantly twirled her hair around her finger. This became so distracting that I forgot to listen to what she was saying. That's hardly the way to be an effective communicator!

Do you always fiddle with your hair, clench your fist, or tap your fingers nervously on the desk? Check out your own body language.

More Body Language Tips

Check out the following chart to see what kind of body language you have.

	Positive	**Negative**
FACIAL EXPRESSIONS	good eye contact smile laughter understanding eyes	glare disgust frown sneer angry look crabby look
VOICE SIGNALS	concerned soft, warm loving	impatient tense whining blaming, accusing sarcastic, angry

TRY THIS!

1. **Start studying other people's body language.** Notice what messages they give out with their facial expressions, tone of voice, gestures, and general body movements. Write in your journal the different things you notice.
2. **With a friend, check out each other's body language.** Please don't take this suggestion in the wrong

Lots of kids make you mad, don't they? Read ahead for tips on how to control your anger and be a happier person.

way—I'm serious. It would be a good idea to have your friend read this chapter first so that he'll understand what you're doing. You can help each other learn how to communicate in a positive way. Use the body language chart for facial expressions and voice signals to try different ways to communicate messages through your body. Pretend that you are a teacher, a boss, or a principal who is receiving these different body language cues. Then have your friend take on the same roles. After you have finished, tell one another how each of the messages affected you as the receiver of the language.

3. **Brainstorm ways you can be more comfortable talking to someone on the phone—especially in situations that are tense for you.** Have you ever noticed how much harder it is to talk to strangers or certain people on the phone? And what about calling up a girl to ask her for a date? Is it so hard because you can't see her body language to know what's the best way to talk to her? Think about voice clues that the other person might be transmitting over the phone.

CONFLICT AND ANGER: HOW TO HANDLE THEM

Life is full of conflict. You won't always agree with your parents, teachers, employers, friends, and classmates. This is a natural part of human relationships. How you handle conflict in your life now determines how successful you will be in the future. If you really work at improving this skill, your life will be a lot less stressful and much more joyful. When you practice dealing with problems with others, you learn more about yourself and how to have better relationships. Just think of dealing with conflict and anger as a "growth experience."

What Do You Believe?

I know this sounds crazy, but before you judge this question to be stupid, be patient and read on. The fact is that before you try to resolve a conflict with another person, it is helpful to know what you believe in, what you will fight for, and why. To fight for your beliefs is a noble thing, but first it's a good idea to see what they really are. Through your years growing-up, you have probably been asking yourself what in the world life is all about. It is natural to have some confusion at this point. Answering the following questions might help you get more clarity. Give these questions a lot of thought. Dig down deep for the answers about what you really believe when you're being objective and honest with yourself.

1. Is it okay to lie in order to get out of a jam with your parents or in any other situation?
2. Do you think it is okay to cheat on an exam or to let a friend copy off of your exam or your homework if either you or your friend is truly desperate?
3. Is it okay to tell a friend or a parent you're going to do something, and then you either forget about it or you just don't do it?
4. Is it important to treat others in your life as you would like to be treated or do you believe in, "Do unto others before they do it to you?"
5. Is it fair to steal your best friend's boyfriend/girlfriend or to steal money from a parent's purse/wallet?
6. Do you think it's okay to always arrive late when you're meeting up with friends or when you're going to class?

Discuss these questions with your parents, your good friends, and a favorite teacher. Get their input to see what they believe. You may not agree with them. Be careful, though, because sometimes people have ideas that are the opposite of what the majority believes. Let me give you two examples.

Case #1. One day while I was taking attendance, I heard a student talking about what had happened to his parents the previous night. His father was mad at his mother because while they were buying a VCR and a television at a local discount store, the clerk only rang up the television and didn't see the VCR. The mother told her she had missed the VCR. Both the father and my student thought she had been stupid to say anything at all. I stopped what I was doing to tell the boy that I thought his mother did the right thing. What do you think?

Case #2. I know a man who always tries to cheat the government, insurance companies, and anyone else he can. He puts down fake deductions on his income tax returns, makes two insurance claims against different companies for the same accident, and tries to get the store clerks to take coupons for things he has not bought. Again, I see this as dishonest, but he doesn't see it that way at all. How about you?

What does the word

integrity mean to

you? Lots of people

say it means to do

the right thing. Can

you come up with a

definition of your

own?

Your job is to take all of the input you have received throughout your life and decide what *you* believe in. After all, it's your life that you are trying to live here, so make the most of it.

Integrity Revisited

Remember in Chapter 5 when we discussed integrity? It's worth repeating here that having integrity is the keystone to being successful and to having a good character. Why is having a good character so important? The main reason is that it benefits everyone. Also, it benefits you because you don't get into unnecessary conflicts when you are honorable and have integrity. Think about it. Would you rather have a life full of problems and conflict or would you rather live life as a good citizen? Remember, when you do the right thing, people trust you and respect you. To get other people's trust and respect is what we all want in life.

Working Through Conflict

The following situation is an example of a typical teenage conflict. You can use these steps to improve communication and solve any problem you have with your parents, friends, teachers, or boss.

The Scenario: Dave, a good friend, is trying to get you to do drugs with him and your other friends. Up to this point you have resisted, but he is pressuring you to start doing it and you are getting angry. Your view is: Whose life is this anyway—mine or his? You're wondering if you have a right to make your own decisions. Here are some steps you can follow to talk to Dave.

Find the right time and place to talk—so that both of you will feel relaxed. No, the hallway after school is not a good time and place! Go somewhere like a park bench, where you know you won't be interrupted by your friends. The advantage of picking a neutral place, where you don't usually hang out, is that both of you can get out of your usual roles and talk openly to each other. Dave will also see and feel how important the friendship is to you.

Before you get together, practice exactly how you want to start out talking. Identify what is troubling you. Be sure you aren't feeling overly emotional. Be calm. You could tell Dave that you are feeling pressured to do drugs, that you feel it is not good for you, and that drugs are not in the game plan for your life. You could tell him that you hope you and he can work this problem out together, because your friendship with him is very important to you.

Give details about how you feel. Get to the heart of the matter instead of discussing past disagreements. Your interest right now is dealing with the pressure to do drugs. You can tell Dave how you feel when he tries to pressure you to smoke marijuana. Say how *you* feel about drugs instead of attacking your friend for what he is doing. Keep the focus on yourself and your feelings about drug use. It's never a good idea to make "you" statements, such as, "You are always trying to force me to get high." Dave will immediately feel attacked and get defensive. He'll hear you much better if you start out saying, "I feel pressured by you to do drugs, and I don't like it."

If you have made Dave feel comfortable and haven't judged him during your drug talk, he may have questions he wants to ask you. Answer them as honestly and openly as you can. If he's a good guy, he'll respect your views and be willing to listen to your concerns.

Tell him what you need from him. This is a key step in resolving conflict because here you have to ask Dave what you need from him. It takes guts to ask because he might tell you to go jump in the lake. You risk rejection, but your bottom line is to take good care of yourself. Why not just go ahead and ask for what you need? You could tell Dave that you need to be accepted regardless of the decisions you make (in this case, not to do drugs). You also need for him to stop pressuring you to smoke marijuana when you're out with your friends. If he is not too far gone as a drug user, he'll respect your needs and back off.

What will Dave's needs probably be? He also will feel a need to be accepted by you because he *is* a drug user. This is a tricky issue because after the strong stand you have taken, he'll know without question how you feel about drug use. It's okay for friends to disagree. Dave will have to deal with his decisions on his own, just as you have your own choices.

Brainstorm ways to resolve conflict. This is the part where you both give suggestions so that each of you comes out feeling like a winner with a role in the solution. If anyone feels he is a loser after the conversation is over, there will always be hard feelings lurking in the background. Both you and Dave will have suggestions to help resolve this situation. Respect each other's opinions and come to a decision about what you will do *together*.

When you have a problem with a friend, talk to her calmly. It's always better to openly discuss your differences.

Why Resolving Conflicts Will Help You Later

Look at what you have just done with your friend:

- You have had the guts to say how you really feel.
- You have had the guts to say what you need from your friend.
- You have given him a chance to change in the relationship instead of just dumping him and moving on.
- You have shown him you really care about him.

Congratulations! You've made yourself vulnerable to another human being because of your courageous and honest stand. You now know what it is like to be teetering on the edge of that cliff, saying what you feel and what you need. The bottom line is this: You never know how someone else will react to your honesty and to your needs, but you will always be better off for being true to yourself. This is one of life's most important lessons. Each of us has to take care of ourselves. No one else can do this for us. Remember, you're in the driver's seat when it comes to your life. The more you assert yourself and ask for what you need, the stronger you will become. You'll be prepared to face life as an adult and handle all of the responsibilities and duties that come along.

TRY THIS!

1. **Map out a plan of action for resolving these conflicts:**

   - Your teacher has accused you of cheating. You are innocent.
   - Your mom and dad have grounded you because you arrived home an hour late.
   - Your friend repeated something you told her in confidence. Now, your other friends are mad at you.
   - You had a party when your parents were out of town. Some kids crashed the party and destroyed a lot of the furniture. Your parents are furious with you.

     After figuring out how you will try to resolve all of the above conflicts, you will probably have questions about whether your plans will be effective. Maybe you could ask a trusted friend, teacher, or counselor for some feedback. After you have thought about new and *good* ways to resolve conflict, compare those ways with how you would have dealt with your problems in the past. Do you see how you can make things better for yourself?

2. **Write yourself a letter in which you describe your feelings about the conflicts you have had in your life.** What effective methods have you used to solve your problems in the past? What ineffective methods have you used to made your problems worse? What would you do differently today? What did you learn from all of your troubles? Identify how conflict causes trouble with your friends, teachers, and family.

Anger—The Acid Effect

- **Anger affects many teenagers.** For some of you, it is obvious that you feel angry, but for others, you stifle your anger because your parents, teachers, and others do not like to see you that way. Your unexpressed anger can sometimes make you a depressed person because you feel powerless to help yourself.
- **What is anger and why do many of us get angry?** I believe it is an emotional reaction of displeasure to the helplessness you have when someone has made you feel inferior, disregarded, or disrespected. When you express your anger to that person, you are asking that she change her behavior toward you and respect you as a valued human being.
- **Express your anger carefully.** The trick to expressing your anger is to separate the person (whom you hopefully care about) from his actions. Yes, he both hurt and angered you, but unless you are careful with how you express your anger with him, your relationship could crash and burn. Learning how to express your anger effectively will help you in all of your future relationships. Put into practice the steps you just read for resolving conflict.
- **Do you cause others to be angry?** We would rather look at how others make us angry than how *we* make *them* angry. An important part of growing up is to acknowledge the harm you do to others and to try to change those things about yourself that need changing.
- **Some angry feelings only upset us.** There are many types of anger that only upset your emotions and your body and really do you no good. Examples: 1) You are in class and a slow student is laboriously answering a teacher's question. You want to scream because it's

Think about what makes you angry. Then think about your part in those situations. What do you do to fan the fire and make things worse? Don't forget—it takes two to have a fight.

taking so long. 2) You are in the lunch line in the school cafeteria and a student is taking forever to get out his money to pay, so you end up with only 20 minutes to eat. 3) Your mother is five minutes late to pick you up after school. 4) Your favorite basketball team didn't win the NCAA tournament. What do all of these examples have in common? They are all things you cannot do anything about. None of them hurts you personally. Be selective about what angers you. Learn to **LET GO!**

Physical Effects of Anger

Twenty to thirty years down the road, you could experience the following physical difficulties if you do not learn how to deal with your anger:

- high blood pressure
- faster heart rate
- depression
- heart disease
- alcohol and drug abuse

TRY THIS!

1. **Find a strenuous physical outlet for your feelings.** Take up running, fast walking, aerobic dancing, or *something* that will get the anger out of your system. I have found that fast, vigorous bicycling is effective for me. Those hills really work all of the negative feelings out of me. I'm too busy huffing and puffing to think about anything else. When I finish the bike ride, I always feel better.
2. **Get a book or videotape on meditating from the library.** Meditation will help you become a more peaceful person. Things will bother you a lot less.
3. **Volunteer to help others less fortunate than you.** Helping others will show you that the things you are angry about are minuscule compared to the problems other people have. While you are angry that your parents won't let you take their car on a Saturday night, there are starving people who wonder where their next meal is coming from. Get perspective on your life and ask yourself, "Do I really have it so bad?"

Whenever I get this "poor me" attitude, I always have to remember people who have it so much worse than I do.

4. **Buy a punching bag and punch away.** Another way to deal with your anger is to get a kiddie plastic bat and beat it on a pillow while you shout out what is making you angry. Some students have used this technique and have told me it is very effective. They have also told me that screaming into a pillow works wonders.

5. **Keep an anger log in your journal** in which you write down what triggered your anger, how you reacted, and what the end result was. Stepping back from your anger by objectively writing about it will help you see patterns and learn how to avoid what makes you so mad. The next time someone makes you angry, tell yourself to **stop!** Become aware at all times of your feelings, and stop them before they get out of control.

6. **Try forgiving the person you are angry with and try to think positively about him.** Remember that your resentment against others can eat you alive and turn you into a negative, angry person. Many times when you forgive that person, you are no longer angry with him. Why let *him* control and run your life? Let it go!

From the six ways to deal with anger, you'll be able to find one or two that you prefer to use. Soon you will learn to diffuse your anger.

CRITICISM—A CORROSIVE COMMUNICATOR

Are you critical of others? No one likes to be criticized. People who are critical of others often go to one of two extremes: they either trash the person or they choose to say nothing. Neither action is good because nothing positive can come of it. When criticizing others, ask yourself why you're doing it. Is it because they are doing something really bad or is it because you don't like the ethnic group they are from, the way they dress, their sexual orientation, or their religious beliefs? Are you being too judgmental and intolerant? Are you playing God, acting as though you know what's right for others?

How do you react when someone criticizes you? There are many ways to deal with criticism. Here's a few, going from worst to best.

1. **You counter-attack by pointing out what's wrong with him.** Attacking others helps no one.

Get lots of exercise. Make exercise one of your top priorities. You'll be able to release a lot of your anger.

2. **You clam up and give the criticizer the silent treatment.** You don't speak on your own behalf. You are allowing yourself to be victimized. You are not showing yourself any self-respect.
3. **You begin to justify yourself and rationalize your shortcomings.** You make excuses for what happened or blame someone else. Are you taking full responsibility here for your actions?
4. **You listen to the criticism and answer without passion** to what the person has just said to you. You are careful not to have an inflammatory tone of voice, body language, or facial gesture. You can find something to agree with, but you can also stand up for yourself and point out where the criticizer is wrong. Remember to keep the focus on yourself and what you do and have done. Avoid pointing out the criticizer's flaws. That's *his* problem, not yours. Take care of yourself, or, as my mother used to say, "Tend to your own knitting."

TRY THIS!

1. **When a friend criticizes you, listen carefully to what she is saying, being careful to keep your emotions under control.** Ask yourself if she is speaking the truth. Are you humble enough to admit you've made a mistake? Can you acknowledge your wrongdoing? It takes a big person, a person with integrity, to say, "I made a mistake and I'm sorry." If you feel that the criticism is unfounded, calmly say so, giving your reasons for feeling you have done no wrong. When you get home, write down what happened in your journal, giving details on how you handled it.
2. **Before you criticize a friend, think about what your goal is.** Do you want to humiliate him or do you want to clear things up between the two of you? Are your motives good ones? How would you feel to be on the receiving end of the criticism you are about to unleash? Are you too angry to talk to him? Would it be better to wait a few hours or even a few days?

SHORTCUT TO ACTION

1. Good listening skills help you get along better with others.
2. Look at the person who is speaking to you while he talks. Give him your undivided attention.
3. Listen to the messages you give to yourself. Make sure you always say positive things.
4. Be honest and kind when speaking to others. Say what you mean and mean what you say.
5. Avoid whining, swearing, and loud talking when speaking. Try not to say, "you know" or "um" constantly.
6. Your body language gives away how you feel. Start to notice how you sit and stand. Ask yourself what messages you're sending others.
7. Use your smile often. It's contagious. Maybe you frown a lot when you're in new social situations because you're nervous. Try smiling more. You will open more doors.
8. Signs of ineffective body language: distracting gestures, yawning, slouching, fidgeting, and wandering eyes.
9. Signs of effective body language: relaxed arms, good eye contact, relaxed posture, smiling and laughing.
10. Anger is a natural emotion. You can learn how to handle it in a socially acceptable way.
11. When you are having a conflict with a friend, talk to him about it, not to another friend. Don't do triangles.
12. Anger has a negative effect on your body. Deal with your anger and let it go. Don't let anger simmer and then boil over later in a massive explosion.

CHAPTER 12

Drugs, Alcohol, Marijuana, Smoking, and Chewing Tobacco

I'm not going to throw a bunch of statistics at you about how dangerous smoking, drinking, and doing drugs can be. You've heard it all before. Instead, I'm going to share with you the physical and emotional effects of these deadly habits on both the user and on her family and friends. Since one of the best ways to understand substance abuse is through firsthand accounts, I'm going to share with you some of my own experiences as well as those of other people whose lives have been touched by substance abuse.

PEER PRESSURE

When you are subjected to peer pressure, your friends are trying to make decisions for you about what you ought to do—like whether or not you should use alcohol, drugs, and tobacco products or engage in sexual activity. Peer pressure can also involve exerting pressure on you to be thin, to be popular, and to feel accepted by your friends. You probably have been subjected to pressure many times in your junior high years and even before then. In this chapter, you will find many ways to get your friends off your back so that *you* can make your own decisions about what's right and wrong for you.

Read the following sections on alcohol, smoking, marijuana and other drugs, and chewing tobacco. For more information on each subject, I've included toll-free telephone numbers you can call. Please approach this chapter with an open mind. I'll give you the facts, but you will have to draw your own conclusions.

ALCOHOL

Alcohol abuse is the number one drug problem in the United States. Many people have a drinking problem but do not realize it. It has been estimated that 10 percent of adults in the U.S. are problem drinkers.

Effects of Alcohol

Inhibitions disappear. The drinker does and says things he wouldn't normally do when he is sober. The morning after, he wonders what happened the night before and if he got into any kind of trouble.

Judgment is impaired. For example, when driving it is hard to stay on the road, to judge the time needed to stop, and to avoid hitting people crossing the road or cars that stop suddenly.

Motor skills are impaired. The drinker will often have difficulty walking and will fall occasionally.

Speech is slurred. Ever heard a comedian imitate a drunk person in a movie or on television? It's not exaggeration—that's how a drinker really sounds.

Some of this might seem hilarious unless you actually know someone who is addicted to alcohol. When the drinker is your father who often doesn't come home at night, is sick a lot and can't go to work, is fired from his job, beats up on his wife and kids, and frequently can't find where he left his car, there is no humor in the situation. Alcoholism is no laughing matter.

In addition, there have been many cases, especially of teenagers and college students, who drink so fast that their brains cannot cope with so much alcohol at once. They die from alcohol poisoning. Alcohol is no joke.

Are You a Problem Drinker?

I have had some students who are problem drinkers. The following questionnaire will help you determine if you might have a problem with alcohol. Answer *yes* or *no* to the following questions developed by Alcoholics Anonymous World Services.

1. Do you miss days or class periods at school because of drinking?
2. Do you drink to overcome shyness or to build up self-confidence?
3. Is drinking affecting your reputation at school or elsewhere?

Alcohol makes a person do and say crazy things. The user cannot function normally. If he drives a car while intoxicated, he endangers his life and the lives of others. DON'T DRINK AND DRIVE.

Be strong when your friends pressure you to do things that are bad for you. Remember, it's your body, not theirs.

4. Do you drink to escape from study or home worries?
5. Does it bother you if somebody tells you that you drink too much?
6. Do you have to take a drink to go out on a date?
7. Do you ever get into money troubles because of buying alcoholic beverages?
8. Have you lost any friends since you began drinking?
9. Are you hanging out with a crowd of heavy drinkers?
10. Do your old friends drink less than you do?
11. Do you drink until the bottle is empty or the beer cans are all "dead?"
12. Have you ever had a loss of memory from drinking?
13. Have you ever been stopped by the police, arrested, or put into hospital or jail because of drunk driving?
14. Do you get annoyed with classes or lectures on drinking?
15. Do *you* think you have a problem with drinking?

A "yes" to one question is a warning.

Answering "yes" to as few as three questions means that alcohol has almost certainly become—or is becoming—a serious problem for you.

Physical Damage Caused by Chronic Alcoholism

Check out what can happen to you down the road if you drink too much alcohol:

- Damage to the liver, pancreas, and kidneys
- Premature aging
- Decreased brain function

Remember, alcohol is an addictive *drug*. You might have seen your parents drink too much. They come home tired from work and have a glass of wine or a beer to unwind. Then they have another drink during dinner and an after-dinner drink. Liquor is served everywhere to celebrate such happy occasions as weddings, graduations, and retirement parties. It seems okay to you, but the harsh reality is that it can cause total chaos in your life if you choose to drink too much. You *do* have a choice.

What to Do When Confronted with Alcohol

The best thing you can do is not go to parties where you know alcohol will be served. Avoidance is the safest choice you have. If you do go and want to avoid drinking, try one of the following ways to say "no" to alcohol.

1. No, thanks, I'm on a diet.
2. Thanks, but I'm on the wagon.
3. No, I'm not in the mood.
4. I'd rather not tonight.
5. Thanks, but I don't drink.
6. I'm an athlete—I can't break training.
7. No thanks, I'd like a soda instead.
8. No thanks, alcohol makes me sick—I'm allergic to it.
9. Thanks, but alcohol turns me into a person I can't stand.
10. I don't like the taste of alcohol.

Alcohol is a drug. Because of its social acceptance, it is deceptively dangerous.

If you say any one of the above lines with conviction, most friends will not press the point. If you say it with your voice wavering, as if to say, "Will you still accept me if I don't take this drink," your friends will keep trying to push it on you. You can be strong and resist if you want to. Make your own decisions. Also remember that your friends might persist in getting you to drink because they know it is dangerous *(and illegal for teenagers).* They will feel better about themselves if you drink with them.

If you do decide to take that drink, make sure that you don't drink and drive. You can kill yourself and others. I know of students who have had their lives ruined because they drove while drunk and were in an accident that killed friends or strangers. Just remember that you can be a weapon if you drive drunk.

A PERSONAL STORY FROM THE AUTHOR

My life has been touched by a drinking and driving tragedy. My cousin, Bob, was driving on a two-lane highway when a drunk driver crossed the center line and hit his car, killing his one-year-old baby in the backseat and seriously injuring him. He spent several months in the hospital recuperating. I shall never forget the tragedy of seeing that little baby in the casket. All I could think about was how his life had been snatched from him forever.

Words From a Recovering Alcoholic

It helps to think about what you're getting involved in *before* you start doing it. Read the following poem written by a recovering alcoholic. It will help you realize what will happen to your life later if you drink too much now.

I drank to be witty—and I became a boor.
I drank to relax—and I couldn't stop my hands
*   from shaking.*
I drank to feel good—and I suffered through
*   sickening hangovers.*
I drank to be happy—and it made me depressed.
I drank to be a good dancer—and it made me stagger.
I drank to be a good conversationalist—and I couldn't
*   pronounce my words.*
I drank to be sociable—and I became angry
*   and resentful.*
I drank to help my appetite—and cheated my body of
*   nutrition by not eating right.*
I drank to be a good lover—and I couldn't perform.
I drank to show I was a man—and I became a
*   slobbering, bawling baby.*
I drank to be popular—and lost my friends.
I drank to enjoy life—and contemplated suicide.
I drank for camaraderie—and drove everyone away
*   from me.*
I drank to escape—and built a prison for myself.
I drank to find peace—and I found hell.

SARAH WANTS YOU TO KNOW

Alcohol used to be my weekend date. I would get together with my group of friends and just drink, drink, and drink. We had fun playing drinking games and just acting like wild and crazy teenagers. Well, one night, too much of that fun left me crawling out of a jeep that flipped over in a ditch.

My friend had sworn she was cool to drive, but at the time I wasn't even in a condition to judge. We left the party in order to get home by curfew. It was a beautiful night. We had the top off, the radio blaring as the night breeze raced through our hair. I remember sitting in the passenger seat with my feet elevated on the dashboard. I was singing along to the radio.

All of a sudden, everything seemed to be spinning. I felt the car swerving left and right, back and forth. Well, the jeep swerved too far off the road, my friend panicked and lost control of the car. We started spinning, going in circles. I was so scared, I couldn't even scream. My body was thrown out of the top of the jeep from my seat and landed on top of my friend. I couldn't believe what was happening. How could I be so stupid? No seat belt and too much alcohol.

I crawled out of a ditch, 10 feet away from a light pole. Luckily I was okay, except for the fact that my spine shifted, causing my pelvic bone and neck to shift. I have to go to the chiropractor for the next five months for therapy. Now all I can think is I could have been killed or paralyzed. That accident made me 100 percent sober, and still two months later I am terrified of that weekend date with alcohol—now we're not even friends.

Alcohol has caused only tragedies in my life lately, it seems. My father, as hard as it is to say, was an alcoholic. My parents divorced when I was three, but it wasn't until a couple of years ago that I found out it was due to his drinking problem. Regardless of his faults, I was still Daddy's little girl. When I was younger and had a nightmare, he would take me on a night drive playing the song "Sarah Smile," which he named me after. He was also my encouragement. I would bring home an *A* test, and he'd say, "That's my girl. You are going to do something great. Make me proud."

As I got older, I began to realize that drinking was high on his priority list. When I was at his house on the weekends, he would go to the town bar after lunch and again in the middle of the night when he thought I was asleep. As time progressed, my visitations decreased. I didn't like to see my daddy wake up with a bottle of Jack Daniels in his hand. It seemed alcohol was more important to him than me, and I didn't want to compete anymore, so I just stopped going to see him. When my older sister had a baby shower, I was forced to go to his home. As I left, I gave him a hug and kiss good-bye.

If I had known he was going to die, I would have held on to him forever. A man of only 48 died of alcohol poisoning. He came home one night, highly intoxicated, and collapsed in the kitchen. Before the ambulance even arrived, he died in my stepmom's arms crying, "Help me up, help me up." I never even got to say I loved him. At his funeral, I went up to the casket, feeling his ice cold hand, looking at the body that was my Dad. I hung over him sobbing, crying so much my eyes were puffy and red. I was so angry. This wasn't supposed to happen. NOT NOW! I was supposed to make him proud. He was going to be there on graduation day, when I was going off to college to do something great.

Now all I have is memories. It is so hard to look at pictures of us or even go to his house without having a breakdown. Sometimes I will be driving and a song will come on the radio and I will start crying. I miss him so much. I would give anything in the world to spend just one minute with him, to see his face, feel the warmth of his touch, to say, I love you. Alcohol killed my father. I wish that he knew when to stop, when enough was enough. This poison stole my father's life, took my Daddy away. Now all I have left is this pain in my heart and tears in my eyes. Alcohol abuse is only a death waiting to happen, and only memories left to embrace.

Don't Drink and Drive

Read the following true story written by a mom who lost her son to an alcohol-related accident.

DIANE WANTS YOU TO KNOW

This is the story about how I lost my son. I want to share it with as many teenagers as possible.

My nightmare began on Sunday, August 23, 1998. At 10:45 p.m., the call came. Every parent knows. The Call. We *fear* it. Our 24-year-old son was driving home that night when he lost control of his truck. It went off the road and rolled over into the ditch. Both occupants were ejected. No seat belts were worn. The passenger was treated and released at an area hospital. Our son was not so lucky. A policeman was right down the road when this happened. He had paramedics on

Drinking and driving are a lethal combination. When you drink and drive, you and your car are a deadly weapon.

the scene within minutes. They started working on Jeff. He was not breathing. They worked on him for about 20 minutes while the CareFlite helicopter was in route.

While they were working on Jeff, our younger son, Dave, drove by. He saw his brother's Bronco upside down. The police wouldn't let him in the area. He finally said, "That's my brother, and I'm going!" He saw about five medics working on his big brother, a sight he sees now only in the darkest dark. One of the policemen found Dave a phone. Our baby was the one to make that most dreaded call. "Dad, they took him to Harris hospital. It's bad, Dad, real bad."

We got to the hospital about midnight. We were ushered into this little room. The doctors came in. They were talking about closed head injuries, brain stem damage. He needed CAT scans, X-rays, tests. Wait and see. We finally saw our son, hooked up to all kinds of machines, on a ventilator, bloody and bruised. But there he was, our Jeffy. I held his hand and touched his hair. I prayed. The blood flow test they did at 1 a.m. was "inconclusive," the doctors said. They would do another one in six hours. They did not think there was enough blood flowing to our son's brain to keep him alive. In 6 hours we would know.

I called my Mom. We all waited. We prayed and cried and drank coffee. Friends came by and called. Still waiting. More coffee, more tears, more prayers. Time was up. The doctors came in. The chaplain came in. It seems like everyone in the hospital came in to tell us that our son was not going to make it. Brain dead they called it. Too much damage. Too young to die.

Jamie came to visit us. She was with LifeGift. Could we think about organ donation? Nothing to think about, I said. Jeff made that decision when he was only 16. He wanted to be a donor. He said it was the right thing to do. We signed the papers and she left to get things started.

We saw Jeff again. I held my son for the last time. I kissed him and told him again how much I loved him. I told him how much I would miss him, but he had places to go, a far greater place than this one. I left my child in that hospital bed. Outside that room, Steve and I held what was left of our family and cried like babies. We went home to make the arrangements. So many decisions: Casket, music, flowers. What did we want him to wear? What time did we want to have the funeral? Over the next two days, all I really remember was family and friends, tears and prayers, and tons of food that no one was eating. It was time. Everything was done. The service was about to begin. A beautiful service for a beautiful young man. I hope he saw it.

Jeff saved several lives the day he died. His heart, liver, and kidney found new bodies to function in. Two people were given the gift of sight that day too. Countless others were helped with the bone grafts taken from my young son's body. All because of a decision this young man made several years ago. Caring? Yes, Jeff cared a lot about people. Wise? No, he was not wise. Jeff made a decision the day he died that cost him everything. He chose to drink and drive. Jeff's blood alcohol level was twice the legal limit for our state. He was too drunk to drive.

We need to help our young people make the *right* decisions. Please share this part of my life with all of your friends. Please show them the way. *Please don't drink and drive.* The next decision you make about drinking and driving may be the same one that makes your parents decide which casket to buy. Talk about it today, for my son's sake and for your own.

For more information:

Alcoholics Anonymous: http://www.aa.org

National Council on Alcoholism and Drug Dependence: 800-NCA-CALL or http://www.ncadd.org

American Council for Drug Education: 800-488-DRUG or http://www.acde.org

The College Alcohol Study: http://www.hsph.harvard.edu/cas/

MARIJUANA

Marijuana is the illegal drug most widely used by teenagers in the United States. This section will provide you with information about the drug and the dangers of using it.

A PERSONAL STORY FROM THE AUTHOR

When I was in college, I dated a nice guy who started using marijuana because lots of his friends "were doing it." It changed his personality completely. Before the drug use, he was a great guy, but little by little, he started becoming more lethargic and stopped caring about his personal appearance. I could see that this was not just a "phase" with him but was his way of coping with the pressures of school. So I said, "Adiós." It was really sad to see him in that condition, but the only person who could change him was himself. I often wonder what happened to him and hope that he got help for his problem.

Short-term Effects of Marijuana Use

- makes you unable to think clearly or to concentrate
- reduces your short-term memory
- decreases your coordination for tasks such as driving
- increases your heart rate
- can give you anxiety and panic attacks
- makes you lethargic—you're too tired to feel like doing anything
- can damage the immune system, making you more susceptible to disease

Long-term Effects of Marijuana Use

- psychological dependence requires you to use more of the drug to get the same effect
- increased risk of serious lung problems, including cancer

- for men, lower sperm counts and difficulty having children
- for women, increased risk of infertility
- diminished or extinguished sexual pleasure

These short- and long-term risks are even greater when other drugs are mixed with marijuana.

PATTI WANTS YOU TO KNOW

Drugs definitely made my life completely unmanageable. The first time I used drugs, I smoked pot. I loved it. It was a great experience. I kept using regularly, and soon enough I was hooked. I couldn't and didn't want to stop, and soon pot was not enough. I started looking for a new and better high, and I found one—I ended up using LSD, cocaine, and alcohol. Once I started using more, I did not care about anything or anyone. My life became a complete disaster. I hated myself, I didn't care at all what happened to me, and it came down to if I wanted to live or not.

At school, I had about a 0.3 GPA. I didn't even go to school most of the time. I would just go get more drugs. Friends stole from me and I stole from them. I lied to them and they lied to me. They talked behind my back and I talked behind their backs. My parents didn't trust me in my own room, or on the phone, or even at school. I definitely knew I had a problem but didn't know what to do. Finally my parents did something. One day they picked me up from school and told me they were putting me in a hospital for inpatient treatment. I was drunk at the time, so it did not really phase me. After I got out of that hospital, I came home and the first thing I did was go downstairs to the basement and huff chemicals.

For about four months, I went from hospital to hospital for treatment and never was willing to get help. One night at someone's house, I drank too much and threw up lots of blood. My parents were called to come pick me up. I woke up the next morning in my family room and wasn't allowed back in my room. My mom was so depressed, she wanted to commit suicide. My dad just yelled and threw me around. I had nowhere to go. I was stuck and I did not know how to get out. I could feel the emptiness in my gut. I was completely numb inside and out. I had a disease and couldn't get rid of it.

Finally after weeks of just lying on the couch, I wanted to change. I wanted to live again. I wanted to feel love and happiness. I was willing to do whatever it took to get sober. Now I have been sober for eight months, I work the 12 steps, and I love my life. And all it took was for me to be willing to be sober. I still have a disease, and I will have it for the rest of my life.

You may think that to be cool you have to do drugs. No. You just have to like yourself to be cool.

For more information:
Drug Abuse Hotline: 800-888-9383
American Council for Drug Education: 800-488-DRUG or
http://www.acde.org
National Council on Alcoholism and Drug Dependence:
800-NCA-CALL or http://www.ncadd.org

SMOKING AND CHEWING TOBACCO

Picture these scenarios:

You and your friends sit down in a restaurant and light up a cigarette while waiting for your food. The people at the next table complain to the waitress. She tells you that it is against the law to smoke in public places, like restaurants, and that if you want to smoke, you'll have to leave the building. You and your friends get up in a huff and storm out of the restaurant.

You can't smoke anywhere at school and are forced to hide in the bushes between classes, even though it is 20° outside.

You are on a flight to Europe that lasts eight hours. You cannot smoke during that entire time and you are *dying* for a cigarette after only one hour.

You go to a new girlfriend's house, and they have a big sign on the window that says, "Thank you for not smoking."

Your boyfriend tells you that he can't stand the way your breath smells because of your smoking. You feel angry, and that makes you want to light up even more.

You look at yourself in the mirror. You're now 40 years old, but look 60. Your face is a road map of wrinkles, your teeth and fingernails are stained yellow, your breath stinks and so do all of your clothes.

These events are your future if you smoke cigarettes. It doesn't seem fair, does it? The sobering fact is that every year more and more restrictions are put on smokers in public places. About the only place you will be able to smoke in peace will either be in your car or at home. The world is becoming more hostile to smokers every day. The United States government has recognized that smoking is a public health issue and has launched an aggressive fight against the tobacco industry.

The Facts About Smoking

The tobacco plant originally grew in the Americas but is now grown in many parts of the world. It is cultivated for its leaves, which, when cured, are used for making cigarettes and chewing tobacco. The part of the tobacco plant that gets you hooked on smoking is nicotine, which is a poisonous alkaloid found in the tobacco plant. Nicotine is so powerful that it has also been used as an insecticide to kill bugs.

Nicotine can create a feeling of relaxation or give the smoker a "buzz." The problem with nicotine, as with alcohol and other drugs, is that the smoker develops a tolerance for

Nicotine is a habit-forming drug. Many former smokers who also had other addictions said quitting smoking was the most difficult habit to break. If you've never started smoking, be glad.

Smoking can cause everything from stained teeth and wrinkles to stomach ulcers and heart disease. Hopefully, you can avoid its grip and breathe healthily for the rest of your life.

the drug and needs more nicotine to make his body feel good. Not only can he not quit, but he will need to smoke more to get the good feeling he had when he first started smoking.

In addition to the addiction-causing nicotine, there are many toxic substances in the tobacco plant that can cause cancer.

Physical Effects of Smoking

You've probably heard about smoking causing lung cancer but there are other negative things that can happen to your body.

- You will physically slow down because your blood carries less oxygen. When you climb up steep hills, you will become short of breath.
- Even if you don't get cancer, you have a good chance of developing emphysema or asthma.
- Smoking causes heart disease.
- You will be vulnerable to longer-lasting and more frequent colds and respiratory infections.
- You will have premature signs of aging, such as wrinkles.
- After several years of smoking, you will have a hacking cough every morning when you wake up.
- You might get throat cancer and have to get your larynx (voice box) removed. You'll speak with the help of a mechanical voice box that makes you sound like you're from outer space.
- There's an increased risk of stomach ulcers.
- The gum disease gingivitis can cause you to lose your teeth

A PERSONAL NOTE FROM THE AUTHOR

My father smoked for many years. He had a hacking cough every morning and a stomach ulcer. He also lost all of his teeth because of gingivitis. When he quit, he told us that he was sorry he ever picked up a cigarette. I'm sorry he did too because the different illnesses caused him a lot of pain and suffering.

Reasons for Smoking

You may be asking yourself why anyone would ever take up smoking. Teens smoke for several reasons:

1. It looks "cool." The Joe Camel and Marlboro ads make smoking look glamorous and sexy.

2. Many kids see their friends smoking and want to be a part of the group.
3. Their parents smoke, and it seems like the thing to do.
4. It's a good way to rebel against their parents. Most parents do not want their kids to smoke, so what better way to make them mad?

The fact is, if people don't start smoking before age 20, they most likely will never pick up the habit. Because of this fact, advertisers go after teenagers with ads that appeal to them. Beware!

The Benefits of Quitting Smoking

If you are already hooked on smoking, there are many benefits for you when you quit.

Your sense of taste and smell will improve. When you bite into a hamburger, it will taste much better than it tastes now.

You'll be richer. Cigarettes cost so much money. Think of all of the money you can save to spend on things that won't harm you.

Your health will start to improve immediately:

- your cough will disappear
- your risk of getting lung cancer will be greatly reduced
- you will have fewer respiratory problems like bronchitis and pneumonia
- your circulatory system will improve
- your lung function will improve

A lot of people in your life, including family and friends, will be glad when you quit because they don't want to see you have health problems. They really care about you. You're worth their concern—just remember that! Even if you feel that no one cares about you, you can feel good that you care about yourself.

Those who quit smoking become evangelists against the habit. They scream the loudest when they have to breathe someone's cigarette smoke. In addition, they will want to tell you how they quit because they're proud to be smoke- and drug-free.

MARY JANE WANTS YOU TO KNOW

I'm a teenager; I like attention; I want to be an individual; we're a lot alike. But there is one difference between you and me—my father died of cancer when I was 12 years old. More specifically, lung cancer as a result of tobacco use and smoking. My dad started smoking when he was 13 and continued until he was diagnosed in 1990 at the age of 47. At that time he had just received a promotion, had three young children, and a loving wife. What he had done in his life was about to come back to haunt him. He suffered a long and painful death and had a huge amount of regret. I am not saying this to scare anyone—it's the truth. As a result of his cancer, he became paralyzed and susceptible to seizures. Being paralyzed was not easy for a high school football star, and memory loss and

Yes, quitting is hard, but you can do it. Millions have quit and are leading much healthier lives because of it. Do yourself a favor. Stop as soon as possible.

seizures didn't come easy to a bright college-educated man. Cancer does not stay isolated; it wants to spread.

I watched my father deteriorate. When you have an adult at home who is dying, it's hard to have your friends over. They don't know how to react. But my father was one of the best, finest, most honorable men I know. Life is still wonderful for me and I am thankful for the opportunity my father's death has given me to mature and understand. I am 17 now and I live a very peaceful and happy life along with my mother, brother, and sister. There are still times when I cry and yearn to ask him questions. I mean, who is going to walk me down the aisle on my wedding day?

All I can say to you is that it isn't worth what you'll have to endure later as a result of smoking. When I see people smoke, it's a slap in the face. And it is *not* cool to be a "Marlboro Man" when you're six feet under.

How to Quit Smoking

Set a specific day when you will not be under a lot of pressure. If you can, find another smoking friend who will quit with you, so that you can support each other.

Be sure to have a lot of healthy snack foods near you at all times. Fruits you can carry, such as apples, pears, oranges, and bananas, are great to have with you. You can also munch on vegetables such as celery or carrot sticks when you get that nicotine urge.

Get lots of fresh air and exercise. When you want to smoke, take a brisk walk around the block or ride your bike to the park.

Drink at least eight glasses of water every day. Try to avoid sugary and fatty foods, or you run the danger of replacing one bad habit with another (overeating).

Keep busy doing things. Clean your room, talk to a supportive friend, take up a new hobby.

If you slip, get right back in the saddle. Don't waste time getting mad at yourself or you will be back in the addiction cycle before you can count to ten. Often, it takes two or three tries before you successfully quit smoking.

Change your habits. Analyze the things you always did when you were smoking and change your behaviors. If you always smoked right after eating, change your habit. Play with your dog or go for a walk after each meal instead of lighting up. Do something different.

Always remember why you are quitting. Visualize the extra money you will have. Think about how much better you will feel physically.

Carry a yo-yo with you. Say what? Yo-yo's are lots of fun to play with and will keep your mind distracted when you've got the urge to smoke. Maybe you can learn some new tricks in your spare moments like "walking the dog" or "around the world."

Keep your mouth busy—chew gum or suck on hard candies.

TERRENCE TAKES A STAND

I'm a smoker. I started by trying to be cool around my friends. Now, I smoke because I need it, not to be cool. It is a very bad habit to me—a nasty habit. I need to quit.

I lost my grandmother due to smoking. She had asthma and emphysema. I never realized that smoking could do so much to the body. It does so much harm, stains your teeth, gives you bad breath, causes gum disease, and damages your lungs.

Even though I'm only 22 years old, I've been through a lot at such a young age. I feel if I can stop at a young age, so can America's teens.

Please take advice from a peer, a friend, a brother, a son, a grandson, even an uncle. I love life. Don't end it early for yourself by smoking.

Chewing Tobacco

Chewing tobacco has many of the same hazards as smoking tobacco. There are a few added warnings about "chew." Instead of lung cancer, the user has a good chance of developing oral cancer—of the mouth, tongue, cheek, and throat. Often the cancers occur where the chewer holds the tobacco in his mouth. Because it is directly in contact with the gums, it causes them to recede. Your teeth will loosen and will eventually fall out.

TRY THIS!

1. **Do you know any drug or alcohol addicts?** What are their lives like? Are they successful? Are they going anywhere? Are they happy and in control of their lives?
2. **Think about the cost of drugs and alcohol.** Put a pencil to paper and figure out how much you would be saving by *not* using. You could buy yourself something really nice at the end of each year—sort of your payoff for not getting hooked.

SHORTCUT TO ACTION

1. Learn how to say *no* to drugs, alcohol, and smoking without making your friends angry. *You* are the one to decide what you want to do. Remember that.
2. Alcohol is a depressant. It has destroyed many lives—not only the user's, but also his or her family's.
3. Chewing tobacco can cause cancer of the throat, mouth, and nose. It also causes gum disease. Eventually the user will lose his teeth.
4. Drugs of all kinds (alcohol, marijuana, cocaine, crack, and LSD) cause the user to do and say crazy things. It also can cause brain damage. Each drug has specific harmful effects on the body.
5. When you drink and drive, you and your car are a deadly weapon. Do you want someone else's death on your conscience for the rest of your life? Do you want your friends to die?
6. People are getting more hostile every day to people who smoke in their presence. Do you want people giving you the evil eye every time you light up?
7. Before you start to use any drug, research the effects it will have on your body. Simply enter the name of the drug in the search box on an Internet search engine and you will find lots of information. It's always better to know what you're getting into *before* you do it.

CHAPTER 13

Preparing for Training After High School

WHERE DO YOU WANT TO GO AFTER HIGH SCHOOL?

Four-year college is not the best choice for everyone. Many students attend two-year community colleges or technical schools or obtain on-the-job training through an apprenticeship or internship. No matter which direction you take, you'll need to check out entrance requirements. Keep career interests and your abilities in mind.

What Degree Will You Need for Your Career?

There are many options for earning certificates or degrees after high school. So, how much education is enough for you and the career you've chosen? If you answered, "Huh?", you'll need to do some research on different careers. Ask your school counselor to give you a list of some good career search books. In addition, he can probably give you a career inventory test that would indicate what types of professions would best suit you. You are still young and have many years ahead of you, so don't get stressed out about finding a career. Actually, think of it as fun and worthwhile—you are starting to carve out your own life, independent of your high school, your teachers, and your parents.

What you choose to do after high school is a big step. Go slowly; ask people about their jobs, read books on different careers, think about what you would like to do. Are you happiest working outdoors or do you dream of buying and selling stocks at breakneck speed on your computer? Do you like working with machinery or would you prefer to have an office job where you could manage other people? You know what kinds of jobs you would hate to do, but finding out exactly what type of job would be best for you will take some work.

Different Degrees and Certificates

Check out the following explanation of the different degrees. After you have finally zeroed in on a career that interests you, gather information on what kind of education you'll need to get after high school.

Certificate. Some occupations require you to have post–high school training that lasts from three months to two years. After you have successfully completed the training for a specific job, you are awarded a certificate that gives you access to jobs right away.

Associate's degree. The associate's degree is generally awarded by junior colleges or privately run career schools. Students typically study half of the number of hours that four-year college graduates need—60 to 64 credit hours. The degree usually takes two years to complete if the student attends full time. This degree prepares the student for a specific career in fields like dental hygiene, criminal justice and law enforcement administration, nursing, mass communications, construction technology, and film and video production.

Associate of Arts degree. This degree is used by students who cannot afford to go to college or whose high school records aren't strong enough for them to get into a four-year college. The Associate of Arts degree usually fulfills the general requirements of most colleges. After completing the degree in about two years, the student can transfer to a four-year college to complete work in his major area of study.

Bachelor's degree. The bachelor's degree is earned after successfully fulfilling all of a four-year college's requirements. There are several different types of degrees: the Bachelor of Arts, with an emphasis on the humanities; the Bachelor of Science, with an emphasis on math and science; the Bachelor of Fine Arts, with an emphasis on art, art appreciation, music, music appreciation, and photography; and a host of other more specialized degrees.

Master's degree. This degree is earned by college graduates after studying an additional one or two years beyond the bachelor's degree in a specialized field. The term "master" signifies that the degree holder has mastered a high level of skill and knowledge in the field he studied in college. Sometimes a student will get a master's degree in a field different from his earlier degree, but he'll have a lot of catch-up work to do before he can successfully fulfill all of the requirements for the master's degree.

Doctoral degree. The doctoral degree is the highest degree attainable. It is generally earned by people who have a specific specialty in their field of study. These degrees are

The degree you need depends on the career that interests you. Once you decide on a career, then you will be able to determine your next steps. You need to do a lot of research, so have fun exploring and figuring out which career program is best for you.

The earlier you start thinking about your future, the better you will be prepared to make the moves needed to start your journey after high school graduation. Remember, graduation is a commencement—a new beginning to your life. You'll be on the threshold of an exciting new life and career.

obtained by doctors, lawyers, college professors, school administrators, or by anyone who pursues study of his field to the highest level possible.

Me Go to College? No Way, José!

For those of you who hate the thought of going to a four-year college, there are many other options for you. Check out the sections on vocational and technical training, apprenticeships, military training, and community colleges. As you will see, many career benefits are gained when you pursue an education or training beyond high school.

TECHNICAL AND VOCATIONAL TRAINING

Technical and vocational schools that offer vocational training are sometimes called trade schools. They offer a wide variety of training and education that lead to jobs in a single career field. I checked in my local phone book to get an idea of the types of schools out there for you. Here's a few ideas of careers you can be trained for: dental and medical assistant, pet groomer, administrative assistant, medical records technician, computer programmer, computer-aided draftsman, welder, travel agent, office administrator, computer network administrator, health information specialist, bartender, veterinary assistant, furniture reupholsterer, auto mechanic, occupational therapy assistant, massage therapist, and a ton of others. Check your own yellow pages to find other professions that you can obtain training for.

Employment Trends in the Future

According to the Bureau of Labor Statistics, by the year 2000, the percentage of **unskilled workers** will have dropped down from 60 percent of the workforce in 1950 to only 15 percent of the workforce.

Skilled labor will increase to a total of 65 percent of the workforce. It stood at only 35 percent of the workforce in 1950.

Professionals will remain constant at the 1950 level of 20 percent of the workforce.

Stephen Blair, President of the Career College Association, says, "These figures show that the majority of the jobs in this country will require technical and career education beyond a standard high school education. Only 20 percent of the jobs will require a traditional four-year college degree. The growth areas are clearly going to require nontraditional technical career education... Without a doubt, a solid high school education is critical for whatever field you wish to enter. Employers are looking for individuals who can read, write, and communicate effectively with their co-workers and customers. The new 'front line' employee will be expected to take on far more responsibility than ever before, and **they will be expected to think and reason in creative ways."** (Source: *Peterson's Vocational and Technical Schools, 3rd Edition*)

Be sure you check out the trade schools that offer the training you're looking for. Attend a school that will help you be successful.

Advantages of Vocational Training

- **Your time in school will most likely range anywhere from one week to two years.** This short term training will allow you to enter the work force quickly.
- **You will train for employment in a specific job.** You should be able to gain employment when you complete the training because your skills will match the job requirements.
- **Your education most likely will not cost you as much as it would to go to a four-year college.**
- **Your teacher will have personal experience in the field he or she is teaching.** He can give you helpful hints for obtaining a job.
- **You will use the knowledge you gain in classes to solve practical problems in laboratories and workshops at your job site.**
- **During your vocational training, you'll get lifelong skills,** such as good work habits, self-confidence, teamwork, and practical problem solving. Training will be hands-on. That is, you'll begin by learning the specific skills necessary for the job.

Possible Disadvantages of Vocational Training

- **You may train for a field for which there are not many jobs available.** You should research careers to see where the jobs are. A helpful resource is the *Occupational Outlook Handbook* of the Bureau of Labor Statistics. You can find the information on the Web at http://stats.bls.gov/ocohome.htm or in your local library. The hottest fields will be in the health and home health care, computer programming and systems, occupational and physical therapy, and paralegal fields.
- **Some vocational schools are better than others.** You must check out each school carefully. Talk to past

Many teenagers choose to become apprentices because they like to work with their hands, want to earn money while they learn, and are interested in the construction trades. For them, apprenticeship is the ideal work situation.

graduates. Find out what percentage of graduates get jobs. Know who you're dealing with. Call the Better Business Bureau to see if there are any complaints against the school. Talk to past graduates. Check to see if they have state licensing and accreditation. Are the courses up-to-date and taught by teachers with the latest skills? Do the facilities have state-of-the-art technology? Does the school have a job placement office? Will you get hands-on training?

- **You won't get as well-rounded an education as you'd get at a traditional college.** You'll be studying only one area. This focus does not have to be a negative, however. You can study additional information on your own by reading books, newspapers, and magazines. Many graduates of vocational schools are avid readers with a lot of knowledge on many topics. Don't buy into stereotypes if you know what field interests you. Go for it!

For more information, read:

Peterson's Vocational and Technical Schools, East and West Editions

APPRENTICESHIPS

According to the *Occupational Outlook Quarterly,* "Apprenticeship is a relationship between an employer and an employee during which the worker, or apprentice, learns a trade. The apprenticeship covers all aspects of the trade and includes both on-the-job training and related instruction in the classroom. Apprenticeships usually last about 4 years but range from 1 to 6 years. During this time, apprentices work under experienced workers known as journey workers—the status they will attain after successfully completing their apprenticeships."

Apprentices are actual employees of a company, which pays them roughly half of what the experienced worker gets. The apprentices get an increase in pay after satisfactorily completing each portion of the apprentice training.

Typical apprenticeships train you for careers as a carpenter, welder, iron worker, electrician, stone mason, and tile setter, among others. Also, there are a number of different things you can do after you've trained for one of these careers. For example, a carpenter doesn't just hammer nails all day. He's the member of a team that builds homes, commercial buildings, roads, and bridges. He also remodels homes and office buildings, installs drywall and cabinets, and completes exterior and interior finishes. Some carpenters specialize in one phase of the trade, such as installing concrete forms, installing acoustical materials, or driving pile. Millwrights handle, clean, erect, install, and dismantle machinery, equipment, and other heavy materials. Cabinet-makers build specialized, fine cabinets, furniture, and other articles for customers.

Typical Requirements for Apprenticeships

1. You must have a good high school attendance record and a good attitude.
2. You must be drug-free.
3. You must have a good work ethic.
4. You must have reliable transportation and access to a telephone.
5. You should have good math and communication skills.
6. You should like physical work, much of it outdoors.

The U.S. Department of Labor Bureau of Apprenticeships and Training mandates that you spend at least 144 hours per year in the classroom. To be an apprentice, you usually must be 18 years old, unless you get special permission from your parents. Then you may enter an apprentice program at 17. In a number of programs, you don't need a GED or high school diploma.

Advantages of Apprenticeships

- **You won't be stuck behind a desk day after day.** You'll go from job to job, meeting new people and seeing new places.
- **You get paid as soon as you start your apprenticeship.**
- **Many apprenticeship programs are affiliated with community and four-year colleges.** Some community colleges will give you credits for anywhere from 34 to 45 hours toward an associate's degree depending on your experiences. Then, you only need to earn 19 to 30 more credit hours at the community college to get the degree.
- **When you advance to journeyperson, your salary almost doubles.** Wages are based on your level of training and years of experience.

Companies are seeking candidates for apprenticeship who have a good high school attendance record and a good attitude. You must be drug free.

Apprentices are proud of the part they have had in building famous landmarks such as the St. Louis Arch, the World Trade Center, and the Sears Tower. Their work takes a lot of hard effort and perseverance—doing the job one step at a time.

Possible Disadvantages of Apprenticeships

- **You will have some periods where you cannot work, due to the weather.** Sounds like a good time to take a vacation, doesn't it?
- **Your education will be limited to knowledge of one trade.** But this is not always true. Many tradesmen read about things other than their trade. You have the power to educate yourself however you see fit.
- **The tradesman sometimes wishes he had gone to college.** Well, there is nothing stopping him or her from going to night or weekend classes. In fact, apprentices are ideal candidates for distance learning classes via the Internet. Check out the end of Chapter 14 for more information.

JOHN GAAL WANTS YOU TO KNOW

As my high school graduation day approached 22 years ago, I had no clue what my career path would be. Fortunately, one thing I did learn as a high school student was to be open-minded. This attribute allowed me to try college for a while and then move into a field I would never have thought of entering five years earlier. Two years after high school graduation, I was accepted into a union carpenters' apprenticeship program.

It was during my apprenticeship that I learned the true value of education. The hands-on nature of my apprenticeship linked the theory from the classroom with the practice in the field. And because of the union contract, I was earning good money while this learning was taking place. As time went on, I often visited the library and read a number of books on the topics of carpentry and construction. The payoff was respect on the job site for my layout and organization skills, which proved to me that our industry needed those with brains as well as those with brawn. My apprenticeship training did more than teach me how to learn—*it taught me to love learning.*

Upon graduating from the union carpenters' apprenticeship program, I entered the field of vocational education. In other words, I began teaching carpentry and cabinetmaking and now serve as the coordinator of the union apprenticeship program I graduated from so many years ago. Since graduating as a union journey-level carpenter, (with the continuous support of my family and friends), I have earned numerous undergraduate and graduate college degrees in majors ranging from construction management to architecture to international business. To that end, I currently sit on a number of national advisory committees that impact the construction industry on local, national, and international topics. My eclectic background of both traditional and nontraditional education has taken me to Mexico, Egypt, and several European countries. To be sure, without my years of education, I would not be able to enjoy the opportunity of sharing my life experiences at two local institutions of higher education as an adjunct professor.

In closing, I wish you success and leave you with some personal time-tested beliefs:

Knowledge is power.
Learning never stops.

It's better to try and fail than not try at all.
Never underestimate the value of your family and friends!

For more information:

Talk to the trade unions in your city or town for more information. Your state will most likely have an office that oversees apprenticeships. You may also contact the U.S. Department of Labor's Bureau of Apprenticeship and Training, 200 Constitution Avenue, NW, Washington, D.C. 20212; telephone: 202-219-5943.

Do some research to find more information. Ask your school counselor for helpful phone numbers and sources of information.

Check out the following Web sites on apprenticeships to get more information:

http://www.prideconstruction.org

http://www.omah.k12.wi.us/CareerWorkshop/apprent.htm

MILITARY TRAINING

For those students who cannot afford post-high school training, the military offers a lot of different options. One of the most common avenues is enrollment in one of the military branch's Reserve Officer Training Corps (ROTC) programs. Your guidance counselor will have more information for you. In addition, the military branches often send a recruiter to schools. He can give you more information.

The Army ROTC awards hundreds of scholarships a year. The Army's scholarships can be worth as much as $64,000. Traditionally, Army ROTC is a four-year program. The first two years are taken in the freshman and sophomore years of college, with an emphasis on the basic courses. The second two years are taken in the junior and senior years. During the summer between the last two years of college, you attend an advanced camp that will give you hands-on training. For more information on the Army ROTC program and all other programs of the military branches, visit the Web site http://www.militarycareers.com, which has links to the ROTC programs for the Air Force, Navy, Army, and Marines, or visit http://www.petersons.com/ugrad.

STUART C. SUCHLAND WANTS YOU TO KNOW

Serving in the U.S. Army has certainly been the most significant influence in my life since childhood. I served on active duty and in the reserves for eight years that

Community college is a great way to start college without breaking the bank. A two-year associate's degree can open up many doors to you for gainful employment.

were filled with high and low points, and I feel I was more impressionable than older soldiers would have been in the same situations.

Probably the most important thing I came away with from the military was self-confidence. I had the fortunate experience to work with some of the best soldiers in the Army, who were also excellent mentors. I was successful at several different schools, on training missions, and in real-life. With every award I won and every successful mission, I gained confidence in my abilities.

I also feel that I now have a different perspective on life, careers, and the rest of the more important things in life. I was put in a leadership position at a young age—much younger than the members of my team were. I had to make decisions and evaluate people in a difficult set of circumstances. I didn't always make the right choice, but the experience was extremely valuable.

The Army put me in the position to deal with others. I was a self-reliant person, but I learned that I had to rely on my team in order to do a good job in the military. I feel that I am much tougher mentally and physically from my experience in the military. I tested and exceeded my personal limits.

COMMUNITY COLLEGES UP CLOSE

Community colleges have an open-door policy—they accept anyone with a high school diploma or its equivalent (GED). They appeal to people who cannot afford to go to a four-year college, to those who want to go to college part-time while holding down a full-time job, to those who did poorly in high school and wish to get their grades up in order to transfer to a four-year college, and to students who are seeking certificate or associate's degree programs.

There are more than 1,500 community colleges in the United States, with an enrollment of 5 million students. Community colleges are sometimes referred to as junior colleges or independent technical colleges. They offer a comprehensive curriculum, including technical and continuing education programs. The highest degree conferred by a community college is the associate's degree.

Benefits of Attending Your Neighborhood Community College

You can try out the idea of college without making a big financial commitment. Often, students don't know if they can survive college. They are more comfortable starting out in a community college. Trying college out this way is a good solution for those who are reluctant to join the four-year college fray.

They offer courses at convenient times and places. As the "people's colleges," they sometimes have satellite classes in the local junior or senior high school buildings as well as their on-campus sites.

They are inexpensive. Annual tuition and fees average 50 percent less than at public four-year colleges and an even higher perecntage less than at private four-year colleges. As an added benefit, because the community college is near the student's home, he does not have to pay room and board. Community college is a great solution for kids who can't afford a four-year college because they can work for two years while they go to school and save up money so they can later transfer to a bachelor's degree program at another school.

The faculties at community colleges concentrate on teaching. There are no "publish or perish" requirements for teachers. They can focus on you and your education rather than on advancing their own careers or keeping their jobs.

Career counseling services help students get jobs. One of the associate's degree program's major goals is to get students employed after graduation. They usually have a close association with companies in the area and often tailor their programs to companies' needs. In addition, they can supply specialized training programs for the businesses. Companies can then send their employees back to school to upgrade their skills.

They have remedial courses for students who need to improve skills. They have courses that upgrade math skills, language skills, and overall learning/study skills.

They enable students to grow up before continuing at a four-year college. Sometimes, students who graduate from high school don't have a clear idea of what they want to do with their lives. They aren't emotionally prepared to continue in school. The community college gives them a chance to mature and gives them the time they need to check out many different fields and to build up the skills they need for four-year college.

Many community colleges offer home instruction. Distance learning is made possible by cable television or public broadcast stations or through home-study courses that can save you time and money.

Community colleges offer day and night classes to accommodate people who have full-time jobs on varying schedules.

For detailed information on two-year colleges, read *2-Year Colleges* by Peterson's, now in its thirtieth edition. It will give you a better idea of the kinds of degrees you can obtain from community colleges.

Maybe you're not sure you want to go away to a four-year college. A community college will give you an opportunity to explore your options and find out what you truly want.

SHORTCUT TO ACTION

1. Finding out what you want to do with your life requires some time and effort. Surf the Web. Talk to people. Take career interest inventories.
2. Your school counselor can help you figure out what you can do after high school.
3. College is not your only option. You can attend a vocational or technical school, enroll in a Reserve Officer Training Corps (ROTC) program, become an apprentice, or attend a junior college.
4. Vocational training allows you to study for a specific career.
5. With an apprenticeship, you earn a salary as soon as you start the program. Your salary rises as you complete each part of the program and the longer you stick with it.
6. Check out the *Occupational Outlook Handbook* published by the Bureau of Labor Statistics. It is a valuable predictor of which jobs will be in demand in future years.
7. ROTC is a college program that enables many young men and women to attend school. You may be able to get a scholarship that will pay for all of your college education.
8. Community college makes sense for a lot of students. It offers many valuable and exciting programs that will lead to future jobs.
9. Your community college has a career counseling office that will help you find a career that suits you. After all, you want to be happy in all of your working years.

CHAPTER 14

On to College

This chapter will benefit those who plan to go to a four-year college. The information will help you attain your goal of getting accepted to the college or colleges of your choice.

WHY GO TO COLLEGE?

The younger you are, the more likely you'll think that you don't want go to college. That's why it's so important for you and your parents to read this chapter right away.

Even if you think you won't go to college, the smartest thing to do is keep your options open because you might change your mind. The easiest and best way to give yourself as many choices in life as you can is to take college curriculum courses in high school, starting when you are a freshman. Most colleges require that you take a certain number of English, math, science, social science, and foreign language courses to qualify for admission. The earlier you get started, the easier it will be to fulfill the requirements. If you're the rebellious type, at least do enough work to get credit for the courses. Colleges will generally give you a break if you "come to your senses" and show improvement over the C's, D's, and F's you got in your freshman and sophomore years.

Are You Ready for College?

Identifying why you want to go will help make it clear to you if you're ready to attend college. Don't skip this step, because it could save you lots of time and money if you learn early in the game that you just aren't ready to get a college degree. Examine the reasons students often give for attending a four-year college, and then decide if you think they're good or bad reasons.

Reasons for Attending a Four-Year College

	good reason	bad reason
1. To be with my boyfriend/girlfriend	❏	❏
2. To prepare for a new career	❏	❏
3. Because there's nothing else to do	❏	❏
4. To improve myself	❏	❏

5. To party every weekend	❏	❏
6. To learn more about my chosen field	❏	❏
7. To get away from my parents	❏	❏
8. For the love of learning	❏	❏
9. To avoid having to get a job	❏	❏
10. To become a well-educated person	❏	❏

If you said the even numbered statements were good reasons for going to college and the odd numbered reasons were not, you have a good grip on things. If you want to go to college to party every weekend, to be with your boyfriend or girlfriend, to get away from your parents, or because you have nothing else to do, **wake up,** because you're on a course for disaster. I'm not trying to put you down if you like any of these reasons, but I am telling you that students with these reasons usually don't perform well in college. Read the next section for a little insight into what you might need to do.

Sabbatical from School

Are you fed up with school? Are you tired of teachers, exams, and stuff you have to do? Do you just need a break from all of it? Are you not really crazy about the idea of another four years in school? If you feel burned out, maybe you need to work for a year and *then* go to college. In all my years of teaching, I've seen many students flunk out of college because they weren't ready go. There is no law that says you must go right away.

IMPORTANT: Sometimes students who don't go to college immediately after high school never go back because they get busy doing other things. They often regret it. College will enable you to get a job that will pay more. You'll need to weigh what is the best thing for you, given your personality and your work ethic. You know what is best. Think about this dilemma, because if you immediately go to college, you must make the commitment to do your best work. If you give yourself a year off, you might be more motivated to succeed, especially after working in a boring job for a low salary. A good compromise would be to take a class each semester at a junior college to stay in the education loop.

TIMETABLE FOR THE COLLEGE BOUND

If you plan to attend college, you'll probably have to take a national standardized exam before you can be admitted. It is a

Don't feel bad if you don't go to college. It isn't for everyone. Maybe you could take a community college course from time to time to keep in the educational swing of things. It's always good to stretch your mind and learn new things.

Plan out your high school career as early as possible, even before you start your freshman year. When it comes time to graduate, you'll be glad you'd stayed on track.

good idea to read the following timetable for your four years at high school. Your school should notify you of the exact deadlines, but this information will help you. Ask your counselor for the ACT and SAT information packets during your junior year. After you read the information from both packets, you'll know what you're required to do. Check out the explanation of these two exams in the section *Making Sense of College Entrance Exams.*

Freshman Year

- **Meet with your school counselor to map out a tentative four year plan.**
- **Read as much as you can to get that extra advantage.**
- **Work hard to get as many language and math skills as possible.** Build up your vocabulary and master your math and science courses.

Sophomore Year

- **Take the PSAT exam or the PLAN exam in October for practice.** That way you'll get a good idea of what you need to study for the test that you will take in your junior year. The PLAN (the pre-ACT) exam is only given during the sophomore year. Your results on the PSAT (the pre-SAT) exam will determine whether you qualify for the National Merit Qualifying Test during your junior year. Talk to your school counselor about all of the details for signing up, where the test will be given, and how much it will cost.
- **Keep reading during your sophomore year.** The more you read, the better your vocabulary and reading skills will be. For suggestions on what to read, look at Chapter 8 for the National Endowment for the Humanities' reading list. Learn all you can in your English, math, social studies, and science classes. Even foreign language class can help you with your English vocabulary. I remember after one of my classes of sophomores took the PSAT exam, they came back excited that they had learned a word in Spanish class that was on the exam: Edifice, *edificio,* building. You never know when something you learn in a class will come in handy some day.
- **Go to career days and college fairs.** Go to college night or college fairs at your school or in your community to get as much information as possible. By visiting college

representatives, you will get a better idea of what kind of grades you'll need and what SAT or ACT scores are required for admission into certain colleges.

- **Start checking out colleges.** Get an idea of what colleges will be a good fit for you and your interests, your GPA, and your ACT or SAT score. Write to them for information or visit their Web pages. Later in this chapter you'll find a detailed guide on how to narrow down your choices. You have a lot of research to do, but it's well worth it to do a thorough job, getting as much information as possible to make a wise decision.

Junior Year

- **Take the PSAT/NMSQT (Preliminary SAT/National Merit Scholarship Qualifying Test) in October.** Keep in close contact with your school counselor so that you know when you have to register for the exam. Deadlines are very important in the precollege game, so pay attention to announcements at school. When you are a junior, you will only have one chance to take the PSAT—in October. It's the qualifying test for the National Merit Scholarship. Taking the PSAT is also a good preparation for the SAT I exam you will be taking later.
- **Take the SAT I in March or May.** You may need to wait until May to be sure you have learned all of the math and science concepts that will be tested. The ACT exam is given in September, October, December, February, April, and June. You may register for the exam on ACT's Web site (http://www.act.org). You can even pay with VISA or MasterCard! If you're near the deadline date, this is a great way to register for the exam.
- **Take Advanced Placement (AP) exams** if you have just finished the course being tested. The exams are given in May. More on AP exams later.
- **Do some research on careers.** Then you will be able to choose a college in a more logical way. If you have no idea what you want to do in the future, don't worry, because some college students change majors three or four times before graduating. Knowing exactly what you want to do with your life is an ideal situation—but not one that many students find themselves in.
- **Talk to your counselor about college possibilities.** He will have a good idea about which schools you should

What do all of these letters stand for—ACT, PSAT/NMSQT, SAT I, SAT II, PLAN? These admissions tests are enough to make you go back to bed and pull the covers over your head. Just be patient, take a deep breath, and read on.

"Senior year, I think I'll take all easy classes," you might be saying. There's no one to stop you, but be careful. Colleges look at the types of classes you take and the grades you get in your senior year.

apply to based on your test scores, GPA, and career interests. Start to get an idea of the kind of college you are looking for to help in the narrowing-down process.
- **Plan college visits during the summer after junior year.** Colleges are not as busy during the summer. In addition, you won't have to miss classes during your senior year. You will have a more relaxed time and can visit longer to get more complete information. After all, you need to keep your senior grades up in order to have the best possible GPA and class standing.

Senior Year

- **Retake the SAT I or the ACT exam if your score was low.** Many students retake the tests because a lot is riding on their score. In addition, you can prepare somewhat for the next time you take the test. It does help to study for the exam as much as possible, if for no other reason than to get psychologically prepared.
- **Get application forms from the colleges you are interested in.** You may want to apply to four or five colleges—one or two you can easily get into, two that you have a good chance of getting into, and one "long shot."
- **Send in applications for early decision by the deadline**—usually November 1 or November 15.
- **Send in the Free Application for Federal Student Aid (FAFSA)** as soon as possible after January 1.
- **Complete all applications by the due date.** Plan way ahead so that you don't panic at the last moment.
- **Take Advanced Placement (AP) exams in May.** AP exams are explained later.
- **Avoid "senioritis" at all costs.** Do *not* get yourself in a bind by taking easy courses your last year or by not studying so you get terrible grades. Those grades you receive will be forwarded on to the college you will attend. I have known some students who were put on academic probation *before they even started college.* Ouch, that hurts.

The College Admissions Exams— The SAT I and the ACT

Virtually all American four-year colleges require that you take the SAT I or the ACT to make it easier for admission offices to choose which students they will accept. Acceptance is not based solely on the exam but also on other criteria

such as grades, extracurricular activities, teacher recommendations, and the college essay. Standardized tests use the
same standards for grading everyone's tests, which helps
level the playing field. Otherwise, students who graduate
from high schools where standards are not strict would have
an easier time getting into colleges than students who go to
tougher schools. Admission personnel also believe that good
test scores mean that you will complete college-level work
successfully and be an asset to their college.

MAKING SENSE OF COLLEGE ENTRANCE EXAMS

The SAT I

**The Scholastic Assessment Test (SAT I) is the favored
exam of most colleges.** It is given seven times per year—in
October, November, December, January, March, May and June.

**The SAT I is a three-hour exam that measures the verbal
and mathematical reasoning abilities you have developed in
your high school classwork.** Most college-bound students
take it for the first time in March, May, or June of their junior
year because they have completed most of the course work
that will help them do well on the exam. This gives you an
advantage because if your test scores are lower than you
need, you can take it over at the beginning of your senior
year. If you had a bad day when you took the SAT I the first
time, you get another chance.

**The highest score you can receive on the SAT I is
1600**—800 for the verbal section and 800 for the math
section. Needless to say, the more competitive colleges
require higher test scores than most state universities. Your
test score on the SAT I will give you a good idea where you
should apply for college admission. If your test scores are too
low for Princeton or Harvard, you may have to give up your
dream of going there for college. Pursue a dream
that's attainable.

**You may register for the SAT I exam online at
http://www.collegeboard.org.** You will need to pay for the
exam using a MasterCard, VISA, or American Express credit
card. This is a great option for all of you procrastinators. You
can also get sample test questions for the SAT I online.
IMPORTANT: If you don't register before the deadline, you
will have to pay a costly late fee.

**College Board will give you a book to help you practice
for the SAT I.** *Free Sample Test and Tips* offers many useful

*Do the colleges you
are applying to
require you to take
the SAT I or the
ACT? Be sure you
check this out,
because you don't
want to take the
wrong test.*

tips. Check it out. Ask your school counselor if he has one. Otherwise you can go online and find out how to get the booklet. It's worth your time.

College Board has several books for sale to help you. *10 Real SAT's* and *Real SAT II: Subject Tests* are books of past exams that can give you a good idea of what you need to concentrate on before taking the tests. Visit the College Board's Web site at http://www.collegeboard.org for more information or call 800-406-4775 (toll-free).

Special provisions for the SAT I. You may take the exam on Sunday due to religious convictions. You also may show up at the exam on standby and pay $30 extra to take the test if you forget to register by the deadline. Even then, you are not guaranteed admission to the exam.

College Board sends all of your scores to colleges. Colleges will see your scores and notice if there is improvement the second or third time you take the test. This could work for or against you. If your test scores don't improve, schools believe the scores demonstrate your actual skill level. If they do improve, your standing with the colleges is improved. I believe that if you study hard for the exam, familiarizing yourself more with the types of questions and taking several different past SAT I exams, you will do better the second time. You will feel more confident and comfortable with the test after a lot of preparation and fine-tuning. You will be more psychologically prepared.

The American College Test (ACT) Assessment

The ACT is a three-hour, multiple-choice exam given six times a year. The exam tests your subject knowledge of English, math, reading, and science reasoning. It also tests such things as English grammar, spelling, vocabulary, organization, and style of writing. The science reasoning section of the exam tests your knowledge of physical science, biology, chemistry, and physics. The mathematics section tests arithmetic, algebra, geometry, and some trigonometry.

You can prepare for the ACT exam because it is more subject-oriented than the SAT I. If you are already taking challenging courses in high school, you will simply need to brush up on your material before you take the exam.

ACT has a free practice test booklet. The *Complete ACT Assessment Practice Test* booklet gives you some useful test-taking strategies.

ACT also has more sample questions and explanations of correct answers online at their Web site, http://www.act.org. You may also buy two sample test booklets for $3 each from

ACT. You will find details in your ACT Packet. You may register for the ACT exam online as well. Payment must be made by VISA or MasterCard.

Special provisions for the ACT. You may take the test on Sunday for religious reasons. Your fee for taking the exam may be waived if you can show financial need. If you have a learning disability that is documented, you may receive additional time (up to five hours) to take the test in October, December, and April. Note that there is no standby provision for the ACT.

ACT allows you to choose which scores to send colleges. When you take the exam, if you do not put down college codes on the score sheet, only you will receive the test scores. Then, after you have taken the ACT two or three times, you can choose which scores you want sent to colleges. This can be an advantage because colleges will never see your first test score. You may have had a bad day, not felt well, or were just not in synch with the test taking. For those of you who suffer from test anxiety, you will feel better because so much will not be riding on the first exam. You may even do great the first time you take it because the pressure is lessened.

IMPORTANT: If you decide not to have your scores sent at the time you register for the exam, there is an additional fee per school to have the score sent later.

Test Tips for Exam Day

- **Get a good night's sleep the night before.** Do *not* go out and party. Don't try to cram for the exam. It is more important that your brain be alert and functional.
- **Eat a good breakfast.** If your stomach is growling or you are starved, you won't be able to do as well. Give yourself an advantage. If you are extremely nervous, at least try to eat a slice of pizza if regular breakfast food turns your stomach in the morning.
- **Take a snack with you for break-time.** Lots of times, breakfast eaters are starved by 10 a.m., so be prepared.
- **Wear clothes in layers.** Some classrooms may be freezing, but others may be hot. You just never know, so it's a good idea to wear clothes you can take off or pile on.
- **If you are having personal problems, leave them at the door.** I have known students who were upset because they've broken up with a boyfriend or had just found out their mother had cancer right before the

The ACT is a more subject-oriented exam. If you do poorly the first time, you can study and hopefully raise your score next time.

A good emotional and physical condition are important when you take the tests. Get enough rest, eat a good breakfast, bring a sweater or jacket to the exam, and ignore other test takers.

test. They didn't do well because they couldn't focus on the exam. Train yourself to focus only on the exam during the testing time.

- **Relax.** If you have prepared yourself mentally and psychologically for the exam and have done some practice exams, you should do okay. It's a fact, though, that if you get terribly nervous, you will not be able to use your full brain power. Check out Chapter 7 for some tips on how you can be more relaxed during the exam.
- **Avoid sitting next to someone you know will distract you.** If you are taking the exam at your school, you might see a knuckle cracker, a sigher, a sniffer, or a gum popper. Sit on the other side of the room. They may be good friends of yours, but sit far away from them.

How to Improve Your Score on the SAT I or the ACT

- **As mentioned, study the SAT I or the ACT packets** that have sample test questions and test-taking strategies.
- **Many companies have published books to help you prepare for the exams.** The more practice you get, the better. These books give you that much-needed edge and also get you psychologically prepared for either exam. Check them out. Some recommended books are four books from Peterson's: *Panic Plan for the SAT, Panic Plan for the ACT, ACT Success* (with software), and *SAT Success* (with software).
- **Sign up for a professional course,** such as the Princeton Review. You will need to do research on these courses to find out how effective they are. Ask your counselor for advice before you spend any money.
- **Work with an individual tutor** who can help you with the sections of the test that are the hardest for you. You can count on this costing you big bucks. Again, ask around for advice on how effective a tutor would be and to get recommendations of people you can hire.
- **Buy a computer program on CD-ROM.** There are many for sale. Ask your counseling office which one you should buy. **IMPORTANT:** Some of the programs can only be used on a PC, so you will need to check this out carefully if you have a Mac.

SAT II

SAT II's are subject tests—one-hour multiple-choice exams that measure your knowledge of particular subjects and your ability to apply that knowledge. They are given on the same day as the SAT I exam with one exception: the Language Tests with Listening are only offered in November. You may take three of these exams in one day. Note that the SAT II: Writing Test has an essay in addition to multiple-choice questions.

Take these exams as soon as you finish the course work. If, for example, you studied chemistry in your junior year, it would be practical to take the exam right away before you forget the material.

Good scores on SAT II tests will impress admission officers when they decide on whom they will invite to attend their schools. In addition, the tests can be used for placement purposes. Many students who take the foreign language exam may have their language requirement waived.

Many competitive colleges want to see your scores on three SAT II exams. If you are applying to schools like Princeton, Stanford, or Harvard, it is a good idea to take three of the SAT II's in your best subjects.

Colleges check to see how difficult your course load has been. If you are trying to get into a highly competitive college, take several AP classes and the SAT II.

Advanced Placement Classes and Exams

Students who take AP courses and exams while in high school have a real advantage when applying to the more competitive colleges. AP courses are like college courses—the workload is heavy and students are expected to perform as if they were in college. In addition, the exams are very challenging. Any student who gets a 3, 4, or 5 in an exam may be able to waive that subject's introductory course when he gets to college. Some colleges even grant college credit for successful scores on the exams. With the high cost of college tuition and room and board, a student can save a lot of money if he does well on the exams.

Colleges will be impressed that you are taking tough courses. Regardless of how each college treats the AP exam grade, taking such rigorous courses will be noted by the college admission offices. It can be the deciding factor when the admission committee must choose between two candidates.

You may be eligible for a fee reduction. At this time, each exam costs $75 to take, but students from low-income families can apply for fee reduction or federal grant money. You will have to show your latest Federal Income Tax Return to demonstrate need. Some high schools even pay the fees for their students, regardless of financial need.

College Credit Courses Taken in High School

Many high schools and colleges have formed partnerships where college courses are taught at the high school. The students, upon successful completion of the classes, receive college credit. I've known many students who took enough college credit courses to be classified as sophomores when they started college. That's a savings of one year's tuition, room, and board! The students were able to graduate from college in only three years.

If your school offers such classes, find out how you can get into them. Often, there are prerequisites and grade requirements because they are more rigorous than regular high school classes. It's a worthwhile goal, if you're interested.

IMPORTANT: Some high school students take college credit courses only to find out later that the colleges they are interested in do not accept the credit. Be sure and find out whether the colleges you want to attend will accept the credit. You could lose a lot of money if they don't.

Are You Still Reading This?

Are you getting stressed out as you read about preparation for college? As I was writing about the SAT I, SAT II, ACT, AP exams, and college credit courses, I was thinking about how stressful your junior and senior years can be, especially if you want to attend an academically competitive college. I know it'd get me stressed. Some of you will cover all of the bases, get good test scores, write a great college essay, get incredible teacher recommendation letters, and still, you won't get into the college of your dreams. I believe that after you have done everything possible to get into the college, you must let go of your expectations and have the attitude that if it's meant to be, it will be.

Someone I know wanted to get into Princeton, as his older sister did. Unfortunately, he didn't get in, even though he had good credentials. He was distraught at first, but he picked himself up off the ground and went to another very good college. He is now a very successful person and is happy with his life. Sometimes students think that there is only one college for them. Beware of that line of thinking, because you have no control over the admissions committee. They may have criteria of which you are unaware. That doesn't mean you're worth any less. It simply means they were looking for someone else. You *are* good enough.

Taking Courses at a Junior College During Senior Year

Sometimes seniors get restless during their last year and need a new challenge. Many students have opted for dual enrollment at their high school and a nearby junior college or college. It's a good way of testing out the college waters and to start earning college credits. You'll have a better idea of what college is like and will be better prepared when you start.

THE NITTY-GRITTY OF GETTING INTO COLLEGE

Criteria for Choosing Colleges

Check out the following things you should ask before you start to make up a list of colleges you like. Get your parents involved in this process because they'll have a lot of good questions to ask.

1. **Academic level.** If you have a high GPA and great test scores, you should look for the best possible choices for your academic level. If you go to a college that is not very rigorous, you won't be challenged enough. On the other hand, your choice of colleges will be different if your test scores are low and your GPA is average. This will help you narrow down the list of possible colleges you will apply to.

2. **The size of the student body.** How many students attend the college? Do you prefer a big school or a small one? What would feel most comfortable to you? I enjoyed going to a large school because my high school had only 400 students, but you may prefer something else. Remember, *your* comfort level is very important because if you pick the wrong college in the wrong setting, you probably won't do as well or be as happy. Base your decision on what would make you happy.

3. **The locale of the campus—in an urban area, in a suburban setting, or in a rural area.** You might like a big city setting because you like all of the cultural activities it offers. On the other hand, you might feel in danger because big cities often have more crime. Do you prefer a suburban setting that is near the city but is still removed from high crime areas? You might prefer a rural area, far away from cities. Rural colleges

You should research each college carefully. Make up a list of things you need from each college. When you sort everything out, you'll be better able to narrow down your list.

offer college-sponsored events and activities, but when no school events are scheduled, your pleasures in life may consist of watching videos, visiting with friends, and studying. That might be what you need, especially if you get distracted when there are too many things to do.

4. **Does the college offer the programs that interest you?** If you are unsure of what your major program of study will be, you will have a wider selection of colleges to choose from. You'll be able to take many varied courses and will find out what interests you the most. You never know; something you thought you would hate might end up being your major. Note, however, that if you have a definite scientific bent, you should try to find colleges that are good in the scientific fields.

5. **Will the college accept your AP test scores and college credit courses for credit?** This could be a big financial consideration for you. If you have already paid for those AP exams and the college credit courses, losing the amount of time, money, and effort you spent would be a crushing blow.

6. **Do you prefer a state school or a private school?** Answering this question will help you narrow down your list quite a bit. This is a matter of preference that only you can answer. You might prefer a college with a religious affiliation, like a Christian school. Check out *Peterson's Christian Colleges and Universities* if that's your interest. I'll mention other special kinds of schools later on in this chapter.

7. **Does the college have study-abroad programs?** Some do not but have an affiliation with schools that do. They'll accept other schools' credits from the year- or semester-abroad programs. If you're interested in furthering your foreign language study, this will be an important question to ask.

8. **How big are the required courses for freshmen?** At large state universities, a basic psychology course may have 500 students with a teaching assistant in charge of your lab. If that freaks you out, you'll have to take it into consideration when choosing a college that's right for you.

9. **Student body composition.** Is the student body diversified? Or does the college give priority to people of one race or religion? Some students may be interested in getting more diversity in their lives while others might want to attend school with a homoge-

neous group. This is an important question you need to ask yourself. Where will you be most comfortable?

10. **Distance from home.** Do you want to be close enough to home so that you can sometimes come home on weekends? How difficult will it be to get home—how far is it and is transportation easily available? You might decide you want to explore a different part of the country because you desire a change.

11. **Financial considerations.** Can you and your parents afford to send you to the college? Does the college give financial aid? Will you qualify? Do not automatically reject certain colleges because their tuition is too high. Often, they have a large endowment and can afford to give out substantial scholarships.

12. **What are your parents' preferences?** You will have to take this into consideration. If you hate their choices, you need to come up with some good reasons why you do not want to go to those schools. Be sure your arguments are based on facts and not on your wanting to do the exact opposite of what your parents tell you to do.

Do you want to go to California to be near the beach or do you prefer skiing in Vermont? Do you want to be close enough so you can go home on weekends or do you want to be farther away? What are you emotionally pre- pared for?

Narrowing Down the List

The twelve questions above were a good starting point for your exploration of colleges. Now comes the task of narrowing down your list. To narrow your list, you should take all of the following steps:

Talk to your counselor. She will know the colleges that will fit your SAT I or ACT scores and your GPA. If you have a certain college that you really want to attend, but your scores and GPA are a bit lower than what the college says it wants, do not be discouraged. You never know when they might make an exception. And don't let your counselor discourage you from applying to certain colleges because she doesn't think you have a chance of getting in.

Get information from your college and career center. In a smaller school, there might be one counselor who is in charge of college applications. He will be the counselor with the most information. Many high schools have research libraries and computer labs for you to explore colleges.

Read four-year college guides. *Peterson's Guide to Four- Year Colleges* is a comprehensive guide that emphasizes standards for admission at most four-year schools. After careful study of the guide, write for more information from

College visits give you more detailed information. Before the visits, the colleges are a vague entity. After you visit them, you will have a much better idea of where you can see yourself living and learning.

the colleges you like. You can go online to ask for this information or even get the information you seek from the school's Web page.

Talk to past graduates of colleges that interest you. Your counselor might know of people you can contact. Often, you can get good information from them because they have been there.

Visit every college that interests you. This is a very important step that you should not ignore. You don't want to get to your college and discover that it's a scary place for you or that you don't like something very basic about it.

The Campus Visit

The campus visit is a key process in deciding your final list of colleges. It is a must because no one can tell you what you will like and what feels right for you. You might think you want to attend Superior College but when you get there, it's all wrong for you. When you visit, you can see the campus, meet and talk to students, see what the social life is like, visit classes, check out the academic facilities, and talk to someone in the Admissions Office.

After you have narrowed down your choice of colleges to five or six, find out when they host high school students for campus visits. If you can visit several of the colleges in the same geographic area in one trip, you will save yourself and your parents a lot of money. Try to coordinate all of the visits so that you will have enough time to spend at each college. Some students I have known have flown from one college to another, feeling that everything was a blur because all of the visits ran together in their minds. You and your parents, if they go with you, will want to spend some time on your own, exploring each campus and talking to people.

Some colleges take the campus visit more seriously than others. Some schools only give you a guided tour of the campus and provide general knowledge. You will already have much of that information from the research you have done, reading college catalogs, talking to people, and visiting the college's Web site. Because you want to see what the campus is like and get a feel for the college, this visit is important—although you will have to fight harder to get the information you want.

Some colleges make a super effort to help you in your quest for information. They also try to personalize the visit as much as possible. Often they will assign a guide to each student who will take you around the campus and answer questions. The guides they have selected are students they trust will give their college a positive spin. Students are often able to spend the night in a dorm, meet lots of students, go to classes, meet some professors from the department they are interested in, and talk to an admissions officer.

Colleges often try to have you schedule your visit during homecoming weekend or another time when some fun activities are going on. Remember, their goal is to recruit students to their college. You will enjoy these fun-filled visits but be sure that you get what you came for—detailed information on the criteria that will help you separate College A from College B in your mind. The more you find out, the better decision you will be able to make for yourself.

When you are on a college visit, try to do some more "snooping around," after you say goodbye to the admissions office and to your student guide. Talk to as many students as you can. Remember, first impressions of a college may be based on one less-than-friendly student or one super-friendly student. Meet as many people as you can. Walk around, just noticing things. Read the campus newspaper. What do they write about? Is there a rapist on the loose who is attacking females on their way home from the library? Is there theft in the dormitories? You can find out a lot about a college's priorities and orientation by reading the newspaper. If the newspaper has a lot of articles on such fluff subjects as the dormitory food, you can wonder how academically serious the school is. If, however, the newspaper has thoughtful articles on substantive issues, such as the environment or any topic important to today's society, you can believe that this school has a lot of potential for you—one where you can learn a lot and get a good education.

After each college visit, immediately write down your impressions. It would be helpful to make up a questionnaire sheet of all the important questions *you* want answered. Fill this out for each college. Also write down your general impressions of each college and of the things that happened when you were there. Did you feel there was an overemphasis on parties or that the college had very little social life? Write down everything you can think of. When all of your college visits are over, you'll be able to compare and contrast the colleges to get an idea of which one is the best for you using the information sheets you have filled out.

Make an effort to talk to people you see in the library, at the neighborhood burger stand, in the dorms—anywhere you go during your visit. Ask lots of people how they like the college and why.

Information You Need From Each College

Check out the following list of things to find out at each college.

- **Diversity.** What is the gender, ethnic, religious, and geographic makeup of the student body?
- **Health services.** What kind of medical care is available to students? Is it easily accessible? Is there dental care? Emergency care?
- **Class sizes.** What is the ratio of students to faculty members? How does the school arrive at that figure? Do they only count full-time faculty members? Does the school count such people as librarians as faculty members to make the ratio look good?
- **Library.** Does the library have a good collection of books in your field? Will you be able to do your research at the college library or will you have to go to other colleges to get the books you need? Ask students their opinions of the library. You can get a lot of good information that way. Be sure to talk to more than one person to get an objective view.
- **Campus police.** Does the college have its own police force? Will they walk you back to your dorm if you're using the computer lab or the library late at night? What are the crime statistics for the campus? What kinds of crimes are reported?
- **Counseling services.** Is there psychological counseling for students who are having a hard time coping with college life? Are there support groups for students with similar problems? How much does the student have to pay to get this help?
- **School calendar.** When does the school year start and end? When are the vacations? Are students given a few days between classes and final exams to study? Does the college offer summer school programs?
- **Dormitories.** Are they located in a safe area of town? Are they close to classes? Are the dorms co-ed? If so, how do they separate the sexes? Are the dorms quiet or noisy? Do they look well-cared for or are they awful places to live? Is there a residence adviser for each floor who helps the students out with their problems? Is alcohol allowed in the dorm? Do the cafeterias serve well-balanced meals? How are roommates selected by the college? Do they give you an opportunity to state your preferences? Are you guaranteed a dorm room for all four years?

A FUNNY STORY

My niece Elizabeth called up her freshman-year roommate during the summer, as all colleges advise. When she asked to speak to Chris, she found out that she was going to be rooming with a *guy!* She was surprised, needless to say. She called up the university and asked them to change roommates. Just imagine if she had not called and went to move in and found herself in that situation. There's a reason why you need to do some preparation work before you get to your college. Take their advice. They're not kidding.

Do you want to be in a fraternity or sorority? Ask those who are in them how they like them. Ask those who are not why they are not in them.

- **Extracurricular activities.** Are there clubs and organizations for students to join? Can anyone join? Get a list of them at each college, if possible.
- **Intramural sports.** Can students join intramural teams and compete against other teams? What sports do they offer?
- **Exercise facilities.** Do students have exercise equipment available for their use? Are the hours convenient? What are the facilities? Is there a weight-lifting room or a swimming pool?
- **Fraternities and sororities.** How many of each are there? Are they active in campus affairs? What is their general reputation on campus? Are their members known only as party animals? Do they participate in hazing? Do they do volunteer work for the community? What percentage of students on campus are members of fraternities and sororities? Do they live in the fraternity or sorority house? Ask students you meet a lot of these questions. They will have very definite opinions.
- **What percentage of the freshman class returns the next year?** What percentage of students graduate from each freshman class? Is the number high or is it low? What is the reason for the graduation rate?
- **Does the college have a career placement office?** How active is it in the placement of graduates? What percentage of graduates get jobs right out of college? What kinds of jobs do they get? Can alumni use the career placement office? Does the college help students find part-time jobs during the school year and the summer? How are campus positions filled? Can anyone apply? Are freshmen eligible?
- **Does the community get involved in college activities?** Does the neighborhood like the college? Do the college and the community interact? How? What kinds of activities may they participate in?

A college education is a major investment of your time and money. Ask lots of questions.

- **Are students allowed to have a car on campus?** Is a car a practical thing to have? Is parking readily available? Can the student get around easily on foot? How many students use bicycles to get from class to class? Are there bike racks for them to lock up their bikes?
- **Social activities.** What kinds of things do students do for recreation? You can't study all of the time. You need to have some fun, too. All work and no play . . .
- **Are provisions made for disabled students?** If you have a particular disability, will the university help you get what you need to get a good education? Ask specifically for help with your disability.
- **Are there remedial classes for students who need them?** What classes do they offer? How do they determine if a student needs them?
- **Are there tutorial services for difficult classes?** For example, are there student tutors who help the students understand and do calculus homework?
- **Does the college have an honors program?** What are the qualifications you need to have to get in the program? What are the benefits to enrollment in the program?
- **What is the school policy on drugs and alcohol?** Is it anything goes or do they have strict rules for controlling consumption?
- **Facilities.** Are the buildings well-kept? Are there plans for expansion? Does the college pay attention to appearances or do buildings look run-down?
- **Does the college have partnerships with businesses?** Are students eligible for internships? What are the internships like? Is there a work-study program while the student attends school?
- **How well is the college endowed?** If it has generous alumni, you have a better chance of getting financial aid.

The Application

Follow all of the steps below to have a humdinger of an application.

1. **Make a photocopy of all applications before and after you complete them.** That way, you can practice on the photocopy. Be sure and make a copy of the completed application in case it gets lost in the mail.
2. **Follow directions for each application EXACTLY.** Imagine not giving them the right information they

requested. They'll think you can't read! Well, I'm exaggerating, but it won't look good.

3. **Be very neat.** Don't have scratch-outs or erasures. Type or print neatly in black ink.

4. **Give as much information as the space allows.** Be specific about your interests, extracurricular activities, your goals for the future, and your interest in this particular college.

5. **Write a great essay on the topic given.** More on this later.

6. **Fill in all of the blanks.** Give information in each space.

7. **If the college says that some of the questions are optional, do them anyway.** If you don't, you might appear lazy. It never hurts to do more than you have to.

8. **If the colleges to which you are applying accept the Common College Application,** consider whether you are at an advantage or disadvantage not filling out their particular application. Perhaps you could attach the special college essay to the Common Application. It would probably be a good idea to ask the college if that is okay.

9. **Put your college application aside for a while.** Then go back and look at it. Have you written something that will make the college admission officer take an interest in you? It is always good to step back from your work.

10. **Make a list of everything you are required to send to each college.** Highlight the deadlines for each item.

11. **Have a separate file folder for each college to which you apply.** If you have papers piled up all over the place, you won't be able to find what you need in a hurry. It pays to be organized. File things as soon as they come in the mail. You won't drive yourself crazy.

12. **Celebrate the completion of each step: after you have written the college essay, after you have sent in the completed application, and when you hear back from the colleges that have chosen to admit you.** The process can be an arduous one. You deserve to kick back, celebrate, and relax. Just don't forget to get back to your senior class work.

The Common Application

Almost 200 colleges recommend the Common Application for undergraduate admission to their schools. This is a fairly basic application that only needs to be filled out once—then you send it to as many schools as require it. It can be a huge

Spend a lot of time filling out the applications. They will give a positive or negative impression of you. Besides, it's always good to do things carefully. You will be more successful in everything you do when you take the little things seriously.

Can you stand the

tension when you

are put on a wait

list? It's risky

business, so be

careful. You have to

accept the possibil-

ity that you may not

get accepted.

time-saver, but it can also detract from your individuality. As I suggested above, if a college allows the Common Application, answer the essay questions on the school's own application as well. You can find the application online at http://www.commonapp.org/.

Early Decision, Early Action, Regular Admission, or Deferred Admission

Colleges select students for admission in several different ways. Each plan has its advantages and disadvantages.

- **Early decision.** Students apply to the college in the fall and receive notification of admission or non-admission before the end of December. Please note, however, that this early decision plan is legally binding, because if you are accepted you must attend this college. Applying for early decision can be an advantage if you are certain the college is your top choice.
- **Regular admission.** Most students apply for regular admission because it has no strings attached. You have to apply by a certain deadline. If a college accepts you for admission, you do *not* have to accept their offer, especially if you get a better offer from another college.
- **Deferred admission.** For a variety of reasons, some students need to take a year off from school. Many colleges will allow you to start school a semester or year late. Be sure to check each college's policy.

If you are placed on a wait list, the college should tell you how many other students are on the list, how far up on the list you are, and the percentage of students on the list who usually get accepted for admission. If it doesn't, call and ask. If you are put on a wait list, you are under no obligation to attend the college if you are later accepted nor to send them money to secure your place on the list. Colleges should inform you of your status on the wait list by August 1.

Teacher Recommendations

Check out the following tips for getting the best teacher recommendations.

- **Ask a teacher who knows you well to recommend you.** Most teachers are pleased to recommend you if they think highly of your work. You will be most successful when you ask a teacher in whose class you excel.

- **Give your teacher the recommendation form,** with all of your information on the sheet, signed by you. Be sure to give him an addressed, stamped envelope. I have had students give me a blank recommendation form. They didn't even put their name on the form.
- **Waive your right to see the recommendation.** Colleges believe that if your teacher does not show you the recommendation, she'll be more honest. I always give the student a copy of the recommendation letter I write because I know how much pressure is riding on those recommendations. Not all teachers will do this, though.
- **Give your teacher the recommendation form at least three weeks before it's due.** Ask the teacher after five days if he has filled out the form. If he has not, tell him exactly when it's due. I never mind when my students remind me. Sometimes I need it!
- **Give the teacher an information sheet.** Write about yourself, telling your teacher about your accomplishments, your extracurricular activities, and your goals and dreams for the future. Recommendation forms always ask the teacher to assess you in leadership skills, your ability to work with other people, your ability to be a self-starter (initiative), and your ability to be a critical thinker. Give the teacher examples if you feel that is necessary. I have always appreciated it when students give me important information I can include on the recommendation form. In addition, tell the teacher what classes you took with him in what years and the grades you received.
- **After you are through with your applications and have sent them off, breathe a sigh of relief.** Then, send a thank-you note to your teachers. They will appreciate your gratitude. It always helps to do nice things for others, anyway.

Writing the College Essay

For many high school seniors, college application essays are excruciatingly painful. Many students try to avoid writing them for as long as possible. All of a sudden, there's only a week left to write them before the application deadline. You'll be super-stressed out. If you apply to ten schools, you may have to write ten different essays. Ouch!

Typical Types of College Essays

- The personal experience essay
- A philosophical topic

Your teacher will appreciate it if you give him an information sheet that tells him who you are, what you have done, and what your plans are for the future. You want him to show your best side, so it is important to take this step. It's in your best interest.

The college essay is

a good opportunity

to find out more

about yourself.

Think of it as your

chance to do some

deep thinking, to get

some direction for

your future, and to

see what you have

done in the past.

- An activity or hobby of yours
- An important person in your life, whether fictional or real
- The creative essay
- An important academic awakening
- Your world view or view of a particular issue
- Why do you want to attend this college?

Sample Essay Topics

From the Common Application:

- Evaluate a significant experience or achievement that has special meaning to you.
- Discuss some issue of personal, local, national, or international concern and its importance to you.
- Indicate a person who has had a significant influence on you, and describe that influence.

From Tulane University:

- Please write an essay describing in some detail some special interest, significant experience or achievement, or anything else that has special meaning to you or has had a significant influence on you.

From the University of Chicago:

- Names have a mysterious reality of their own. We may well feel an unexpected kinship with someone who shares our name or may feel uneasy at the thought that our name is not as much our own as we imagined. Most of us do not choose our names; they come to us unbidden, sometimes with ungainly sounds and spellings, complicated family histories, allusions to people we never knew. Sometimes we have to make our peace with them, sometimes we bask in our names' associates. Ruminate on names and naming, your name, and your name's relationship to you.

From the University of Massachusetts Amherst:

- Provide information about your achievements, personal qualities, goals, or anything else that will help us to learn more about you.
- The University is actively committed to enrolling a multiculturally aware student body. How can you contribute to or benefit from this environment?

From Macalester College:

- What factors have led you to consider this college?

- Transcripts, test scores, and a list of awards provide at best only a partial sense of a candidate for admission. For this reason, we ask that each applicant submit an original piece of written work to complete his/her application. This essay is your chance to give us more than the inevitable admissions facts and figures and to demonstrate your ability to organize thoughts and express yourself. You might want to focus on an experience, a philosophy, or a significant event or devise a topic of your own. Our goal is to receive an essay which will help us to know you better as a person and as a student. The rest is up to you. Do remember, however, that your essay should be carefully prepared as it represents a major component of your application to Macalester.

As you can see, essay topics can cover any number of areas and vary in specificity. Read on for tips on how to write the best essays possible.

Suggestions for Writing a Good College Essay

Take the essay seriously. If you are being compared to other students who have similar SAT scores, good faculty recommendations, and a good GPA, colleges will look more carefully at essays to determine who gets admitted. An excellent, interesting essay could tip the balance in your favor. Take it seriously, especially for the more competitive colleges. Check out Peterson's *Writing a Winning College Application Essay* for some pointers and examples of student essays.

The purpose of the college essay is to find out who you are. Through your choice of topic, the expression of your ideas, and your conclusion, the college will get a better picture of you. The admissions committee will also know if you can write well—an important concern for all colleges.

Think over the essay topic for several days before you begin to write it. I have found that I can write something more easily if I have mulled the topic over in my mind for a while. Don't jump in and start to write. It will probably be lackluster and boring. You must find a way to personalize it, making it more interesting.

Put the essays into categories. If three out of five colleges want you to write about a personal experience, you can use the same essay for all of the applications. If the question has a different twist to it, but still asks you to write about yourself, you probably can use the same personal experience

Before you write each essay, think about it for a couple of weeks. You will come up with more ideas if you give yourself time to absorb it, to toss it around in your mind, and to see where you want to go with the essay topic.

In your essay, be yourself. Be careful not to write a boring, formal paper that looks great but doesn't tell the person reading it anything about you. The admission staff wants to know more about you, so now's your chance to shine.

you wrote about for the other essays. Perhaps you will only have to perform minor surgery, changing your beginning paragraph or your conclusion. Look for ways to minimize your workload while still doing a good job.

For a personal experience essay, think, think, think. This type of question will make you question who you are, what makes you special, and why you are good enough to get into the colleges of your choice. You might have to question what your values are, what you believe in, what your aspirations are, or what makes you different from other students. Think of this as a great opportunity to get a fresh perspective on your life, to develop goals for your future, and to see what you need to do to make yourself a better person.

Have a positive attitude about writing the essay. Don't waste your time moaning and groaning about the essay. It's not going to go away—you still have to do it. Make it a pleasant experience. You might even find that you enjoy writing it.

Don't be afraid to toot your own horn. Colleges want to know what makes you special. You don't want to brag, but you don't want to minimize the good things you have done. This is your time to shine. When you reflect over all you have done in your life, you will probably find that you've done lots of neat things. Start writing them down and keep adding things that you have accomplished.

Have a beginning, middle, and end to your essay. Many writing teachers advise their students to tell your audience what you're going to say, say it, and then tell them what you just said (your conclusion).

The college essay is the most personal part of your application. In the rest of your application, you have given the factual information the college has to have. Imagine yourself as an admissions officer reading thousands of essays. This is your chance to grab his attention. Unless you take time to write a good essay, yours will be a vague memory, along with loads of others. Catch his attention by showing your personality—your unique perspective on the topic. If you have a great sense of humor, show that in your writing. If you are very serious about social issues and intend to devote your life to making a difference, let the school know. Don't be afraid to be humorous *and* serious at the same time.

Write in a relaxed tone. Some students feel they have to write a formal, stiff paper that sounds more like an academic research article. Your goal in these essays is to present yourself in a positive way. You don't want them to think you have a board holding up your back. Just be yourself.

Do not use profane language, slang, or bad grammar. If you do any of these things, you'll turn off your reader. Use good judgment here. Know your audience. It's not for your teenage friends.

Use examples in your essay. Instead of using generalities, cite specific instances in your own life that were significant and that deal directly with your topic.

Don't repeat yourself in the essay. Don't dilute your ideas by repeating yourself. Your essay will be boring for your reader.

Have good transition sentences that link each paragraph. Don't abruptly jump from one idea to another. Lead into your next idea smoothly and with panache.

After writing the essay, check your "mechanics." Do you have any spelling errors? How's your punctuation? Does the essay flow well? If you were reading this essay, would it interest you? Do you use the correct verb tenses? Is the essay forceful and persuasive?

Have someone else proofread the essay. Often, other people will see things you don't see because you're too close to it. Have several people read the essay. They will have a different perspective than you and might be able to help you make the essay more interesting. **IMPORTANT:** Pick your readers carefully. Ask someone who is objective and who has your best interests in mind.

Make a copy of your essay to be safe, both on paper and on a computer disk. You may need to send it again if your application gets lost in the mail.

A Student's Essay

A student named Brian wrote the following essay for his application. He was asked to write on the following topic: **Sharing intellectual interests is an important aspect of university life. Describe an experience, book, class, project, or idea that you find intellectually exciting and explain why.**

BRIAN'S WINNING ESSAY

"Ah, mi joven, es que aquí trabajamos para vivir—ustedes viven para trabajar—aquí estamos contentos." She delivered her message to me so plainly, an unintended gift, wrapped with sincerity and tied with simple ingenuity. Something I had pondered at great lengths attempting to discern, what many spend lifetimes searching to find, my Spanish home-stay mother served me as an epiphany along with the usual Spanish olives, paella, and seafood. On the surface, Antonia had explained to me her dime-a-dozen analysis on the fundamental differences between Spanish and American culture. In reality, my Spanish "temporary

It's always a good idea to write the essay and leave it for a few days. Then, come back and read the essay as if you were an admissions officer. Do you sound like an interesting person or do you come across as boring? Keep revising it until you like it!

If you're a good athlete and have decent grades, maybe you can get a sports scholarship. Read Peterson's Sports Scholarships and College Athletic Programs for more information.

mother" had given me an intuitive insight on how both I and other Americans lead our lives almost masochistically. Her words rang translated in my ears, "You see, my dear child, here we work to live—you live to work—here we are content." Suddenly I began to question what I have always perceived to be my inherent way of living. Could it be that the prize we win pursuing our fast car, fast food, fast service, fast-lane–oriented culture is nothing but a shortcut alley to a life with too fast an ending? After eating lunch that day, I rose from the table and pensively walked to my bedroom, which lacking of all adornments, proved that Antonia was right. Even the bedroom that this generous family had offered me for my five-week foreign study was blessed with a sacred plainness, garnished with nothing excessive; it was modest in its nature. This family indeed worked only enough to sustain life, but unlike Americans, they elected to truly "live" the rest. Overwhelmed from realizing that this life-loving culture was omnipresent in this quaint Spanish town called Conil de la Frontera, I resigned quietly to studying for the next day's test with a clouded and perplexed mind. The passage of the five weeks I spent last summer in that handsome village incited feelings that were a combination of comfort, isolation, fascination, and aggravation. I found myself prejudged as a pretentious and overworked American whose monetary priorities exceeded nearly all other matters. Although I was somewhat ashamed to be associated with what American culture embraces, I eventually found it difficult to live "al español," the Spanish way. Surprisingly, I couldn't relax in the same fashion as they did. I couldn't savor the day without preoccupations for tomorrow as they did nor foresee me ever adapting fully to their ways. Frustrated, I yearned to emulate them and to be able to relish every moment of life as they so genuinely did, seemingly without worry or care. I noted, however, that American culture, although not nearly as relaxed, holds a more secure future for its followers. Since Conil, I more attentively analyze the contrasting priorities and values among human cultures. I thank wholeheartedly that simple woman on the opposite hemisphere. Antonia not only set me on an eternal quest for the ability to "love the day," but she also taught me how to make one darned good bowl of gazpacho.

This essay helped Brian get accepted to Stanford University, where he's now a student. *As you can see, he took his assignment seriously, and it paid off.*

Sports Scholarships

If you are a talented athlete, you have a good chance of obtaining an athletic scholarship if do the following things:

Get good grades. Many colleges will not take a chance on athletes who get mediocre grades. They will fear you won't be able to do well in your college courses while participating in a sport.

Take the SAT or ACT in your junior year. Read the section on these tests to see how you can improve your scores if the first ones are low.

Take school seriously. Some high school athletes think of only one thing: their sport. They dream of being another Michael Jordan or Mark McGwire. But both of those stellar athletes graduated from college first. Keep your focus on your schoolwork.

Get out and promote yourself. Don't expect the schools to come find you. Some will, some won't. It might be the schools that don't come looking for you that will be the best fit for you.

Send videotapes of yourself in action in your sport. Ask your parents to help you with the taping. In addition, send newspaper accounts of your exploits and your coach's comments about your skills.

Register with the NCAA Clearinghouse. They will certify your eligibility to play.

Keep your coach informed about what you are doing. He might know college coaches who would be interested in you. Keep him involved in the process because he's your best advocate.

Have a reputation for a good attitude as an athlete and as a person. Some athletes are known as prima donnas who will be hard for a college coach to handle. Have some humility about yourself. You do not walk on water, so don't act like you do. Be known by your fellow athletes and your coaches as a hard worker. A good work ethic could be the deciding factor for you to get the scholarship.

Okay, so you have an eyebrow ring. Is that so bad? Not if the rest of you looks neat and clean. And get that hair out of your eyes. It makes you look dopey.

The College Interview

You must prepare for each interview with the college admission officer. Be prepared with information about each college in order to show that you are serious about your interest in the college. Ask questions that show you are a thinking person. Don't ask questions about social life or how the dorm food is. You can ask the students those questions.

Dressing for the Interview

- Make sure your clothes are neat and pressed.
- Carry your interview clothes with you; you can change right before you get to the campus. You want to look fresh, not wilted.

    Guys: Wear a dress shirt with a nice pair of pants. Save the jeans for while you're traveling.

    Girls: Wear a simple dress or a blouse and a pair of nice pants. Don't wear skirts that are too short.
- Things *not* to wear: Hats, tight clothes, faded jeans with holes in them, too much perfume, tee-shirts, dirty shoes, or lots of makeup.
- Get that hair out of your eyes. You may be a serious student and have your act together, but adults often irrationally judge you harshly when they can't see your eyes. Save that look for when you're at home.

The Interviewer

Interviewers come in all sizes and shapes. The vast majority of them want to put a good spin on their colleges and are competent interviewers. Remember, colleges are trying to sell *you* on the idea of attending their school.

- The good interviewer will give you a chance to talk about yourself. He'll have a good picture of who you are by the end of the interview. In addition, he will answer any questions you have about his college. You will do most of the talking, while he listens.
- You might also get a gabby interviewer who talks to you the whole time. This guy won't have much of an impression of you. He likes to hear himself talk. In addition, you won't learn much about the college. Do your best to get some of your comments in. The interviewer will have to come up for air once in a while. Steer the conversation toward some things you want the college to know about you.
- You might also find yourself in an interview with a person who sizes you up the minute you walk in the door and forms a negative opinion of you before you have had a chance to say a word. The only thing you can do with this interviewer is to go ahead with the interview, make a good impression, and hope that he realizes he judged you incorrectly. Sometimes the interviewer does this on purpose, to see if you can keep your composure and hold your ground. Don't let any interviewer psych you out!

Likely Components of the Interview

- **He will probably have your test scores in front of him.** If you didn't have your test scores sent to his college, it is a good idea to bring them with you, along with a record of your GPA. He will most likely ask questions to clarify some points. He will also attempt to get new information about you.
- **He will ask you why you want to attend his college.**
- **He will give you enough time at the end to ask any questions you have.** This is your time to ask for information about the college that you have not been able to find in any of the college's literature. You can also ask what your chances are for admission, given your test scores and your GPA.

- **He will tell you what procedure will be followed by the admissions office.** You probably will find out when you will hear whether or not you've been accepted by the college.

How to Have a Good Interview

- **Get as much information on the college as you can before you go in for your interview.** Having good information about the college shows that you are serious about your desire to attend the school.
- **Get to the interview on time.** You don't want to make a bad impression on the admission officer. If you have a true emergency and are delayed, call ahead to his office to inform him why you will be late. Calling shows you care and that you respect the interviewer's time.
- **Listen carefully to the interviewer.** He will guide the interview where he wants it to go. Follow his cue. Concentrate on what he is saying. Don't get distracted by a fly on his forehead or his nervous tic.
- **Be pleasant and smile at appropriate times.** Try not to be so nervous that you appear to be too serious, without a sense of humor. Be your true self. Relax. Look at the interviewer when you talk to him. Speak clearly—not too fast or too slowly.
- **When you are asked a question that stumps you, take a few seconds to think before you speak.** Sometimes, an interviewer will ask you an absurd question, just to get your reaction. It is better to think before you speak. A snap answer will be much worse than a well-reasoned answer.
- **Bring along a notebook to write down information.** If you are on a trip to several colleges, it would be a good idea to take notes so that you don't get the colleges mixed up. You will also give the impression that you are seriously considering the college.
- **Don't sit rigidly in your chair and don't slouch.** Don't look like you have a board up your back or like your spine has crumpled. A good, relaxed posture will give the interviewer a favorable impression of you.
- **Toot your own horn, but don't brag.** Sometimes it is difficult to find the right balance. If you simply state the accomplishments you have attained, you won't come across as a braggart. Actually, most students tend to downplay what they do instead of bragging. Be sure you strive for a balanced approach.

Always be honest in interviews. If you tell wild stories about your accomplishments, the interviewer will get suspicious. If your stories are true, bring evidence to back them up, such as newspaper articles, essays, and notices of awards.

*If you prepare your-
self before the inter-
view, you won't be
flustered or caught
off-guard by any
questions the inter-
viewer might ask.*

- **Don't be negative.** Put everything in your life in a positive light. If you had terrible freshman and sophomore years, tell the interviewer what you learned from the experience. Be humble and acknowledge that you messed up. The interviewer will respect your honesty.
- **Always tell the truth.** Don't exaggerate the things you have done in your life. Stick to the facts.

Possible Questions You Will be Asked and How to Prepare for Them

Most questions will all be a variation of the following themes. Be ready for anything, however, because each interviewer will have his pet questions. You can't totally anticipate what he'll ask but you can prepare beforehand to get used to being asked a wide variety of questions. Have a friend ask you the following questions and any others he can think of. That way, you will feel more comfortable and confident when you walk into the interview. Many students are nervous about these interviews but do not need to be if they prepare in advance. If your friend is also applying to colleges, you can return the favor and ask him questions, so that he can be better prepared.

- Why do you want to attend this college?
- What do you have to offer the college?
- What are your goals for the future?
- Why do you want to go to college?
- How would your friends describe you?
- What do you want to say about yourself?
- What are your strengths?
- What are your weaknesses?
- Tell me about your proudest moment.
- Is this college your first choice?
- Who is the person in your life who has influenced you the most?
- What are your hobbies and interests?
- What do you think about the latest news in _____? (This question will be to see if you read the newspaper and know what's going on in the world).

After the Campus Visit and Interview

Write down your impressions from the campus visit and interview. If you write down your thoughts right away, you won't get the colleges mixed up. Many students go to several colleges in two or three days. It is easy to forget important points about each school if you don't write them down. Take good notes. When the time comes for you to decide what college you will attend, your notes will help you in your decision.

Send a thank-you note to the admissions officer. Make the note personable, indicating the things you learned from the interview and what impressed you about the college.

FINANCING COLLEGE

Free Application for Federal Student Aid (FAFSA)

You must apply for financial aid using the FAFSA form. All students who wish to apply for financial aid from the federal government and colleges must first fill out the FAFSA. You can find the form in your school's guidance office or on the Web at http://www.fafsa.ed.gov. Students must use this form to apply for federal student grants, work-study money, and loans. Colleges also use the information from the form to calculate the amount of aid they are willing to give you, based on your parents and your income.

You and your parents are required to give a full disclosure of your income and assets. The FAFSA asks both you and your parents to fill out your own sections in which you state your income, your assets, your debts, and your net worth.

File as soon as possible after January 1. It is a good idea to file the FAFSA form as soon as possible after January 1. Some schools also have specific deadlines for completing the FAFSA. You may apply over the Internet at http://www.fafsa.ed.gov.

After your FAFSA form is processed, you will receive a Student Aid Report (SAR). The report will include all of the information you supplied, including a calculation of your expected family contribution (EFC)—what you and your family can afford to contribute to college expenses.

On the FAFSA form, you can designate six colleges that you want the financial information sent to. Colleges use this information to offer you financial aid for the school year.

You and your parents must resubmit the FAFSA form every year, in case your financial situation has changed. This will be to your advantage if your family incurs major medical expenses or if one of your parents loses his or her job.

Be sure your information on the FAFSA form is completely accurate. If you are caught giving erroneous information, you can be fined. Colleges *can* and *do* check

Your parents will complain about filling out the FAFSA form. It asks for detailed information about their finances and takes a lot of work to assemble all of the information. Bake them some cookies or make dinner to say thanks.

Get as much information as you can on financing your four years of college. You can save money if you know all of the ins and outs of applying for aid.

information given on the form. In addition, the college in which you enroll may ask for copies of your family's income tax return.

Check out the following Web sites for financial aid information:

http://www.collegeboard.org

http://www.fafsa.ed.gov/ (to download the FAFSA form)

http://www.finaid.org (for financial aid information)

http://www.ed.gov/offices/OPE/ (for information on Federal Financial Aid

http://www.ed.gov/offices/OPE/Partners/ed.html (for useful Web addresses to two-year, four-year, and historically black colleges)

http://www.uncf.org/programs/programs.htm (for United Negro College Fund Scholarships)

Aid from the Student Financial Assistance Programs

Your financial aid will most likely include funds from these student financial assistance programs. The programs are administered by the U.S. Department of Education. They provide 70 percent of all student financial assistance (more than $40 billion a year). Read the following information on the different kinds of financial aid you can receive from the U.S. government, all based on the results of your FAFSA.

Federal Pell Grants. These are available to undergraduate students. For the 1998–99 school year, awards ranged from $400 to $3000. These grants do *not* have to be repaid.

Federal Stafford Loans. These loans are available both to undergraduate and graduate students. First year undergraduates may receive loans up to $2625. The amount received through the Stafford Loans increases every year, but will not exceed $5500. The interest rate is variable but never exceeds 8.25 percent. These loans can be either subsidized or unsubsidized. If you qualify for the subsidized Stafford loan (based on need), the government will pay the interest on your loan while you are in school. When you leave college, you will have a grace period of six months, during which you do not have to pay interest on the loan. After the six month period, you will then need to start paying off the loan plus any interest that accumulates.

Federal PLUS Loans. These are subsidized loans made to parents that must be repaid. If you do not receive any financial help from your parents for college expenses or your parents cannot get a PLUS Loan, you are then eligible to borrow additional Stafford funds. The interest rate on these loans is variable but never exceeds 9 percent.

Supplemental Educational Opportunity Grants (SEOG). These are only available to undergraduates. Awards range from $100 to $4000.

Federal Work-Study. Work-study provides jobs to undergraduate and graduate students who are paid an hourly rate at minimum wage or above.

Perkins Loans. Undergraduate students receive up to $3000 and graduate students receive up to $5000 for these low-interest loans (5 percent).

In addition to federal student aid, you may also be eligible for a Hope or Lifetime Learning income tax credit. For more information about these tax credits and federal student aid, visit the U.S. Department of Education's Web site (http://www.ed.gov/studentaid).

A college education is not out of your reach if you have the drive, ambition, and desire to learn. There are agencies out there that will help you finance it.

State-Run Tuition Savings Programs for College

Many states have tuition savings programs for college. Ask your school counselor if your state runs one. You and your parents might benefit from such a program.

Other Ways to Fund College Expenses

ROTC scholarships offered by the Army, Navy, Air Force, and Marines. Students study in participating colleges from all over the United States. The ROTC student agrees to a course of special study relating to the branch of the military that offers the scholarship and to take part in military drills. In exchange for this scholarship, the student agrees to go on active duty for a prescribed period of time after graduation. The ROTC program pays the full amount the student needs to attend school—including money for room, board, and books.

Scholarships from private organizations. Check scholarship books to see if you qualify for private scholarships. Does the company your mother or father work for award a college scholarship? Are you available for minority scholarships? Is one of your parents an alumnus of a college that gives reduced tuition to children of its graduates? Turn over every stone to see if you qualify for more awards.

Check out the following books on scholarships: *The Scholarship Book* by Daniel Cassidy and Peterson's *Winning Money for College* and *Scholarships, Grants & Prizes.*

Your high school college and career center or counseling office has a wealth of scholarship information and applications for you.

Turn in the FAFSA and any other financial forms as soon as possible. Sometimes those who send them in early get the best scholarships. Ask the financial aid officers of the colleges for more information.

Questions for a College's Financial Aid Officer

You should ask the following questions to the financial aid offices of the colleges you're applying to:

1. Does your college require other forms besides the FAFSA?
2. What are the deadlines for submitting financial aid forms?
3. How soon will I receive word of the financial aid award?
4. If I request financial aid, will this have a negative impact on my admission to your college?
5. Does your college participate in a special tuition payment plan—such as installment payments each month?
6. What is the nature of the scholarship? Will this be a yearly award or is it just for your freshman year? What are the requirements to keep the scholarship? Is there a GPA requirement?
7. If you receive a scholarship from an independent source other than the college, will the college lower the financial aid you will receive?

You could find yourself with several college scholarship offers. Having the financial information from each college's financial aid department will help you and your parents evaluate all of the college's offers.

Attention, Parents!

You will have to fill out a form for your senior student based on your assets and income during his junior year. January 1 in the junior year is the beginning of the tax year that will affect your child's financial aid for college in his freshman year. If you have funds saved in your child's name instead of your own, he or she will be eligible for less aid. If the money is in your name, you will be penalized much less. Read the latest version of a book on financial planning for college for more details. You could save yourself a lot of money. Check out The College Board's *The Parents' Guide to Paying for College* and *Meeting College Costs*.

THE SUMMER BEFORE COLLEGE

You will probably be feeling a lot of emotions the summer before you go to college. The vast majority of incoming freshmen have a lot of fear about how well they will do, both in the classroom and socially. Read the following tips to help you prepare for a big change in your life.

Get yourself mentally prepared to have more responsibility. You are used to your mom and dad being a strong force in your life, but now you'll have to make your own decisions. Whether you get through college or not is up to you. Did you know that only 50 to 60 percent of students who start college complete their four years and graduate? Your parents won't be able to guide you through all of the problems that will come up. This doesn't mean that you will have more problems than you have now, but that you will be the person who will have to make the decision on how to handle them. If you have a positive attitude about your new power to control your own destiny, you will be well on your way to succeeding in college and to becoming an adult.

Read lots of books over the summer. Check out the National Endowment for the Humanities reading list in Chapter 8 for the names of good reading suggestions. You'll be reading in much higher volume in college than in high school, so doing lots of reading now will get you prepared. Think of it as basic training for college.

Start to reconfigure your thinking about school. In high school, your teachers have probably hounded you to get your assignments in on time and to be responsible. Your college teachers will not do that. They will assume you know what you're doing and can handle it yourself.

Realize that in college you won't have umpteen quizzes and tests. College class grades are sometimes determined by only one or two grades. Many students crash and burn because they don't study until right before the test. *Cramming is a big mistake!* I taught for many years in a university and saw this happen frequently. It is important to keep up with the reading for class, to take good notes on what you read, to go to class, and to take good notes in class. Listen carefully to what your professors say because most college professors won't give away the content of an exam like your high school teachers did.

When you read books during the summer, think critically about what you're reading. What does that mean? You should look beyond the obvious (plot and characters) and think about what motivating force is driving the characters to act the way they do. Ask yourself, "What does this book teach me about life?" Try always to look beyond the superficial. Start to dig deeper.

Read the following books to get psyched up for college: Peterson's *The Ultimate College Survival Guide* and Suzette

Lots of high school graduates go crazy waiting for the summer to end so they can start in college. They're usually nervous and can't stand the wait. Get busy doing some of the things suggested in this section. You will be more mentally prepared.

College is not like high school. Expect things to be different. You won't have teachers and parents hounding you to do your work. You are in charge. Enjoy your new power and use it well.

Tyler's *Been There, Should've Done That: 505 Tips for Making the Most of College.* Both books are loaded with useful information to help you get acclimated to college.

Read all of the letters from your new college. Take their advice on things you need to do before you get to college. They will have great suggestions that will help you be more comfortable when you start school in the fall.

ADVICE FOR SURVIVING THE FIRST YEAR OF COLLEGE

Be sure to attend all orientation programs sponsored by your college. Take the opportunity to learn all you can *before* classes start. Then, you won't have to waste precious time finding out things like where important places are and where you go to change your schedule.

Avoid the Freshman 15. Often, dorm food is starchy and fattening. Be sure you eat lots of fruits, vegetables, and grains every day to avoid gaining weight. Don't forget to drink milk every day, too.

When you have a problem in a class, ask for help. Most professors will be happy to help you. My nephew had a hard time in his freshman year English composition class. He kept going back to his professor for help and ended up getting a *B.* His persistence paid off. Other students didn't go see the professor for help. 40 percent failed the class.

See your adviser to help you make class scheduling decisions. Often, your adviser will know the ins and outs of the college and can help you formulate a good game plan for getting the best possible education. He can also help you avoid classes you would be well-advised not to take.

Keep track of your spending. Write down everything you spend. Balance that checkbook every time you write a check. Record every ATM withdrawal to keep track of your balance. Avoid those credit cards.

Keep on top of all of your course work. Don't wait until the night before to read 500 pages of a novel or study ten chapters in a history book. Do some of the work every day to avoid the stress of last-minute hysteria.

Get to know your teachers. A friendly chat from time to time, coupled with questions about the course work, will help him remember who you are, especially when you need a recommendation for graduate school or for a job. One of the best parts of the college experience is the exchange of ideas with others. Your teachers are a good place to start.

Exercise regularly. If you sit around constantly and never exercise, you will become sluggish and will have less energy. Get that body moving.

Get involved in all of your classes. Cultivate an attitude of enjoying learning.

Ask for information when you need it. Ask lots of questions as often as you can. Obtaining lots of information and meeting lots of people will help you get more out of your education. Don't let things happen to you. Make your own success happen.

REASONS TO TRANSFER TO ANOTHER COLLEGE

When you start your freshman year, hopefully you will be pleased with the college you chose. Sometimes, however, you will need to transfer to another school. You should ask yourself if you have truly given the college a chance. Be aware that you may lose some or all of the credits you have gained in your freshman year, so don't make this decision lightly. Here are some reasons why you might need to transfer:

The college does not have a good program for your major. You may have decided after you got to college what you wanted to major in, unaware that the college does not have a very strong department in that major.

The college is not difficult enough. If you are not getting the challenges you need and find yourself goofing off and not learning as much as you would like because the class work is so easy, contact another college to find out their requirements for admission. As a possible solution to avoid the transfer situation, research who the better, more difficult teachers are. All colleges have good teachers who demand more from their students. Check around for more information before you decide you're not getting a good enough education and need to transfer.

The college is too difficult. Have you really worked hard enough to succeed in your courses? Do you just want party all of the time? Think hard before you transfer out of a difficult college. You will be happy when you graduate that you did the extra work necessary to succeed.

You cannot afford to continue attending the college. Perhaps your father lost his job and your parents cannot continue to send checks to the college. Before you make a quick decision, find out if you can find alternate ways to finance your education. Talk to your college's financial aid office. Maybe they can increase the money you receive from

If you are miserable in your new college, give yourself some time to get acclimated. Maybe you're just homesick. Maybe you miss your girlfriend or boyfriend. Maybe college is a big change for you. Sometimes, it takes time to adjust. Don't have a knee jerk reaction and try to leave immediately.

Independent study comes in handy when you need to pick up a course for graduation that is not offered the semester you need it.

them. If not, you can return home to live with your parents to save money and go to the local state university.

OTHER WAYS TO "DO COLLEGE"

Independent Study (Correspondence Courses)

What is independent study? It refers to individual instruction by mail. Instead of learning in a college classroom, you can do your course work at home. You can enroll at any time and work at your own pace. Independent study is a flexible way to take college courses and even high school classes while working a full-time job. This type of learning is flexible and geared toward busy people who have special needs that do not allow them to attend classes on campus, a rotating schedule that keeps them from attending class on a regular basis, or other obligations that keep them from going to school.

How does independent study work? The assignments are usually completed at home and evaluated by a faculty member who designs the instructional materials and guides your course study.

Is the U.S. mail the only way to communicate with the universities? Independent study has changed dramatically in recent years. Before, the postal service delivered course materials to the student, who then returned his completed work by mail to the professor. Now, colleges communicate with students via videotaped lectures, audiotapes, and e-mail. E-mail allows the student and teacher to communicate more swiftly, enabling the student to fulfill the course requirements more rapidly. In addition, many resources on the Web help the student get more information for his education. Students who do not have a computer can access e-mail and the World Wide Web at their local library.

Where can I get more information? Peterson's *Independent Study Catalog* is an excellent resource for more detailed information on 13,000 correspondence courses at more than 140 accredited schools. The book also gives you all of the information you need to make wise choices regarding choosing accredited schools, transfer policy for accepting the credits, and financial aid.

Distance Learning

What is distance learning? Distance learning provides educational programs to off-site students through the use of technologies such as cable or satellite television, videotapes and audiotapes, computer modem, computer and video conferencing, and fax. Students may receive the classes in the workplace or even at home.

What students are mostly likely to benefit from distance learning? If you quit after high school and later on during your working career decide you need more education, distance learning is an ideal way to gain new knowledge. Often, students who have been away from college for a few years or more have families to care for and cannot afford to quit their jobs, move to a college campus, and simply be a student.

Why has distance learning suddenly become so popular? The demand for better access to educational resources and the improved technologies have driven the rapid development of distance learning. In 1994, fewer than 100 institutions were providing this type of education. Now, more than 850 accredited North American colleges provide distance learning classes. It's the latest trend in education. Many students take distance learning courses for credit that may be applied towards a degree, to update their skills in this ever-changing job market, and to receive professional certification. Many corporations are forming partnerships with universities to bring college courses to the workplace to encourage employees to continue their education and update their work skills.

Who are the most likely distance learners? Most are adults who are more than 25 years old, employed, and have some previous college experience. They generally are highly motivated. In fact, their completion of course work exceeds that of students taking courses on campus.

Where can I get more information on distance learning? To get a general idea of courses offered by colleges, check out the Western Governors University (http://www.wgu.edu). It electronically delivers classes developed by accredited schools in sixteen western states. In the south, the Southern Regional "Electronic" Campus has also recently been developed, which includes courses from fifty colleges and universities in fifteen southern states (http//www.srec.sreb.org). You can also take a look at another Web site, http://www.hoyle.com/distance.htm, which gives general information on distance learning, or you can read Peterson's *Guide to Distance Learning.* This book provides information on 850 individual colleges and their delivery methods (from

Do you have small children and can't afford to hire a babysitter and go to college? Or do you live in a small town, far away from a college, and cannot afford to leave your job? Distance learning could be the ideal solution for you.

videoconferencing to computer-based), subjects, requirements, tuition, fees, registration information, application
contacts, and financial aid.

What kinds of colleges offer distance learning courses?
Highly rated colleges are starting programs via distance
learning, to meet the needs of today's busy students. You can
earn everything from an M.B.A. at Duke or Syracuse to an M.S.
in engineering at Purdue.

SHORTCUT TO ACTION

1. Make sure you have good reasons for going to college. If you aren't psychologically prepared for all of the work you have to do, you'll have a hard time succeeding. And your parents will have wasted a lot of money sending you there.

2. You *can* prepare for the SAT I and ACT exams. There are many resources you can use that give practice exams. You'll be less nervous if you prepare.

3. Keep a high energy level when applying to college. If you take the applications one step at a time and start on them well in advance, you won't get so stressed out.

4. Research colleges before you apply. You will need to narrow down your list according to the criteria you set up beforehand.

5. Make the campus visit and interview important parts of your decision. Seeing the campus and talking to lots of people will help you decide which school is the best fit for you.

6. Fill out each application as if you were taking a final exam. Check it over carefully for errors before submitting.

7. Teacher recommendations are important. Pick teachers who know you well and who respect your work. Thank them for their recommendations.

8. If you have to write college essays, think of them as an adventure, not a noose around your neck. Have fun writing them. Be sure to put your personality into each essay. The essay shouldn't be too stiff, but it also shouldn't be too loose.

9. Prepare for each college interview. You don't want to make a bad impression. Practice with a friend who has to go through the same thing.

10. With your parents, get as much financial aid information as you can. College is expensive. It's important to make all of the right moves.

11. Prepare yourself mentally and emotionally for college the summer before.

12. To survive your first year of college, read Peterson's *The Ultimate College Survival Guide.*

Dear Students,

I would appreciate any comments you have on *The Ultimate High School Survival Guide* and welcome your suggestions for the next edition. What parts did you like? What would you like to see me change or improve? You can reach me via e-mail at dueber@stlnet.com.

Thanks for any feedback you can give me!

Sincerely,

Julianne Dueber

INDEX